*The Completely Revised*

^ **HOW TO
*RUN* YOUR BUSINESS
SO YOU C^N**

...ion

J...

Ed... ... Carroll

First Edition with Irv Sternberg

**Business Enterprise Press**

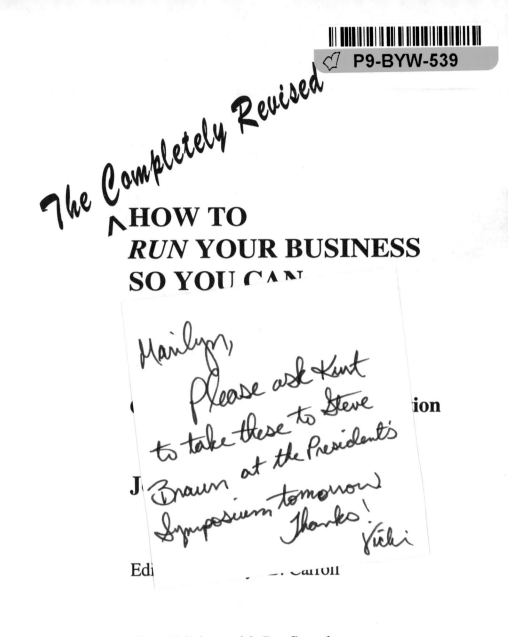

*(handwritten note):* Marilyn, Please ask Kurt to take these to Steve Braun at the President's Symposium tomorrow Thanks! Vicki

# The Completely Revised

# HOW TO
# *RUN* YOUR BUSINESS
# SO YOU CAN
# *LEAVE* IT IN STYLE

**Completely Revised Second Edition**

*Library of Congress Catalog Card Number:  96 - 80008*

Brown, John H., 1947-
   *The completely revised how to run your business so you can leave it in style/John H. Brown*
      *p.  cm.*

   *ISBN 0-9655731-1-7*

   *1. Business enterprises--United States. 2. Estate planning--United States. 3. Business enterprises, Sale of--United States. 4.Business enterprises--Taxation--United States. 5. Inheritance and transfer tax--Law and legislation--United States.*

*First BUSINESS ENTERPRISE PRESS paperback edition 1997.*

# DISCLAIMER

*This publication is designed to provide information in regard to the subject matter covered. It is sold with the understanding that while the author is a practicing attorney, neither he, his law firm, nor the publisher is engaged by the reader to render legal, accounting or other professional service. If legal advice or other expert assistance is required by the reader, the services of a competent professional should be sought. The purpose of this book is to educate. Neither the author nor Business Enterprise Press shall have any liability or responsibility to any person or entity with respect to any loss or damage caused, or alleged to be caused, directly or indirectly by the information contained in this book.*

*If you do not wish to be bound by the above, you may return this book to the publisher for a full refund.*

To my first employers
from whom I learned so much
–my parents,
**Harold** and **Helen** Brown

# CONTENTS

# About the Author

**John Brown** is a shareholder of Minor & Brown, P.C., a Denver law firm he co-founded twenty years ago. Minor & Brown, P.C. specializes in business transition planning–helping owners first prepare for the day when they will transfer their businesses and then guiding owners through the selling or transfer process.

John's expertise in business succession planning is well known throughout the Rocky Mountain Region. He has worked with the area's most successful entrepreneurs and business-owning families as they prepare to and do leave their businesses in style. Since the publication of John's first book in 1990, he has represented and consulted with business owners across the United States.

John is also a co-owner of JD Ford & Company, L.L.P., a Denver based, private investment banking firm that provides financial advisory services to established, mid-sized, closely held companies and entrepreneurs. Its services include mergers and acquisitions, business unit divestitures, management buyouts, valuations and other corporate finance transactions.

John wrote this book to share his experience in representing hundreds of owners in successfully leaving their businesses in style.

# Acknowledgements

The source for almost all of the information in this book is the thousands of clients my firm has represented over the last twenty years. To them I give my unqualified gratitude.

The first edition of this book could not have been written without the consistent help--in writing, editing and thinking--of my original ghostwriter, Irv Sternberg. This complete revision was done without his capable assistance--so he is finally off the hook. Any errors in substance or style are mine alone.

For this revision, I had, it seems, a cast of thousands who reviewed and commented on this book. My fellow shareholders: Ned A. Minor, Barbara J. Wells, James A. Thomas, Jr. and John A. Logan; several associate attorneys in my firm including: Anthony A. King, Laura L. Breaker and Lisa A. D'Ambrosia; my fellow professionals: David C. Cribari, CPA, Craig L. Hayward, CPA, and William Holben, CPA. They corrected mistakes, but more importantly, contributed many planning strategies and tactics. I must also thank the hundreds of business owners and their advisors who attended my seminars and workshops, asked the probing questions, clarified my thinking and refocused my efforts to better reflect their experiences and their needs.

Finally, to the extent this new book is well organized, consistent and readable, full credit belongs to Kathryn Carroll, my editor.

*Preface to the Completely Revised Second Edition*

The reason that this Completely Revised Second Edition exists has more to do with what I've learned from business owners over the past seven years than it does with any changes in the law. Although there have been some changes to the laws that affect business owners and the planning they need to do to leave their businesses in style, none is dramatic enough to require the publishing of a second edition.

Seven years of countless conversations with business owners across the United States have had a profound impact on my view of leaving a business in style. I learned that there is more interest than I imagined in using a sale to a third party as the ticket to financial security. Readers and seminar participants had specific questions about using transaction advisors, what they charge, what they do and how they do it. I wanted to answer these questions in a second edition but since this is not my area of expertise, I called upon one of the Rocky Mountain region's leading investment bankers (and a partner of mine) Joseph M. Durnford of JD Ford & Company, Ltd. He not only wrote Chapter Nine devoted solely to third party sales, but he also provided significant revisions to Chapter Two concerning business valuations and Chapter Eight regarding transaction advisors. His input added a strong dose of real world experience to the topic of third party sales.

As a result, this Second Edition is a "completely revised" book. I've added chapters, case studies and more checklists at the end of each chapter. I've deleted material and reviewed and revised everything that remained. Finally, I've made it easier for you to find me and the information you need from me by including a Request Form at the back of the book. I hope you will use it and the infomation in this book to successfully leave your business in style.

# Part I

# Creating and Preserving Value Within the Business

Creating and preserving value for your ownership interest is fundamental to leaving your business in style. Chapters 1 through 5 show you how to create and preserve value. These chapters follow a logical sequence.

First, you must create your "Exit Plan" based on a proven process. This requires learning certain "owner skills" and developing exit-based objectives with the help of a solid team of advisors.

Secondly, you must know the worth of your business. After all, much of your exit strategy is based on converting business value to something a bit more useful–cash. Consequently, it is essential to know what your business is worth as you begin to execute your Exit Plan.

Next, every owner can preserve business value by learning how to avoid unnecessary litigation and other business hiccups by practicing "preventive maintenance" through the use of a legal audit and other methods. You will be introduced to the year-end review–the most effective way to use your advisory team and to keep your Exit Plan on track.

A critical element in creating and preserving value in your business is knowing how to motivate and keep your key employees. All of Chapter four is devoted to this topic.

Finally, familiarizing yourself with the basics of tax planning enables you to preserve value in your business by minimizing taxation. Chapter Five will not make you a tax expert but it will give you the tools you need to make business decisions with taxes in mind.

# 1

# When You're Too Busy Fighting Alligators

*How to get what you want when you leave.*

You own a profitable and growing business that provides a lot of what you desire: income, wealth, an identity, challenge, stimulation, satisfaction, and pride. By all conventional yardsticks, you are a success. Well done!

But wait a minute. Despite these positive signs, your business may be failing you in an unexpected way. Let's consider an owner-based definition of success—one that measures success in business not by how well the business operates under your ownership and not by the benefits it provides, but by the rewards it will bestow when you leave it. Because in the end, what you really want and need from your business is *the ability to leave it—under the most favorable conditions.*

There are few universal truths in business life. This is one: *You will leave your business.* There is only one way you, as an owner, can do so successfully: You must create an Exit Plan as early as possible and stick to that plan as long as you maintain your business.

But you *do* plan, you say. True. You plan your day-to-day operations. You create production or service schedules, devise marketing strategies, plot sales efforts, compile projections, generate organization plans. But this is traditional business planning; it is not the kind of planning that business owners must do for themselves. What is the difference? Let's look at a case history.

## A Tale of Two Partners

*In the late 1980s, I met with the two major owners of a thriving construction company in Denver. Despite the downturn in the local economy, this firm had been able to maintain profits and income because of the wide experience and extraordinary personal efforts of the owners.*

*When we set up our meeting, I assumed we would be discussing typical fiscal year-end matters: income taxes, business continuity, and estate planning. When we met, however, the owners' first words were, "Can you review this auction agreement? We're going to sell all our equipment and get out of the business."*

*I was shocked.*

*The owners, both in their early forties, explained that their efforts to maintain the business had drained them. For years they had complied with government regulations and braced for and adjusted to the changing tax code that dramatically affected the tax benefits of their multi-million dollar investment in construction equipment. Now they no longer had the patience, desire, or stamina to continue; they convinced me they were serious about giving up their business. So we began to explore alternative ways of getting money for the company, other than through an auction of the equipment.*

*First, we considered a sale to a third party, but the business was too large to be bought by any company other than the larger national construction firms. Feelers to those companies revealed little desire to acquire a construction company in the then depressed Rocky Mountain region.*

*We discussed the possibility of transferring ownership by selling the firm to the employees or offering a buy out to key managers. Both ideas were rejected because, although there were important employees, none had ever been groomed to accept greater responsibilities in the organization. There was simply no one ready to take over and run the business, nor had anything been done to create funding for the owners' buy out.*

*The two owners had retained control of all of the key functions. Unless they continued in those roles, the business was unlikely to remain successful. Since the owners were unwilling to keep fighting the battle that had worn them down, they sadly decided to liquidate at auction prices, despite years of profitability.*

This story illustrates an important point: A business can be both growing and profitable, even highly profitable for a long period of time, and yet have little worth beyond the "fire sale" value of its tangible assets: machinery, vehicles, office equipment, furniture, buildings, and inventory.

The Denver construction company was both profitable and growing, yet little value had been created or preserved. And this was a $30 million in annual sales company, not a mom-and-pop store.

How did these hardworking, experienced, knowledgeable, and successful partners find themselves in this predicament after years of dedicated involvement in building their company? They never took the time to plan for and create a market for their stock. They had no Exit Plan.

For years they devoted themselves to the day-to-day management of the business, personally handling hundreds of details, dealing with crises, putting out fires. The intensity the owners generated and the energy they expended in avoiding the alligators and making their company a success eventually led to their burnout—and inevitable liquidation. Reluctantly, they gave up their business and the hope that someone else was available to keep it going.

The business disappeared. Dozens of employees lost their jobs. The owners settled for the cash raised from the sale of their tangible assets—an amount far less than the company's value as a going concern. All of this could have been avoided through proper planning. The problem was, they simply did not know they needed an Exit Plan.

That's why I wrote this book. First, to convince busy owners of the need to plan. Second, to show them how to plan and third, to motivate them to execute their plans.

### *Developing Your Exit Plan*

What exactly is an Exit Plan that will allow you to leave your business in style and **how** do you create it? Certainly there is an almost infinite variety of businesses and business owners. Consequently, each owner's exact Exit Plan will vary, yet almost all contain common elements. These elements form the essence of this book.

To give you an idea of where you stand in developing your Exit Plan, take the following quiz. I have framed each of the basic steps in developing an Exit Plan as a question. If you can answer "yes" to all of the questions, this book will serve as an affirmation of the decisions you have implemented. If you are like the vast majority of business owners, however, these questions will highlight areas you have neglected. Take the quiz now:

1.  Do you know your primary planning objectives in leaving the business, such as:
    a.  Departure date?
    b.  Income needed to achieve financial security?
    c.  To whom you want to leave the business?

2.  Do you know how much your business is worth?

3.  Do you know how to increase the value of your ownership interest through enhancing the most valuable asset of the company – the employees?

4.  Do you know the best way to sell your business to a third party which maximizes your cash, minimizes your tax liability and reduces your risk?

5.  Do you know how to transfer your business to family members, co-owners or employees while paying the least possible taxes and enjoying maximum financial security?

6.  Have you implemented all necessary steps to insure that the business continues if you don't?

7.  Have you provided for your family's security and continuity if you die or become incapacitated?

If you are like every business owner I have ever represented, you will only be able to answer "yes" to a few of these questions. If you are going to successfully exit your business, you must be able to say "yes" to each and every one. The rest of this book is dedicated to getting you to "yes."

## Planning for Yourself as an Owner

All businesses do some kind of planning. It may be a simple discussion or a document. Most planning, however, is done at the business level, not at the ownership level, and covers the operational aspect of a business, such as a managing work flow or developing a budget or marketing plan, and perhaps organization or administration plans for adding personnel and equipment as a company expands.

But this is not the kind of planning we're discussing here. There are numerous marketing, management, and accounting resources and advisors available to help the business owner achieve his or her goals in these areas. The kind of planning I'll discuss is **owner-based**. It is not based on business needs as much as it is on the goals your business must achieve before you can leave in style.

These goals are nothing more—and nothing less—than getting to "yes" on each question I've listed immediately above.

Generally, these owner-based goals (or objectives) fall into three broad categories or Parts:

I:   To create and preserve the value of the company;

II:  To provide a means to exchange that value for money with the least tax consequences possible;

III: To meet personal and family needs by providing security and continuity to your business and for your family either upon your planned departure or if disaster strikes—upon your death or disability.

This book is divided into these three Parts.

## Creating and Preserving Value

Although the purpose of business is to make money, an objective generally perceived as being worthwhile and useful, most entrepreneurs are so dedicated to this purpose they have little or no time to spend on creating and preserving value for their businesses. Nonetheless, it is time you must find . . . time to plan to meet specific objectives. Creating and preserving value is the subject matter of Part I.

## Exchanging Ownership for Money

Inevitably, every business owner will sooner or later leave the business. Yet, few owners think about that event as they build and run their businesses. In no other area is the need for planning so obvious and the lack of planning so evident.

For now, you should be aware of the need to plan for your eventual departure because one of the following scenarios is going to occur:

1.  You will transfer ownership of the business during your lifetime because you've decided you want out. Without planning, you may well have to liquidate; with planning,

you will be able to sell the business to a third party, to key employees or co-owners, or to family members—all at minimal tax rates.

2. You will die or become totally disabled, and the business will have to be liquidated unless some type of business continuity arrangements have been planned and documented.

## *Meeting Personal and Family Needs*

Unlike sellers of IBM stock, you have no readily available market to which you can sell your business. This is an especially serious problem if you unexpectedly die or become permanently disabled before all of your planning is completed. After all, your business and family must continue on even if you don't. Business continuity planning, estate planning and personal wealth accumulation, all reviewed annually then, are critically important (see Chapters 10, 11, 12 and 13).

Your personal planning requires that your business interest be converted to cash—if you are to leave your business in style. Much of this is accomplished through a well-designed lifetime transfer of ownership. But, you must also address other risks.

A business continuity plan (Chapter 11) provides the mechanism for dovetailing (i) ownership transfer events (e.g. death, retirement); and (ii) valuation and provisions for payment. Personal financial planning sets the agenda for reaching financial security. Without financial security and independence, you will never be able to leave your business—and the title of **your** book would be "*How To Run A Business and Never Leave At All!*" Finally, estate planning provides the mechanisms to continue the business and your family's lifestyle should you depart from the business (and this Earth) unexpectedly.

*For Business Owners Only.*

Planning for these goals and objectives is a function that only you, the owner, can and should perform. But you don't need to do it alone; you can obtain help.

Before leaving this first chapter, let us examine in detail this first step in exit planning: *Determining your departure objectives.* In other words, in order to leave the business in style, first decide what that means, what has to be achieved. The rest of the planning process and all tax planning and implementation is dedicated to reaching the objectives you establish. Appendix 1.1 sets forth a list of typical departure goals most owners share. The purpose now is not to have you irrevocably determine all of these goals before proceeding with the rest of this book. You will need the information I've tried to pack into the book to flesh out the detail of your objectives. But you must get a grasp on your goals before setting course on your journey. Keep in mind that the rest of this book deals with how to refine and attain each objective. Spend time now and fill out these initial departure objectives. You'll have many opportunities to revise as you progress.

## Summary

The importance of ownership planning as opposed to conventional business planning cannot be overemphasized. What is the difference? Ownership planning is concerned with four major areas:

1. Planning for yourself—as an owner.
2. Creating and preserving business value.
3. Transferring ownership and control successfully.
4. Making sure personal and family needs are met.

The sooner you start this process, the sooner you will finish.

## Appendix 1.1:  Initial Owner-Based Departure Objectives Checklist

I.    Financial Exit Objectives

Leaving the business in style means, for me, having $_____ of annual after-tax income for the rest of my (and my spouse's) lifetime.

II.    Personal Exit Objectives

    A.  I plan to work until _____, _____ .  At that date I will no longer be an employee of the company, although I may well want a large portion of my income stream to come from the business.

    B.  I intend to transfer the business to:

        ❏  the following child or children:

        _____

        _____

        _____

        _____

        ❏  the following key employees:

        _____

        _____

        _____

        _____

☐  my co-owner(s)

☐  a third party, known or unknown.

C.  I intend to pursue the following activities after my departure:

_____

_____

_____

_____

# 2

# Making a Molehill Out
# of a Mountain

*Valuing your business to maximize what you get and to
minimize what the IRS takes*

Winston Churchill once described Russian actions as "a riddle wrapped in a mystery inside an enigma." And so must business valuation seem to most owners.

Valuation of privately owned businesses may generously be described as an inexact science. There are many guidelines; there are tax court cases discussing business valuation factors; there is an entire business appraisal industry. Yet, the IRS can use its valuation factors to establish and justify high values for transfer tax purposes and your professional can equally well justify high or low values–depending on the purpose of the valuation–using the **same** factors.

Given this quagmire, why on earth do I suggest, as I do, that valuing your business is a vital first step in the exit planning process? There are several reasons.

First, to exit the business in style, you will need cash. That source of cash is the business. To determine the amount of cash you will receive, we must know the value of the business. Two of your most important business objectives–departure date and financial security–are dependent on the amount of money you receive for your business.

Second, if you intend to give the business to children, the business must be valued and that value must be used for gift tax purposes.

Third, the business typically comprises the great majority of an owner's total wealth. The IRS knows this just as surely as you do. Determining the value now, allows you the opportunity to design an Exit Plan taking your business into account with the goal of minimizing the IRS's take.

Fourth, as you will soon see, well-designed key employee incentive compensation planning is central to increasing business value. Business value is often used as a measuring rod for such plans.

Fifth, if an owner goes through this exercise well before the business is sold or transferred, he or she will be able to pinpoint the factors that are crucial to measuring and increasing (or decreasing) the worth of the business. Your annual year-end meeting is a good time to revalue your business (see Chapter Three).

### Determining a Value

Business owners often ask me and their accountants, "How much is my business worth?" I tell them the question is totally irrelevant and that a much better question would be: "What is the most I can get for my business under the most favorable terms and conditions?"

Answering this more practically requires following one of two approaches. The first is to employ the valuation techniques described on the following pages. This valuation is likely to be performed by your CPA or a business appraiser. The methodology is consistent with the approaches sanctioned by the IRS.

The second approach or methodology is that of the marketplace and must be used when you decide to sell to a third party. It is described in Chapter Nine.

Please realize that business valuation is a process that is absolutely nonabsolute. In fact, there are a number of different methods of valuing a closely held business, each involving a variety of factors with varying degrees of importance and each rendering a different value! I usually recommend an exercise that incorporates several techniques to arrive at a valuation range of fair market values.

The actual sale price of the business is not to be confused with determining fair market value for purposes of gifting, estate taxation, and general planning. Not that fair market value and sales price are unrelated. Not at all. Fair market value determinations are invaluable, but they proceed on a *hypothetical assumption* of what a willing, hypothetical buyer would pay a willing seller when neither is under a compulsion to buy or sell. As such, it is only an educated guess, for we cannot ordinarily go into the real market place and determine what a *real buyer will pay you for your actual business, today.*

If you've decided to sell to an outside third party, you need to know, to the extent possible, what your sale price is as you begin the sales process. You use the value arrived at by the methods described in this chapter as a starting point. But you must gain access to what the market is really going to do with your particular business. For that you must go to the marketplace. Since you have no experience and your advisors likely have insufficient experience, you must use another specialized guide. Depending on the size of your business (and therefore the type of purchaser interested in acquiring it) you will use a business broker, an investment banker, or a merchant banker. Again, for this type of value determination, look to the discussion in Chapter Nine.

Assuming you are not yet ready to sell the business, you still need a valuation for all the reasons just described. So, where do you start?

### *Standard Valuation Methods*

Surprisingly, one place to look for guidance is the IRS. In 1959 it issued Revenue Ruling 59-60. This ruling is still cited extensively today by the IRS and by business appraisers when placing a value on your business. For our purposes it provides a useful starting point.

The major items listed by this revenue ruling are:

- The nature of the business and its history from inception.
- The general economic condition and outlook of the specific industry.
- The book value of the stock and the financial condition of the business.
- The earning capacity of the company.
- The dividend-paying capacity.
- Whether or not the enterprise has goodwill or other intangible value.
- Prior sales of stock and size of the block of stock to be valued.
- The market price of stocks of corporations engaged in the same or similar line of business whose stocks are actively traded in a free and open market, either on an exchange or over-the-counter.

In addition to the IRS's valuation standards, the Courts have, over the years, contributed their own ideas on how to determine a business's value. These include:

- Capitalization.
- Diversification of production.
- Labor policies.
- Quality of management.
- Importance of the selling owner to the success of the business.
- Net value of underlying assets.
- Prospects of creating a market for the stock.
- Restrictions on voting power or the transferability of the stock to be valued.

Other than simply listing these elements involved in arriving at a business value, neither the IRS nor the Courts will tell you which of these factors carry more weight than the others in a particular business. That's as far as they go in providing guidance.

So far I think I've been a pretty good lawyer: I told you that your original question was irrelevant, but that it can be answered in an infinite variety of ways and there is no one correct answer. I've told you that both the IRS and the Courts have come up with many ways to value your business. Now, a good lawyer would say, "No more" and simply hand you the bill. However, unless you've borrowed this book from the library, you've already paid my bill. Therefore, let me help you to wade through this morass and to arrive at a reasonable valuation range for your own business. To do this, let's visit a junkyard in central Wyoming.

*Marcus E. Hamilton Enterprises, Ltd., was so successful, it made me wonder why I didn't go into the junkyard business after high school rather than fritter away time in college and law school. Marcus, in his mid-fifties, had recently decided that southern Florida was more compatible with his winter lifestyle than central Wyoming. He also knew that there was no one in his junkyard business with either the savvy or finances to purchase his ownership interest. So when he met with us, he wanted some idea of what he might expect to receive upon the sale of his business to an outside third party.*

*First, we looked at the value of the assets within the business. This involved examining the book value of all assets, then adjusting those assets to fair market value. This is a necessary step if the cost of those assets, as reduced by accumulated depreciation, is not indicative of the true worth of the asset.*

*In the case of the junkyard business, this was particularly true. A wrecked pickup truck that might have been purchased for $50 could over time yield $1,000 worth of parts. Fortunately, Marcus kept good records (computerized, yet!) of the annual cost of purchased junks. Comparing that with the annual revenues, we were able to come up with a good adjusted fair market value of the original cost of the inventory.*

*The adjusted book value of his business looked like this:*

| Assets | | Liabilities | |
|---|---|---|---|
| Cash | $ -0- | Accounts Payable | $ 138,954 |
| Accounts Receivable | $ 210,490 | Accrued Taxes | $ 6,252 |
| Inventory (adjusted for | | Other | $ 3,973 |
| fair market value) | $ 1,380,000 | | |
| Prepaids and Other | $ 1,888 | Loans (current) | $ 182,302 |
| Officer Note | $ -0- | Notes payable | $ 186,717 |
| | | Mortgages (real) | $ -0- |
| Accrued interest | $ -0- | | |
| Real Property | $ 118,479 | Mortgages (chattel) | $ -0- |
| Equipment and Fixtures | $ 450,000 | Deferred Compensation | $ -0- |
| Notes Receivable | $ 750 | | |
| Cash Value Life Insurance | $ 17,925 | | |
| Total assets | $ 2,179,532 | Total liabilities | $ 518,198 |

| | |
|---|---|
| Total assets: | $ 2,179,532 |
| Less total liabilities | <$ 518,198> |
| Adjusted book value: | $ 1,661,334 |

The total fair market value of the assets (less liabilities) was $1,661,334. If Marcus did nothing but slowly liquidate his business, eventually he could expect to receive approximately that amount less the ongoing cost of operations. On the other hand, a quick liquidation would result in substantially less money than this because the cost of moving his inventory–hundreds of junked cars–would be too expensive and there was no immediate market for that many used cars in central Wyoming. Only by continuing the operation in place could Marcus realize maximum revenue.

After going through these calculations, we obtained one of the two numbers needed to come up with the full fair market value of the business–the net fair market value of the assets. Our evaluation work was, therefore, half completed. In addition to the net fair market value, we also needed to account for the *going concern value.*

Generally, the going concern value is also described as the "goodwill" or "blue sky" value of the business. It's a value beyond asset value. Reducing that value to a supportable number is more difficult and subjective than determining the fair market value of assets. The best approach to take is the one most people would take when buying any income-producing asset. First ask, "What is the replacement value of the asset?" Then ask, "What is the demonstrated earnings capacity of that asset?"

If the earnings capacity is no greater than a reasonable yield or return on the fair market value of the assets, then there is no excess earnings capacity and no going concern value. On the other hand, if there are excess earnings, then there is a going concern value. To demonstrate this, study the following exhibit. Try to work through it and then I'll explain it.

### *Exhibit 2.1* **Going concern value.**

---

(1) Average annual net earnings of the business: total compensation (including bonuses, personal use of corporate assets, and excess rents) paid to owners by the business plus the amount added to retained earnings or annual net income (the average annual net earnings of the previous three years is used generally with greater weight given to the most recent year and less to the initial year) ............................ $ 575,000

(2) Less estimated annual replacement salaries for all owners and their family members ......................... $ 65,000

(3) Less earnings on book value @ 17% annual return on $1,661,334 ....................................................... $ 282,426

(4)  Average net annual excess earnings due to "good-
     will," past activity, and risk of capital [(1) above,
     minus (2) above, minus (3) above – $575,000 -
     $65,000 – $282,426]............................................. $   228,574
(5)  Multiply (4) above x 6 years ................................ $1,365,464
(6)  Add the adjusted book value (tangible assets) ....... $1,661,334
(7)  Total value [(5) + (6)] ........................................... $3,026,798

---

We arrived at a value of slightly more than $3 million as a
sales price for this business. That amount is subject to several other
considerations that we'll discuss below, but it is a supportable value.
And it means more money in your pocket than if you were to sell on
the basis of asset value or some insupportable formula. To make it
supportable, however, you need to understand how we arrived at each
of the line item totals.

First, the *average annual net earnings* of the business is
computed. You have considerable flexibility in determining
"average." You can decide to go back one year or five years. You can
give greater weight to the more recent years or simply have a true
average of all years under consideration. This becomes part of your
bargaining or negotiation when you begin discussions with a potential
buyer. Purchasers are interested in the trend of earnings history, and
they will invariably give greater consideration to more current earnings
of the business. For this reason greater weight must be given to more
recent earnings history to obtain a realistic earning "average." If your
earnings history has been steadily increasing for many years, it will
reflect that increased value under line item (5) by increasing the
number of years–the capitalization rate in effect–of the annual net
earnings.

Purchasers also want to know how much money the owner
has really been taking out of the business. That's why it's critical to
*recast* the financial information of the company to give the buyer
that understanding.

Prudent tax planning for the business owner means that his use of the company's income stream has involved more than simply drawing a salary and, perhaps, a bonus. The planning can involve a variety of other factors, such as leasing personally owned assets to the company in return for high rent, the use of medical expense reimbursement plans, making highly favorable retirement plan contributions, using company assets such as cars and airplanes, and employing a spouse and children at higher-than-expected salaries or wages.

All these amounts must be recast as earnings available to the business owner. It behooves you, then, to start now with your accountant to keep track of these excess earnings.

In line item (2) of the chart, the net earnings are reduced by the *estimated replacement salaries* after your departure. What will it cost to replace you? The answer will be found by looking to industry standards, the salaries paid to key members of your management team now in place, and to what you think is reasonable.

In item (3), earnings on book value are multiplied by a percentage amount. Theoretically, this amount can be anything you want it to be. Realistically, it's the rate of return a reasonable person would want on his capital, subject to the risk factors of that capital. In other words, if I were to loan your business $100,000 to buy inventory, what rate of return would I insist upon having to cover the possibility that you might default on that loan?

Keep in mind also that my loan would be subordinated to any type of bank financing available. Consequently, this rate of return must be higher than any outstanding indebtedness the business has with any financial institution. Typically, a reasonable person (especially the potential buyer of your business) would want a rate of return between 15 percent and 20 percent.

The greater the return expected on the assets, the lower the going concern value of the business. The percentage in this line item will decrease if there is a stable earnings history, if the company has been in business for many years, and if the assets are readily salable and hold their value over time.

Other factors unique to your business may affect the upward or downward movement of that percentage rate. Again, it's in your best interest to begin a list of those reasons supporting a lower percentage rate. The list would indicate the amount of risk an investor would have if he put money into your business. Obviously, this rate would never go below the rate on long-term treasury bonds which is considered a risk-free rate of return.

Line item (4), earnings on goodwill, computes the effect of goodwill. It's what is left over after everything else has been taken from the earnings. This is often referred to as "excess earnings."

Line (5) multiplies the net annual earnings on goodwill by an amount of years. For Marcus E. Hamilton Enterprises, Ltd., that number of years was six. How did we arrive at that number? Much of our analysis was similar in nature to looking at what rate of return an investor would want if he invested in the assets of the company. In closely held businesses the multiple can range from zero to ten. A typical range is two to five times the annual excess earnings capacity or going concern value.

One way of looking at this is to ask, "For how many years would a new owner be willing to give you the excess earnings capacity of the business in order to purchase that earnings capacity from you?" As in the analysis to determine the required earnings on book value (line item (3) above), the first factor is risk. Here the risk is the ability of the business to continue to earn excess amounts above the expected rate of return on the book value. In most businesses that risk is greater than the book value.

In computing the risk multiple with respect to the excess earnings capacity, the analysis must include five factors. We'll discuss each in turn.

*1. The degree to which the excess earnings are transferable to the buyer.* In other words, what do you take with you when you leave the business?

In the case of Marcus's company, the answer was very little. The earnings of the company were based on the inventory–the junked cars–not Marcus's unique abilities. On the other hand, the ability to transfer earnings capacity to a new owner would be much more difficult for a small manufacturing representative's business with one or two employees, little or no inventory, and where all relationships with both customers and the manufacturer's lines were maintained by the owner. That's why, in smaller businesses especially, you can often get more money by finding a co-owner or employee who has the ability to continue the relationships while buying you out.

In later chapters we will discuss creating business value. If you are unable to have in place a strong organization structure that can exist and thrive independently of you, you may be able to look only to the adjusted book value of the business for valuation purposes. Sometimes this can be enough (see the construction company example in Chapter One). However, for businesses that are not capital intensive, excess earnings capacity is the primary component of value. If that's your situation now, you must do everything possible while you are still active in the business to ensure the permanency of that earnings capacity. (That usually means finding, keeping and properly motivating key employees.)

*2. History of profitability.* This is self-evident. I would only add that a stable (and increasing) earnings history, as opposed to a "peaky" earnings history, is more reassuring to the prospective buyer and his advisors.

*3. Market share.* Most closely held businesses will not dominate their market. However, with Marcus E. Hamilton Enterprises, Ltd., that was not the case. Marcus had a lock on the junkyard business for an area of several hundred square miles. He was not only an important source of junk parts, but his business was the first one thought of when it came to disposing of unwanted vehicles.

How dominant in your market is your business? In answering this question, it helps to determine first just what is your market. For example, I have a friend who owns a much smaller junkyard in a major metropolitan area. Yet he, too, is a dominant player in the market. In his case the market is Mustang and Camaro used parts.

The total number of his junk cars is perhaps five percent of Marcus's. But in the Mustang and Camaro used parts market, my friend has a much higher percentage, even in the more populous metro area. This places a premium on the value of this business.

4. *Industry trends.* These can be important if your business is in an industry clearly in decline or is a front-runner in the current hot technology. Otherwise, trends are not terribly relevant.

However, the location of your business could be a factor. For example, while Marcus's original business location was far away from civilization (even as that term is loosely defined in Wyoming), over the last twenty years a town grew up within sight of his junkyard. This has served to increase the value of his business for two reasons: He's closer to his customers, and any would-be competitors would have a hard time getting zoning approval for another junkyard so close to town.

5. *Items unique to the business.* For example, another client has been the printer for a weekly newspaper for more than 15 years. While there is no written contract, the newspaper has become very reliant on my client. A change to another printer would be costly and time-consuming. Thus, a new owner would be assured of a continuing, profitable revenue stream–unless he totally mucked it up. Most businesses, however, do not benefit from long-term contracts. Since 1980 our economy and business practices have become more competitive and fluid, and in a fast-paced, fast-changing business world, long-term contracts and relationships have a lesser role to play.

There may be similar factors in your own business, which should go into this formula determination. I hope the above discussion persuades you to avoid blindly using any "industry standards" in valuing your business. Often we have clients tell us, "Well, my business is worth the gross annual revenues," because that is what they have read or heard from friends in their industries. At best, those "industry standards" provide only useful comparisons to a more proper valuation. At worst, they are misleading and an obstacle that must be overcome in presenting your value to a prospective purchaser.

There is a real value difference between a company grossing $1 million and earning $50,000, and a company in the same industry earning $150,000 in profit on the same revenues.

A final note on Marcus E. Hamilton Enterprises, Ltd. In arriving at the value for his business, we wanted to be reasonable, yet optimistic. We did not ignore negative factors, which would exert downward pressure on the value. Going through the valuation formula well before selling the business enabled us to highlight the important areas and concentrate Marcus's business efforts on areas that would enhance his valuation.

The above example, though lengthy, is elementary. In my experience, it does account for the two primary components of business valuation–the true value of the underlying assets and the excess earnings capacity (going concern value) of the business.

By going through the valuation exercise at the end of this chapter, you will discover the areas of your business that need additional attention in order to maximize value under this formula. You will find this exercise worthwhile, even if you have no immediate plans to sell or transfer your business.

Now you know why valuation is critically important and you've learned **how** valuation methods are commonly used. The next question is this: Do you want to sell your business for as much cash as you can get or do you want to use the lowest defensible value?

## When Less Is More:  Getting The Most Money Using The Lowest Value

The reason for starting with valuation is simple: The typical owner's net worth is largely made up of the value of his closely held business. Somewhere between 65 percent and 85 percent of most owners' net worth consists of their businesses.

And remember, to exit your business in style you must convert this illiquid, unmarketable ownership interest into cash, and lots of it.

That being the case, you will need ordinarily, to sell your *ownership interest* for the **least** (yes, least) amount of money possible.

To see why a low value is instrumental to getting the most money from your business, you must appreciate the huge role played by the IRS. Consider the following two transfer objectives.

If a primary objective is to gift the business to children, valuation is critical, for a major cost of transferring the business will be the gift taxes on the value of the business interest transferred. You need to know **now** what that value is. If you wish to transfer the business to the children by lifetime gift or at death, is a low or a high value desirable?

If a primary objective is to transfer the business to a key employee or employees, or to sell to children, or to sell to a co-owner, ask yourself: "Do these potential buyers have any money? And if not, from where are they going to get it?" Will they not need to earn money from the business, pay income tax on it (tax #1) then pay the balance to you to buy the business–at which time you will pay a second tax on the gain (tax #2)? The higher the business value, the greater the purchase price. The greater the purchase price, the greater the double tax bite.

Working through these questions will lead you to the rather startling conclusion that you will seek the highest possible value for your ownership interest only if you are selling the business to an outside third party; otherwise, *you must make every effort to develop the lowest defensible value for your ownership interest if you wish to receive as much money as possible.* This is why valuation is so critical to the transfer of your business. Remember, if you decide to sell to an outside third party, it will be for cash and you'll want all you can get via a high value. But your children, your employees, your co-owner don't have much of that green stuff. Their source of money, or cash flow, is the same as yours–the business. Therefore, it is vital that the cash earned and distributed by the company, and given to you as you leave, be taxed as little as possible.

It bears repeating that if company earnings are distributed to the purchaser (for example a key employee), it will be taxed to her as compensation–salary or bonus money. She will then pay the after tax money to you (say 65 cents of the original dollar of earnings). You in turn pay a capital gains tax on the 65 cents received (assume little or no basis on your ownership interest, therefore a tax of about 25 percent). The net is less than 50 cents on each dollar earned and paid out by the company.

In other words, all purchasers, other than outside third parties, need to look to the earnings of the company for money to pay to you because they have no money of their own. This results in a *double tax paid on the money received by you* (taxed once as the employee/ purchaser earns it and once when you receive it for your stock). The higher the business value, the higher the tax, the more difficult it is to accomplish a successful transfer . . . the less likely you will leave your business in style.

What is needed is to devise methods to *maximize the income stream to you by minimizing taxation*. Taxes are kept as low as possible by having the money you receive taxed only once. Since **all** the money is produced by the business, *the key is to have you receive the money directly from the business and taxed once to you, have that money be deductible by the business* (which means it cannot be for the purchase of your ownership interest), *and to then sell the ownership interest to the employee/purchaser for a nominal amount* (because that income stream is taxed twice). Chapter Seven explores several techniques you can use to receive money directly from the business after you have left it.

For example, assume you wanted, over time, $1 million for the business. A sale to an outsider for cash will net you $750,000 (25 percent capital gains tax reduces the amount received). To receive the same amount from an employee purchaser (child, co-owner or key employee) would mean that *the business* would need to earn $1,600,000 after you have left the business, which it distributes over time to the key employee. The employee pays taxes of about 40 percent as this sum is received, leaving a total of $1,000,000. This million dollars is paid to you and you pay the same 25 percent capital gains rate as before. The bottom line is that the company needs to earn $1,600,000 for you to net $750,000. Not very appealing, and it makes the sale of the business to anyone other than an outside cash buyer very difficult.

An alternative to this is to value the business as *low as your tax advisor can justify.* Assume, for purposes of illustration, the business could be valued for one dollar. Also assume through a variety of planning techniques (discussed at length in Chapter Seven) that you are able to receive money *directly from the company, on a tax deductible basis* to the company and ordinary income to you. Your tax rate will likely be lower than today . . . so assume an effective rate of 30 percent. For you to receive the same $750,000 after-tax amount, the company needs to earn, then pay to you (and deduct) less than $1,100,000 ($1,100,000 <30% tax> = $750,000 net to you) more than $500,000 less in total business earnings than if the business is sold to you for $1 million. After, or as, you receive this money, you sell the business to the purchaser for one dollar.

Of course, you can not use a business valuation that you can not justify. I'm simply trying to illustrate the need to value the company as low as possible to maximize the net dollars in your pocket. To recap, the key to maximizing cash to you is a two step process: First, value the business as low as your valuation expert deems proper; second, receive the bulk of the cash you need in the form of deductible payments from the business to you. Since all of the money you'll receive when you sell to children, co-owners or key-employees will come from the earnings stream of the business after you've left it, it behooves you and the buyers to have that income stream reduced as little as possible by unnecessary taxes–taxes caused by valuing the business more than is necessary.

### Using Other Advisors to Value Your Business

When the decision is actually made to transfer your business, it's critical that you consult with your accountant, your attorney, and perhaps your financial advisor. Undoubtedly, you will get suggestions regarding valuation techniques to be used for your business. In addition, you and your advisors should determine if it is necessary to hire a business appraiser to formally value your company. Involving a good independent business appraiser early in the process can help to maximize money you'll receive for your company. He can help not only on the current value, but also on ways to enhance it (or reduce it) under specific formulas and valuation techniques.

## Summary

It is important to appreciate the methods of business valuation and the need to place a high or low valuation on your business depending on what type of buyer you have targeted as the new owner. Remember, if you want to sell to a buyer outside of your company, you will want to establish a high value. If you prefer to sell to an "insider" (a key employee, co-owner or shareholder) you will want to establish as low a valuation as possible.

It is also critical to value the business early in the transition process. If you choose to sell to an "insider" and consequently need to establish a low value, you will need time to implement the techniques described in Chapter Seven to get an adequate amount of cash out of the business.

### Appendix 2.1:  Going Concern Value

1. Average Annual Net Earnings           $_____

2. Annual Replacement Salaries           <$_____>

3. Book Value Earnings @ _____%         <$_____>

4. Net Average Annual Excess
   Earnings, etc.
   [ (1) - (2) - (3) = (4)]              $_____

5. (4) x three years                     $_____

6. Add Adjusted Book Value
   (tangible assets)                     + $_____

7. Total Value
   [ (5) + (6) ]                         $_____

# 3

# Avoiding Lawyers and Other Roadblocks to Success

*How to use your advisors to reduce risk, preserve business value, and reach your owner-based objectives.*

If you're like my clients, you view lawyers as the carriers of some deadly disease. Consequently, you call your lawyer only when your business life depends on it.

But just as physicians have learned to control smallpox with measured doses of vaccine, owners of closely held businesses should use lawyers (and other advisors) in controlled amounts to avoid the scourge of litigation and other ills that could otherwise destroy a healthy company.

You will be wise to obtain immunization against the various business litigation viruses which increase your liability. Take the very thing that is the agent of the disease–lawyers–and inject them carefully into your business. Like many vaccinations, this dosage of lawyers should be administered in measured, regular intervals.

The first dosage should be in the form of an initial legal audit, followed by annual fiscal year–end reviews. Interim booster shots may also be necessary from time–to–time to build up your business's resistance in those areas where it may be most vulnerable.

Let's examine more closely just how these injections of your advisors will provide you the protection you need.

## The Legal Audit

Most business people are familiar with the audit performed by their accountants. The purpose of an accounting audit is to verify the accuracy of the financial information appearing on a company's financial statements. A legal audit is similar in that the legal affairs of a business are subjected to an independent rigorous review by a trained professional who reviews the business's existing practices, procedures, and documents to uncover potential legal problems.

The legal audit begins with a review of basic corporate documents: the articles of incorporation, bylaws, minutes of shareholder meetings and board of director meetings, and the stock book showing all past stock transactions. The audit then looks at operating documents: contracts with third parties, loan documents, leases, and a host of agreements regarding employment, trade secrecy, and the transfer of stock, to name a few.

Next, the audit examines *ongoing practices and procedures* for potential liability. These would include hiring and firing practices, insurance coverage, environmental issues, and workers compensation and unemployment compensation issues. Exhibit 3.1 is a partial list from the exhaustive checklists that my firm uses to help make certain that clients possess either signed originals of any document requiring a signature or photocopies of signed documents.

## Exhibit 3.1  Legal Audit Checklist

| | Description | Last Revised | or | Date Reviewed |
|---|---|---|---|---|
| ❏ | Partnership or LLC Agreement | ———— | | ———— |
| ❏ | Corporate documents<br>   1.  Articles of incorporation<br>   2.  Bylaws<br>   3.  Minutes<br>   4.  Wage continuation plan<br>   5.  Medical reimbursement plan<br>   6.  Stock certificates<br>   7.  Subchapter S election<br>   8.  Incentive stock option plan<br>   9.  Non–qualified stock option plan | ———— | | ———— |
| ❏ | Change of registered office/agent | ———— | | ———— |
| ❏ | Employment agreements for owners | ———— | | ———— |
| ❏ | Employment agreements for employees | ———— | | ———— |
| ❏ | Trade secrecy/covenant not to compete agreements | ———— | | ———— |
| ❏ | Buy/sell agreements | ———— | | ———— |
| ❏ | Deferred compensation plan | ———— | | ———— |
| ❏ | Office and facility leases | ———— | | ———— |
| ❏ | Equipment leases | ———— | | ———— |
| ❏ | Authority to do business in other states | ———— | | ———— |
| ❏ | Bonus plans | ———— | | ———— |

| Description | Last Revised | or | Date Reviewed |
|---|---|---|---|
| ❏ Loan agreement with banks, other lenders, and between the company and owners | _____ | | _____ |
| ❏ Guaranty and indemnity agreements | _____ | | _____ |
| ❏ Contracts and other agreements with third parties including invoices | _____ | | _____ |
| ❏ Qualified retirement plans | _____ | | _____ |
|    1. Profit sharing | | | |
|    2. Money purchase | | | |
|    3. 401(k) | | | |
|    4. Defined benefit plan | | | |
|    5. ESOP | | | |
| ❏ Split dollar agreements | _____ | | _____ |
| ❏ Purchase agreements for original acquisition of business | _____ | | _____ |
| ❏ Other | _____ | | _____ |

To continue the medical analogy, a legal audit is like a complete physical examination aimed at discovering problems while they are easily treatable. Most of us, however, are far more attentive to our body's physical signals than we are to the warning symptoms in our businesses. When the legal audit uncovers a problem, remedies can almost always be administered quickly, economically, and completely. If the problem is allowed to fester until a third party–a disgruntled employee, an irate vendor, the IRS–brings it to your attention, the solution is seldom cheap and is usually found only after negotiation and involvement of other parties such as lawyers, accountants, and members of your work force.

Avoid being consumed by the time and money demands of legal problems. Listen to Benjamin Franklin, the consummate businessman, "An ounce of prevention is worth a pound of cure."

Let me emphasize here: This legal audit is a precursor to a more extensive "due diligence review" that will be undertaken whenever a business is sold to a third party. Since this book assumes that you will exit the business, the legal audit and likely more extensive "due diligence review" is inevitable. No one will want to acquire the business if it is rife with litigation exposure, potential environmental claims, unsigned corporate documents, missing stock certificates and the like. Undertake a legal audit **now** by having your legal counsel work through a legal audit checklist with you. If you would like a copy of the comprehensive legal audit checklist that my law firm uses, please complete the Request Form at the back of this book. Save your company hundreds (and very possibly thousands) of dollars by gathering and organizing the documents ahead of time.

### The Fiscal Year–End Review

The second, and most important, linchpin of the business protection program is faithful adherence to the fiscal year–end process. This step is the single most important prevention and planning tool available to the closely held business owner.

The concept is simple. Once a year, about forty–five days before the business's fiscal year–end, your attorney should provide you with an agenda and send copies to your other advisors–your CPA and your financial or insurance advisor. I start with the agenda shown in Exhibit 3.2 and modify it as experience dictates. (I have indicated the Chapters where further information on these topics can be found.)

About twenty days before the fiscal year–end a meeting is then held with you and your advisors. This allows the accountant to review eleven months of operation and to make tentative determinations of projected income tax liability for your company and for you personally.

**Exhibit 3.2.    Fiscal year–end outline** (Indicating Chapter where concept is discussed.)

I.      Review of Business Income Tax Status.

       A. Initial determination of income tax liability. (5)
       B. Existing methods of reducing income tax liability. (5)
       C. Consideration of new methods to reduce income tax liability as appropriate. (5)

II.      Additional Corporate Considerations.

       A. Business value. (2)
       B. Business continuity. (2, 11)
       C. Business expansion/contraction. (2, 3, 4, 6, 11)
       D. Employee considerations including key employee "perks" and incentive plans. (4)
       E. Business contracts, including liability insurance contracts. (3)
       F. Banking considerations. (2)
       G. Exit Planning and strategies. (1, 6, 7, 8, 9, 10)
       H. Miscellaneous. (1, 2, 3, 4, 5, 6)

III.      Individual Planning Considerations.

       A. Current income tax status and methods to reduce income tax liability. (5)
       B. Financial planning considerations. (12)
       C. Estate planning considerations. (2, 10, 11, 12, 13)

IV.      Review of Owner Based Goals.

     The primary purpose of the meeting is communication. You need to know your tax exposure and any income tax and legal developments that have occurred during the year that might affect your operation. Your advisors need to know not only what you have accomplished during the year, but also your future plans. Finally, each advisor must learn what the other advisors have been doing for you and what suggestions they have. This ensures coordination of your legal, tax, and financial planning objectives. The meeting also allows you to obtain input from all of your advisors on specific topics, rather than trying to reach each of them individually for their views–not an effective use of their time or your money.

In short, the fiscal year–end meeting is an important and unique way to use your advisors to elicit and exchange vital information. I can't emphasize enough the importance of this need to communicate, to plan, to prevent problems from arising, and to resolve small problems before they become insurmountable.

## How To Use The Year End Agenda

Let's review the fiscal year–end agenda in some detail. The example included above is one my law firm developed and has refined over several years. I suggest you present a copy of this agenda to your advisors and ask them if they would be willing to meet as a group to engage in the fiscal year–end process. You might even suggest that they not charge you their full fees for the initial meeting, because the meeting may be as helpful to them professionally (as a learning experience) as it is to you. Actually, your advisors should be sufficiently astute to realize that this meeting will likely result in additional work for them as well as foster a more secure relationship with you. They should be happy to attend the meeting at a reduced fee.

### Review of Business Income Status

The planning process starts here. Advisors like to say that taxes shouldn't drive business decisions, but that sound business decisions drive themselves. In fact, a major part of the advisor's job is to minimize your tax consequences at every level.

The first item we like to see is your projected taxable income. We compare it to the projection made at the last fiscal year–end meeting. This gives us a quick idea of how close the business came to meeting its projections. If it fell far short of its projected taxable income, the causes must be examined as we proceed through the agenda.

When we look at income tax liability, we would like to project future tax liability as well as look at the past two years' tax bills. It does little good to move a potential income tax consequence to a future year if it results in a greater tax liability. Similarly, it may do a lot of good to create a large tax loss in the current year if we can carry that loss back to a previous year in which significant taxes were paid.

For an example of this, let's head out to a certain ranch I recall in southeastern Colorado.

### Home on the Thibodeaux Ranch

*The five members of the Thibodeaux family were all in their forties or fifties when they became interested in buying their mother's share of the family ranch–Thibodeaux Ranch, Inc. (TRI). Their father had died about a year and a half earlier, and at the time I met them, the business was a substantial operation.*

*Shortly before the father died–and since then–the mother had been selling off equipment and stored crops and had leased all the land to local farmers and ranchers.*

*Before I began serious planning, I followed my own advice and immediately involved a good CPA firm. We needed to determine the value of TRI so that we could establish a fair purchase price and plan a way for the offspring to buy the ranch from their mother with the least amount of taxes possible. In reviewing the financial information, the accountant quickly discovered that TRI had paid about $250,000 worth of taxes in each of the preceding two years.*

*When the elder Thibodeaux was alive, normal farm operations were usually break–even because he was able to juggle income from* *crop sales and cattle sales from year to year as needed to minimize taxes. Before designing the purchase of Mrs. Thibodeaux's stock, we decided to recapture the $500,000 in taxes paid in the preceding two years.*

*This was accomplished by creating a large tax loss for the current year as well as planning for a large tax loss the next year. Of course, it does no good to create a loss unless the loss itself is useful to the owners. In this case, because the children had been performing substantial services without pay, including selling equipment and crops, managing leases, and overseeing farm operations, we made them paid employees. It was determined that they could be paid relatively high salaries to reflect not only their ongoing services, but also their past, uncompensated contributions.*

*At the same time, we implemented a defined benefit retirement plan that, because of the relatively older ages of the children, allowed us to contribute a significant amount to the plan. The combination of high salaries and large retirement plan contributions created a $250,000 annual tax loss at the corporate level. After two years of large losses, our plan was to convert the regular corporation to an S corporation and proceed with normal farm expenditures. We believed that our plan to attack the large tax liabilities of the past was aggressive but defensible. All of the loss at the corporate level was used to directly benefit the family.*

*The net result was that the government each year wrote a check for repayment of past taxes paid to the company that was used as a large downpayment for Mrs. Thibodeaux's stock! Our clients thought their advisors were brilliant, but I knew that the Thibodeaux family was lucky. Usually, the victims of non–planning have little recourse.*

One of the purposes of ongoing planning is to avoid extreme peaks or valleys in corporate taxable income. If you are able to anticipate large increases through proper tax planning, much can be done to minimize the actual tax cost. These methods include:

- Shifting income taxation from one year to the next.

- Implementing tax reduction devices, such as qualified retirement plans, medical expense reimbursement plans, and the payment of large bonuses.

- Increasing deductible payments to shareholders, such as rents for equipment or buildings that may be owned individually by the business owner and leased to the business.

If these methods are already in place, see if you can increase their use to reduce tax liability. Before reducing corporate taxes, however, you must first determine how much money must remain at the corporate level to fuel future business growth. This is called accumulating capital within the business. The emphasis on minimizing taxes should not replace the clear need to ensure that the business has adequate capital to conduct its business and to grow.

## Additional Corporate Considerations

Up to this point, you've determined your tax consequences and the amount of capital you need to sustain both future growth and existing operations, and you've started the planning process. Now you must review some additional corporate issues.

*Business valuation* is considered for purposes of the buy and sell agreement (as discussed in the following section "Business Continuity") as well was for any other contemplated transfer events such as gifting or sale.

*Business Continuity.*

Foremost among these corporate issues is business continuity. The fiscal year–end process is the time to reexamine your business continuity arrangements. (The business continuity agreement, also called a buy–and–sell agreement, is the subject of Chapter 11.) Are there additional owners or potential owners who should be included as part of the arrangement? Has the business increased in value? Are your arrangements still appropriate? Failure to review the critical components annually will, invariably, cause the buy–sell to depart further and further from reality until if finally favors one party or the other unreasonably. That may not be a problem in most cases, since the parties will most often simply negotiate a more fair agreement at the time of sale. But, if there is acrimony, the party that is the unintended beneficiary of an old buy–sell may attempt to legally enforce the agreement, notwithstanding its unfairness.

If the value of your business has increased, do you need to consider an increase in the funding of a death or disability buy–out? By reviewing business continuity arrangements, you and your advisors have an opportunity to make sure that your business objectives and goals are still consistent with each other. For example, continuity arrangements may require modification if one owner is more anxious to sell his interest, or retire, than the other.

Often the most valuable result of these fiscal year–end meetings is that business owners get the chance to discuss the problems they have with each other, or with the business, in the presence of impartial third parties who can offer suggestions and mediate differences.

A large part of my professional life is spent serving as a sounding board for a dissatisfied owner. Over the years I've found that like most of life's problems, those affecting relations between owners are best resolved at an early stage. Experienced advisors can help you and your partners resolve problems that may threaten your business.

Take, for example, the business buy-in I helped structure for a young key employee. The intention was to have her eventually buy out an older majority shareholder's stock. As a result of the buy-in, the business prospered. In fact, it began growing too quickly for the older shareholder's comfort, and the younger shareholder grew concerned that she would have to pay the older shareholder for the increase in value–an increase due mostly to her efforts.

Little was said between them, however, because they both felt obligated to live up to the terms of their agreement. Instead, in their frustration and discomfort, they grew distant. Eventually, they shared their feelings, separately, to one of the members of their advisory team. Thereafter it was a simple matter to redesign the buy–in to everyone's satisfaction and relief. We came up with a plan to accelerate the buy–in process while still giving the older owner a small piece of the future appreciation.

Even if the idea of transferring your interest is only wishful thinking, it should be brainstormed at the year–end fiscal meeting, because that's where the process starts. For example, thinking about exiting the business will lead to analysis of **when** to leave, **how much** money you'll want, and **who** will be able to continue the business as the new owner. Avoid the roadblocks to your eventual retirement by starting to plan early thus forming the basis of a sound exit plan.

*Business expansion or contraction* is also considered annually in connection with capital needs. If expansion appears likely, you and your advisors should consider banking and capital accumulation needs as well as the purchase of a larger building or the leasing of additional space. On the other hand, if contraction seems likely, your advisors can help you make difficult choices to reduce your overhead. They may suggest layoffs, the sale of some equipment or other assets, a reduction in salaries, or other measures that may be too emotionally painful for you to undertake alone.

During a period of contraction, most businesses dig themselves into a deeper hole, not by cutting expenses too rapidly, but by hanging on too long to the existing operation, primarily because of pride or a deep aversion to laying off loyal employees. Business owners also don't like to admit they are cutting back; the American way is to grow, grow, grow. Yet we've all seen businesses that spend themselves into bankruptcy. One of your most important goals must be to preserve value for the business in difficult times. Your advisory team demonstrates its greatest value when it helps you face hard facts and then helps you translate your decisions into action.

*Employee considerations* are another item for fiscal year–end review. I usually suggest that the business require key employees to sign contracts that restrict competition, protect trade secrets, and fully describe the compensation structure.

When owners balk at this, I describe some of the scenarios that could happen. This tends to change their thinking.

- A top salesman leaves with key accounts in hand.

- A top manager leaves, with former employees, to start her own business.

- An employee who has access to key information about the company leaves, joins a competitor, and uses that information in a manner that hurts the business. (This information might include anything from a business plan to manufacturing secrets; pricing policies, or internally developed business forms, systems, methods, and procedures.)

Don't only learn from your mistakes; learn from the mistakes some of my other clients have made. Keep in mind that employees are your primary means of making money. They are also your primary means of losing money. I approach the subject of employee agreements by asking, "If a particular employee left, what could he or she take that could damage the business?" The employment agreement is designed to prevent the employee from taking that valuable asset.

Sometimes such protection is not possible and the risk must simply be borne. If so, plan to have other employees become involved in the same functions as the key employee. When he or she does leave, the business will be able to continue that key employee's work or function. You can then assure your key accounts that your service to them will continue uninterrupted.

Other, more pleasant employee considerations to discuss at this meeting involve methods of motivating and retaining key employees. I know of few successful businesses, other than the corner hot dog stand, which don't owe much of their success to one or more key employees. Business growth–and value–is necessarily limited unless key employees are provided financial incentives to perform well and to stay long term with the company. This meeting provides a forum for evaluating the need for establishing incentive–based plans or to monitor and adjust existing plans. These plans may be cash-based or equity (ownership) based. They are fundamental to your efforts to find, keep and properly motivate your business's most valuable resource: its key employees.

This idea is so important that it is the subject matter of the next chapter. But for purposes of our fiscal year–end discussion, remember that these plans work best if they fit into the design of the whole business and if they are periodically reviewed by your team at the fiscal year end meeting.

Compensation arrangements for key employees, in particular those whose compensation is not exclusively salary, should be part of your discussion of "employee considerations." Since your advisors represent hundreds of other closely held businesses, use them as a valuable source of information about salary levels, compensation structures, and, in general, what other businesses are doing to motivate and retain their key employees.

Extract as much information from your advisors as you can: that's what you're paying them for. Arrive at the fiscal year–end meeting prepared with your own list of questions. Make this meeting a vehicle to learn as much as you can.

*Business Contracts.* Don't forget to mention any new contracts or forms you are using and a review or audit of your property, casualty, and liability policies is another wise step. This is normally done by a casualty insurance agent who typically does not attend fiscal year-end meetings. However, the agent should supply a written summary of your coverages for review at the meeting, enabling you and your advisors to detect any areas left uncovered by current policies. This can be critical not only to the profitability of your company, but to its very existence.

A case in point is what happened to one of my clients who sells heavy equipment. He had sold an item worth $200,000 and was storing it until delivery in a warehouse. A warehouse fire destroyed the equipment. My client's insurance covered only machinery "in transit"–not machinery in storage–and the warehouse owner's insurance covered only his building fixtures and equipment. My client suffered a $200,000 lick to his bottom line. Don't let this happen to you. Obtain a summary of your insurance coverage and have it reviewed by your advisory team at the year–end meeting.

*Banking considerations* are often a topic at the fiscal year–end meeting. Your advisors normally know which local banks are interested in working with your type of business. Your accountant should know whether your financial condition satisfies the lending requirements of your bank and of its competitors, as well as whether the bank can meet your anticipated borrowing needs.

Frankly, it's darned hard to find a good bank for the closely held business owner. If you have one, keep it, even if you're paying a point more than might be necessary. If you don't have a good banking relationship, finding one should be a goal to be accomplished by the next planning meeting. Again, your advisors can help you locate, evaluate, and select a good bank for your business.

*Exit Planning and Strategy. Of course* your meeting with advisors should discuss the subject matter of this book. The annual advisor meeting is the time to review and revise your exit goals: financial security, departure date, who are your potential buyers or transferees. It is also a time to make sure your are on course to reach your exit goals on time. I suggest you ask the same questions that I asked of you as you began to formulate your Exit Plan in Chapter One:

1.  Do you know your primary planning objectives in leaving the business, such as:
    a.  Departure date?
    b.  Income needed to achieve financial security?
    c.  To whom you want to leave the business?
2.  Do you know how much your business is worth?
3.  Do you know how to increase the value of your ownership interest through enhancing the most valuable asset of the company – the employees?
4.  Do you know the best way to sell your business to a third party which maximizes your cash, minimizes your tax liability and reduces your risk?
5.  Do you know how to transfer your business to family members, co–owners or employees while paying the least possible taxes and enjoying maximum financial security?
6.  Have you implemented all necessary steps to ensure that the business continues if you don't?
7.  Have you provided for your family's security and continuity if you die or become incapacitated?

*Miscellaneous.* When you find miscellaneous other matters to review with your advisors, jot them down; the fiscal year–end meeting is the time to bring them up.

## Individual Planning Considerations

The fiscal year–end meeting is also the right time to consider your personal planning: your individual income tax status, your financial planning, and your estate planning.

*Current Income Tax Status.* Your individual income tax issues must be reviewed in conjunction with the business's tax status. The primary focus should be a balancing act between corporate and personal income taxes: Should the income be left in the company? Or taken out? If taken out, a variety of techniques can then be used to reduce taxation at the individual level. These techniques are discussed in Chapter Five.

The fiscal year–end meeting presents an opportunity to coordinate the planning of your current and future years' income taxes. Unlike businesses, individuals can't go back and recapture their past taxes. Therefore, it's important that you never pay more taxes than necessary.

*Financial Planning Considerations.* Your company's fiscal year–end is also the time to look at your personal financial plan to make sure it is consistent with your business and personal objectives. The financial plan, which is fully discussed in Chapter 12, shows you how to diversify and increase your assets. The meeting gives your financial advisor access to information and ideas from your other advisors that will allow him to keep your plan current and coordinated with your business. He'll have the chance to ask your other advisors questions that will enable him to make the more accurate predictions and informed investment recommendations you'll need to meet your personal planning goals.

A good financial advisor also recognizes the value of a team effort; he'll want to include your lawyer and accountant in that process, especially when you address estate planning considerations.

*Estate Planning Considerations.* Much of a business owner's estate is tied up in the business–directly in the value of the business and indirectly in the income stream that builds up personal wealth and allows for payments of life insurance premiums. As your net worth increases, it may be necessary to make adjustments to your estate plan to reduce estate taxes. An estate plan is designed to attain certain objectives after your death, such as distribution of your assets, transfer of your business interest, education for your children, and income for your spouse and heirs (see Chapter 13).

For many owners this part of the fiscal year–end meeting requires almost no time at all. If their businesses have not increased much in value, their individual net worth remains unchanged and if neither tax law nor their wishes have changed, this part of the meeting may be brief indeed. Nevertheless, reviewing the estate plan in the fiscal year–end meeting provides the chance to reaffirm that the plan is still the best plan for you.

### Review of Owner–Based Goals

Recall the Seneca quote: "When a man does not know which harbor he is heading for, no wind is the right wind." It is at this fiscal year end meeting where the rubber meets the road. Review objectively your long term goals and what was done this year to move forward. What still needs to be done to meet this year's objectives?

I like to adjourn the fiscal year–end meeting at this point and reconvene at a local tavern or restaurant. Take time to wind down from your formal meeting and relax in a comfortable environment. To accomplish that, tell your advisors not bill for this part of the meeting.

Once you get settled in a more relaxing atmosphere, explain what you think about the future of your business as well as your *own future in that business.*

- Begin with a review of your objectives.
- What are your retirement plans? And timing?
- What exit strategy, if any, are you considering?
- Does the business opportunity look strong?
- What is your forecast for business revenues, sales, possible relocation?
- Is the business mature?
- How are the partners getting along?
- Are you pleased with your employees? product mix? the advice and input you're getting from your advisors?

Your advisors, if they've taken seriously the fiscal year–end agenda previously mailed to them, should contribute with their own questions. They should give you the benefit of their recent experiences with their own business clients. As experienced advisors to hundreds of business owners, they can provide valuable input on what other owners are experiencing–key employee compensation, availability of key personnel, bank credit availability, etc. Use their experience distilled from hundreds of their clients to further your business goals.

Sometimes the information I gather at this part of the meeting is off the top of the owner's head but sometimes it is obviously well thought–out. In short, this informal part of the year–end meeting helps me find out where the owner wants to go and allows me (and his other advisors) to help him get there; a process that may take three, five, or ten years. The earlier we can embark on that venture, the more certain its success.

And that, after all, is the purpose of the fiscal year–end planning process–*to ensure the owner's success through planning, communication, and implementation.*

Speaking of implementation, a criticism many clients have of their lawyers is the failure to complete and return work on time. Whether it is an estate plan, a business contract, a buy–and–sell agreement, or a retirement plan, some lawyers seem to be habitual procrastinators. The fiscal year–end process can serve as an effective prod to your "bovine" attorney, or to other advisors for that matter.

With all of your advisors present, you can establish a timetable to execute legal documents, purchase financial planning products, and deliver income tax projections or financial statements. It's one thing for a lawyer to promise a client a document on time; it's quite another to make that promise in front of fellow advisors. Professional peer pressure can work in your favor. If your attorney consistently fails to deliver documents on a timely basis–even under these circumstances–it is time to change law firms.

Another major problem with implementation is making the decision to turn words into actions. Suppose your insurance advisor suggests your company buy additional life insurance for you. Although this idea is simple, its implementation can be delayed because of the need to coordinate and communicate among all of the advisors. To make the premium payment more tax effective, a split-dollar agreement is often used. (Essentially, this is a method of having the company pay the bulk of the premiums in exchange for the right to the cash value.) The accountant may want to do an analysis to ensure that the business can afford the additional premium, and your attorney may have an opinion regarding the overall impact of additional insurance on your estate plan.

If there is no meeting where all of this can be coordinated, the process of fact–finding among your advisors–and between them and you–can be time–consuming and costly. By reserving those decisions for the fiscal year–end meeting, when all your advisors are present, your decision–making will be quick and less expensive.

Developing and implementing your exit strategy requires the close involvement of your advisory team. Each step toward leaving your business in style can be made only with the counsel and assistance of your team of advisors. Review your advisory team now that you see what is expected. Many lawyers draft documents, CPA's crunch numbers, insurance agents sell, financial planners sell products vs. meeting every problem. To get you where you want to go takes education, training and healthy doses of experience–I can say that now that I'm very experienced.

## Assembling your Advisory Team

Where do you look for this help? You turn to your advisors. Because your team of advisors is such an essential element in your business (see also Chapter 12), let's review that concept now–the who, what, why, where, and how of it.

Let's start with the why.

Unless you've spent half your lifetime earning professional degrees, it's not likely you possess all the knowledge needed to achieve the objectives I've identified. Your astuteness and energy notwithstanding, you still require the services of experts whose education, training, and experience will supplement your own background and expand your knowledge. Since your decisions will be based on information, the more quality information you obtain the better your decisions will be.

Whom should you ask to join your team?

The typical entrepreneur needs the help of an accountant (preferably a CPA), a lawyer, a financial planner or business insurance specialist, and, periodically, a specialized business consultant such as a business valuation expert. All should have extensive experience in dealing with closely held businesses as opposed to being generalists in their respective fields.

Specific skills or experience each of your principal advisors should have are listed below in each advisor checklist. (Use these checklists when interviewing prospective advisors.)

### Exhibit 3.3 Checklist for Legal Advisor

Has knowledge or experience in:

1.  Employee incentive plans

    ❑ Non–qualified deferred compensation plans
    ❑ Stock option plans
    ❑ Stock bonus plans
    ❑ Section 83(b) plans

2.  Buy and Sell Agreements which deal with the following transfer events:

    ❑ death and divorce
    ❑ disability buy out
    ❑ retirement of owners
    ❑ involuntary transfers
    ❑ business disputes
    ❑ valuation

3.      ❏ Legal Audit.

4.      ❏ Qualified retirement plans.

5.      Estate Planning.

      ❏ wills and trusts
      ❏ powers of attorney designed for business owners
      ❏ business continuity provisions in estate planning documents

6.      ❏ Tax expertise, negotiating skills and all–around experience in transferring a business to a third party or to co–owners, employees or family.

It is a rare attorney who can do all of this. I wrote the book and I don't profess to do it all–or even most–but *my firm can*–and so should yours.

### Exhibit 3.4 Checklist for Accounting Advisor

1.      ❏ General knowledge as a Certified Public Accountant.

2.      ❏ Tax planner not just a tax preparer. Someone who gives you ideas, makes suggestions and doesn't just respond to what's already happened.

3.      Familiar with:

      ❏ Key employee incentive–based compensation
      ❏ Valuation techniques
      ❏ Employee benefit planning
      ❏ Non–qualified deferred compensation plans

4.      ❏ Financial planning capabilities (or willingness to work jointly with a financial advisor.

5. ❑ Overall willingness to work in the same harness with other advisors (legal and financial/insurance).

6. ❑ Emphasizes tax **planning**. Proactively minimizes income taxes

7. ❑ Can help you choose best entity structure for your business (Subchapter "S," regular corporation, etc.) for ultimate transfer of ownership.

8. ❑ Audit experience.
   (important if you are planning a sale to a third party)

## Exhibit 3.5 Checklist for Insurance/Financial Advisor

1. ❑ General knowledge and experience in the field.

2. ❑ Facilitator, not just provider of product. Can coordinate activities among advisors and you which saves you significant professional fees.

3. ❑ Can provide basic business valuation via software.

4. ❑ Understands fundamental estate and business continuity planning for business owners.

5. ❑ Ability to sell a variety of products.

6. ❑ Knowledge of qualified benefit plans including retirement plans and employee benefit plans.

7. ❑ Experience in use of non–qualified deferred compensation plans for key employees.

An expanded discussion of the role of a financial advisor and selection ideas begins on page 254 of Chapter 12.

Obviously, few, if any, professionals will be sufficiently experienced in all of these areas. And that's not necessary. What is necessary is a broad understanding of these specialized practice areas and the ability and **willingness** of your advisor to obtain the needed skill from within his or her firm or, if necessary, to find *for you* the specialist in her profession to help you with the particular task at hand. Also, not enough can be said for experience in these areas, it counts for far more than "book learning." Of course, it is easy for me to say this now that I've practiced law for almost 25 years. All the while, your advisors, individually and as a group, must keep their fingers on the pulse to ensure the planning process moves forward.

*What will they do for you?*

With your active input, they can help you gain ownership perspective, identify your ownership objectives, and show you how to go about achieving those objectives through ownership planning. As impartial observers of your business, they can provide the objectivity you need in a variety of situations. Perhaps most importantly, once your exit strategy is devised, they will stay with you to see that it is continuously implemented and finally accomplished.

*Where do you find your advisors?*

All reputable professionals are members in good standing in their professional organizations. You can obtain the names of lawyers and accountants from their respective associations and societies in your state. But this, frankly, won't get you very far, because there is no specialty recognized by the Bar Associations or CPA Societies for anything remotely close to "Business Transition Planning." The best course is to seek out names from existing advisors. It is likely you already have one or more trusted advisors who now represent the business. Ask them to help you fill out the advisory team. Just be sure to use the Checklists in this chapter to be sure that they have the requisite experience.

In addition, ask your fellow business owners to suggest names. Their referrals can be the best, because your colleagues may have developed long–term relationships with other professionals. Just be certain those professionals are performing the type of planning work we're talking about here. Consider interviewing one or more in each discipline before making your selection. Although, depending on the size of your community, you may not have a lot of choices.

### *How do you make this team work?*

Once you've identified the team members, bring them together for a team meeting. Let them get to know each other. Observe them as they interact; it's important that the chemistry be good. What you're looking for are team players who listen to you and to each other so that they will translate your wishes into action. Now you know **what** to do: Develop a business Exit Plan with the help of key advisors centered on owner based goals. How you reach those goals is the subject matter of the rest of this book.

### Summary

Most litigation between business owners and their employees, customers, vendors, and co–owners results not from fraud or deception by one side, but from failure to communicate, to understand and to think through all of the possibilities.

An important reason to conduct a legal audit is to review how you document your business relationships. When your lawyer makes a suggestion to improve your documentation, think hard about implementing it. Don't wait until you've suffered losses that could have been prevented.  The fiscal year–end meeting continues the communication process–communication between co–owners and their advisors that serves to prevent problems.

Finally, use the Advisor Checklists to help select a team of advisors experienced in business transition planning.

# 4

# How to Motivate and Keep Key Employees Through Ownership

*Creating value in your business through key employees*

The one indispensable component of a valuable business is its top employees. Think about it: your key employees are even more important than you are for purposes of *creating value* for your ownership interest. The more valuable *you* are to the business, the *less value* you will receive when you leave it because you leave behind a less valuable business. What you need to do is leave behind key employees who add significant value to the business.

So when you ask yourself, "What is the most effective way to create and build value in my business?" the correct answer is: "Finding, keeping, and motivating key employees." There are several important reasons:

1. Properly motivated by a profit-based incentive plan, key employees do increase the value of your business.
2. Key employees often become potential owners when you decide to retire or move on to another venture.

3.  If you decide to sell to a third party, the continued existence
    of a stable, motivated management team will increase the
    purchase price.

What are you doing to motivate your key employees so that
they will want to remain with your company? Chances are, your
reward system for key employees is nothing more than a salary and a
bonus that you, and you alone, determine at the end of each year. As
we will see, this is only one of many possible reward systems, and it
is usually the least beneficial to the Company.

This Chapter explores a variety of incentive packages designed
to help your key employees reach their financial and psychic goals–
if they stay with you. As your key employees attain their goals, the
particular design of these incentive packages will help you to achieve
your ownership goal of building business value (and eventually
converting that value into money).

## The Key Employee

Before we discuss specific measures, we need to distinguish
between the majority of your employees and those we've termed key
employees.

Most of your employees are attracted and motivated by the
usual items–a pleasant work environment, a stimulating job, good
wages and benefits, and job security. The really key people want
more. They think and act more like you. They are eager to be given
responsibilities and challenges. Like you, they want to see the business
grow and prosper, and they want to grow and prosper along with it.
They take pride in being identified with, and contributing to, a
successful business. In short, they act like owners. Unless your
company has several hundred employees, it is unlikely you will have
more than two or three key employees. Their continued presence in
the business is necessary if the business is to thrive.

Identifying these unique employees and nurturing their desires
is like nurturing your own. That's why it is important to distinguish

key employees from employees in key positions.  If your employees in key positions don't respond favorably to the incentive plans described in this chapter, I question whether they are truly key employees.

### The Purpose of Incentive Packages

Good business owners are interested in more than simply motivating their key employees; the owner also wants to keep those key employees forever.  The advantages of motivating and retaining key employees are many.  Initially, there is the obvious one of making the business more profitable.  This is where most business owners stop thinking; this is where you must begin.  A stable, motivated management team is an asset that potential purchasers will pay a lot of money for.  Further, this same key employee, or group of key employees, is also the most likely candidate to purchase your business when you reach retirement age, or your second childhood, and you decide to try something else.

Motivating and keeping your key employees is absolutely necessary if you are to achieve your exit objectives of financial independence, of transferring the business to the right person at the right time and, as we will see, of having the business continue if you don't.  In short, it is no exaggeration to say that the future of your business is in large measure tied into how securely the key employees are tied to your business.

There are several aspects of providing incentives for retaining and motivating key employees.  At the outset one overriding principle must be mentioned.  As we say out here in Colorado, "Don't bet the ranch on the best-looking horse."

True, all business owners make mistakes, especially concerning personnel.  And reading this book won't prevent you from doing so, any more than writing it will ensure that I never again make a mistake in hiring or promoting my own employees.  But if handled properly, personnel mistakes should be no more than temporary setbacks to the business.  However, if you have promised or given an employee stock or some other nonforfeitable right and you lack the means to retrieve that stock, you have made a costly mistake–one that may permanently affect the future course of your business.

Contrary to the stereotype of a business owner as miserly and condescending, almost all successful owners are, in fact, characterized by a spirit of generosity and a desire to be liked by their employees. Your business is a major part of your life, and you want to feel good when you interact with your fellow workers. Thus, a fundamental element in key employee arrangements is *protecting you from your own generosity*, especially when it is misplaced.

Simply installing a key employee incentive plan will not ensure success in motivating and retaining your key employees. Managerial and leadership talent must also be present. Likewise, having the talent is insufficient without a carefully planned, documented, and implemented incentive program that is specific to the needs of your business.

The elements of successful incentive programs are:

1.  The plan *provides financially attractive awards to key employees.* As a rule-of-thumb, the plan should create a potential bonus of at least 10 percent of the key employee's annual compensation. Anything less than this will not be sufficiently attractive to motivate the key employee to modify his or her performance to make the company more valuable.

2.  The plan is *specific*; that is, there are determinable performance standards, such as the company reaching a certain net income or revenue level.

3.  The plan is structured to *increase the company's value* such that, as the key employee reaches measurable objective standards, the net income of the company increases.

4.  The incentive reward is *vested*–payment is linked to tenure thus encouraging the employee to remain on the job in order to receive the reward. Sometimes called "golden

handcuffs," the vested reward may be in the form of an ownership interest or compensation that is deferred until a specific future event.

5. Even good plans fail when there is ineffective communication. To be successful, any incentive arrangement you offer must be thoroughly understood by your key employee; the plan *must be in writing* and, if complicated, must contain a written summary that is easy to read. To ensure that a plan is understood, conduct a face-to-face meeting with your key employee so that you or your advisors can explain it and answer questions.

### Stock or Cash-Based Bonus?

Although there are many ways to provide incentives, most owners offer either stock or a cash-based bonus. (If your form of business is a limited liability company or partnership, substitute the term "ownership interest" or "partnership interest" for "stock.") Both methods are strong stimulants for key employees and can be used effectively to motivate them to perform well and remain on the job in order to achieve their personal goals of job security, job satisfaction, and a pot of gold at the end of the rainbow.

Before learning how and why you should issue stock to key employees, know also why you should not: All too often, issuing stock to employees makes litigation lawyers wealthy. And this author–also a lawyer–doesn't like litigation lawyers messing with his clients! But that's beside the point. The main issue is this: Strange things can happen when you decide to give stock to that invaluable key employee.

Take the case of Centennial Contractors, Inc.

*Not long ago I met with two talented, hardworking owners of a contracting business. Starting from scratch, they had built the business to a book value of more than one-half million dollars. Each of the partners owned 45 percent of the company, and they regarded each other as being equally valuable to the organization. The problem was that they had a third owner.*

*Shortly after founding the company, they had given an employee, Jim Jakeaway, a ten percent share of the company because they felt he was one of the best estimators in the industry. Indeed, he proved to be a tremendous estimator. Unfortunately, as the business grew, a problem surfaced: No one was willing to work under him. His personality was so abrasive that he was incapable of managing what became the estimating department. He also refused to work under anyone else. The only alternative was to let him go.*

*When the majority owners told him he was being discharged, Jim reminded them that he owned ten percent of the company. "What are you going to do about that?" he asked. The other owners belatedly realized that there was no buy-back agreement to require Jakeaway to resell his stock upon termination. Since he paid nothing for the stock, he had little incentive to sell it. Besides, his ten percent ownership represented a controlling vote should the two primary owners ever disagree. This "control" aspect was far more important than the ten percent equity interest. He had the majority owners over a barrel, and he knew it.*

*After the meeting, Jakeaway went to his lawyer and learned that, as a minority shareholder, he was entitled to attend all shareholder meetings and to review the company books and records–including the financial data of the company–at any reasonable time. By nature Jakeaway was prickly. He felt he had been wronged by the other owners, who did not fully appreciate his qualities. He felt humiliated at being fired when he considered himself an equal owner with the other owners. In short, he wanted his pound of flesh–and he got it. Eventually, the two majority owners settled for a cash payment of $100,000–more than half of the company's taxable income for that year.*

This example illustrates several typical problems encountered when ownership is haphazardly awarded to key employees.

1.  The majority owners offered stock ownership to someone to whom they probably did not have to offer ownership. A simple cash bonus plan based upon the company's

profitability probably would have been a sufficient incentive.

2.  The owners made no provision to buy back the stock in the event things turned sour.
3.  There was no mechanism for fixing the value of the stock in the event of a repurchase.
4.  The owners were totally ignorant of the substantial rights that a minority shareholder has in a corporation.
5.  They made a mistake when they thought Jakeaway was a long-term key employee. When the business was grossing $500,000, he was important; when the revenues grew to $5 million, however, he was no longer critical to its success. Indeed, he had become a hindrance.

The majority owners had good intentions when they offered Jakeaway a small ownership interest in the company. But their plan backfired. Instead of benefiting from the capable services of an outstanding estimator for many years, they had to fire him. In the process they learned a lot about "rights" and "obligations"–the rights of minority shareholders, the obligations that majority shareholders have toward a minority owner, and the rights of disclosure enjoyed by all shareholders.

Think about this: When you relinquish any ownership in your business–even one share out of a million–you unwittingly give the new shareholder substantial legal rights. The changes in the company's operations can be the difference between benevolent despotism and democracy. Even an inconsequential minority shareholder has certain statutory rights such as access to company books and records, the right to be informed about the financial condition of the company (including your salary and "perks") and often a right to be consulted and given the opportunity to vote on major decisions of the company.

Further, majority shareholders have a fiduciary duty to deal fairly with minority shareholders, and as directors they have a duty of due care and loyalty to the company which can be used by minority shareholders to attack any self-serving actions, real or apparent. For example, a majority owner may think he has the right to drive a company car–and selects a Mercedes-Benz. However, a minority owner could allege the majority owner was disregarding his duty of exercising due care for the welfare of the company–that a Ford Escort would be a more appropriate vehicle!

Thus, issuance of stock–even a small amount–gives the shareholder a right that is far greater than merely sharing in the growth of the company. With forethought the problems associated with these rights can be limited or even eliminated.

Two other interesting phenomena–one intended, the other unintended–can occur when stock is given to a key employee.

First, the image that an employee has of her role in the company can suddenly change. Now she is an owner and concludes that her status relative to her co-workers has been raised. She becomes more loyal, more motivated, more eager to see the profits of the company increase in order to expand the value of her stock. That's exactly what you hoped would happen.

At the same time, however, that employee's colleagues may become jealous, apprehensive, or resentful. Until now they had seen themselves as her equals. Suddenly she has acquired new status. Soon they are demanding ownership in the company as well. Failing to get it, they may quit their jobs or become so disruptive they must be fired. In attempting to reward a key employee, you have inadvertently antagonized other competent and potentially key employees.

The moral? Don't shoot yourself in the foot. Consider the ripple effect on those not included in the incentive program before your magnanimity threatens your company's success.

Does the Jakeaway example mean that owners should never offer stock in their companies to key employees? I have to answer with my favorite lawyerlike response: "It depends." Circumstances will determine whether this is the right incentive for the situation.

The reasons for transferring stock to key employees are:

- It ties the key personnel to the company by making them part of the company.
- The employees pay for ownership, thus investing, quite literally, themselves into the company;
- Requiring employees to pay for the stock demonstrates their dedication and commitment to the company.
- It provides strong incentive for increasing the value of the company and, therefore, increasing the key employee's benefit.

The best time to award stock to a valued key employee is when all four of the following conditions are present:

1. You have identified a key employee or group of employees who have been with your company at least two years.
2. The key employee or employees would be more motivated by receiving stock than cash.
3. You are prepared to award the employee or employees a *meaningful* amount of stock.
4. You are willing to bring the employee into the company's confidence and provide the employee with access to *all* information regarding the company (including your total compensation!) and allow the employee to participate in major decisions concerning the company.

Having listed these conditions, I now offer some words of caution.

Suppose you decide to offer stock because you have insufficient cash flow to offer money as a reward? It's seldom a good idea to give stock to an employee who prefers cash; he'll only want to convert the stock to cash anyway, perhaps by quitting. Moreover, as we shall see, there are ways to provide for deferred cash incentives that are more attractive to such employees than stock.

In the third condition above, I use the word "meaningful" advisedly. Nothing is worse than offering an incentive award the recipient regards as inadequate. If you are unable or unwilling to make a substantial commitment of stock ownership to a key employee, make certain the lesser amount will be perfectly acceptable before you make the offer; otherwise, consider cash or deferred compensation as an alternative compensation package.

One word of caution, however, when deciding on the amount of stock to award a key employee. As mentioned earlier, minority shareholders (like majority shareholders) have the right to vote on major decisions affecting the company. Awarding stock to a key employee without first fully understanding the voting percentage requirements placed upon corporations by law, or by the company's articles or bylaws, owners may unwittingly tie their hands regarding decision-making for the corporation. Such decisions may include the future sale of the corporation.

Unquestionably, providing the opportunity for stock ownership is one of the most powerful motivating–and retaining– factor a closely held business can offer to a top employee. For that reason it can often backfire for the majority owners if the employee's expectations are frustrated, and it can serve as a powerful disincentive to your key employee if not planned carefully.

Let's look now at a case of misplaced generosity.

*I recall the time I met with Nels Olinger, the owner of an engine rebuilding business he had started twenty years earlier. Nels wanted to begin the transfer of stock to his son, who had already taken over the operations. In the ensuing conversation, I learned that soon after he formed his company Nels had given ten percent of the stock to his secretary, Anna. And he had made no provision to repurchase the stock when she left the company.*

*Two years after receiving the stock, Anna quit. When we tracked her down 18 years later, she was able to produce her stock certificate. After considerable negotiation she agreed to sell her stock back to the company at ten percent of the current book value of the company. That came to $30,000. Had she been less friendly, the damage could have been far greater. Still, it wasn't easy for Nels to pay $30,000 to an employee who hadn't worked for him in 18 years.*

*He estimated that $30,000 probably equaled her earnings during her entire term of employment with the company. Moreover, it reduced Nels's retirement fund by that amount because there was that much less money available from the company to pay him for his stock.*

*In retrospect it was a careless transfer of stock to a good employee, but certainly not a key employee; Anna could not substantially increase the overall profitability or worth of the business. In addition, Nels's generous gesture was made without any consideration of what it would cost him to reacquire the stock after it appreciated in value. And, finally, it even failed as an incentive to motivate and keep Anna as an employee.*

So far I've bombarded you with tales of unsuccessful stock incentive plans. So many plans fail, I believe, for one or more of the following reasons:

- The plan is not directed toward any of the proper owner-based planning objectives, such as increasing the value of the owner's stock, transfer of ownership to another for maximum profit and minimum tax, or providing for the owner's departure via personal financial and estate planning. Transferring stock to a key employee must further owner-based objectives if it is to be ultimately successful.
- Stock is given to the wrong person, often someone who joined the company in its early years but whose importance to the company diminishes as it grows.
- The stock plan is incomplete. It contains deficiencies. For example, if no method is provided by which the receiving employee can obtain additional stock (or, at a minimum, receive periodic notices of changes in the stock's value), the employee will eventually come to view the stock as a reward for past performance, rather than as an incentive for future performance.

- Communication is poor. The key employee never really understands the purpose, terms, and conditions of the plan. As a result, the plan not only fails as an incentive; it actually becomes a disincentive because owner and employee do not have identical expectations.
- From the outset, the majority owner does not fully understand the legal and practical implications in awarding stock to an employee.
- A "damage control instrument" is missing. Even the best-laid plans can go wrong and your key employee may leave for any reason. At that time you need a buy-back agreement that obligates the employee to sell his stock back to you at a predetermined price and upon predetermined terms.

Careful planning can–and does–produce successful results when stock incentives are employed correctly. Take the case of Lindsay Mining, International (LMI).

*LMI was an international mining company based in Australia. It had established a United States subsidiary in Colorado with offices in several other states. To attract and keep the best talent in the industry, it had to offer more than high salaries. LMI soon discovered it needed to offer ownership, financial incentives, and some form of "golden handcuffs."*

*Over the years, LMI provided bonuses of stock in the U.S. subsidiary to its American managers, a small group ranging from three to six individuals. The company also provided a cash bonus plan based on the annual profits of the U.S. subsidiary. The stock and cash bonuses were rewards for that year's performance.*

*Because of the company's financial success and the valuation formula for its stock, the American managers enjoyed current cash bonuses as well as substantial growth in the value of their ownership interests. Moreover, LMI had a written plan that required the company to issue additional shares of stock to the key managers if certain increases in the value of the American subsidiary were attained. These "performance standards" were realistic, achievable through strong effort, and determinable.*

*By their actions the American managers were able to increase their personal wealth while simultaneously increasing the overall wealth of the business enterprise. Everyone benefited.*

*This plan worked because it suffered none of the weaknesses described earlier. Later, one key employee of LMI left the business upon the request of the other key managers. His stock was repurchased according to a fixed formula with a fixed payout. His employment agreement also provided for a fixed severance payment amount.*

*By having everything in black and white, both sides knew the exact cost of that person's departure. The damage control instrument worked, and at this printing the business was stronger than ever.*

## How to Transfer Stock to Key Employees

Once you've determined that stock is an appropriate incentive package for that favored employee or employees, how do you go about awarding it? There are two principal ways, each with its variations and peculiar tax and ownership consequences. Let's review each method.

### Issuing Stock

Stock can be issued to an employee either through a "non-qualified stock bonus" or by allowing him to purchase the stock at either its fair market value or at a discounted price.

With the **non-qualified stock bonus** the employee receives, at no cost, stock from the company. The fair market value of the stock is determined and the value of that stock is taxable to the employee as ordinary income in the year he receives it. The company receives an income tax deduction for the value of the stock bonused to the employee. Thus, if you decide to have the company issue 100 shares to a key employee, and each share of stock is worth $500, the employee's income increases by $50,000 and the corporation deducts $50,000.

The primary economic benefits to the key employee are that the employee acquires stock worth $50,000 at no cost, and the employee receives future growth in the value of the stock.

A stock bonus can and should be part of a formal stock bonus plan. The plan fixes how much stock the employee is to be issued on an annual basis–for example, the employee could be awarded $5,000 worth of stock over a period of five years. In this plan, at the end of five years, the employee would have received $25,000 worth of stock.

Another alternative is to grant the employee the full $25,000 worth of stock in the first year of the plan and tie the stock to a five year vesting schedule. This type of stock bonus plan is called a **"restricted" stock bonus plan**. When stock is awarded to an employee under a restricted stock bonus plan, the employee receives all the economic benefits of owning the full amount of stock up front, subject only to the vesting requirements. In addition, the employee has the option to elect to include the full value of the stock awarded to him in his income, as compensation, in the first year he receives the stock, and thus pay tax on only that amount. This may have the added benefit of reducing the tax burden to the employee because the employee will not be required to pay tax on the appreciated amount of the stock from year one to year five, as may be the case when stock is awarded over a period of time. For example, in a straightforward stock bonus plan, if the per share stock price doubles from year one to year five, the key employee would pay tax on twice as much of a bonus in the fifth year while receiving the same number of shares.

All stock plans must provide a formula for valuing and repurchasing the stock. Then, if the employee later leaves, the stock is repurchased by the employer. If the stock value increased while held by the employee, he realizes its increased value upon the sale of the stock back to the corporation.

Finally, performance incentives and a "golden handcuff" feature should be built into the plan so that stock is given only upon the attainment of defined performance goals, such as certain profit levels, revenue increases, or some other measurable fiscal event. Periodic (usually annual) awards of stock can create this "golden handcuff" feature because your key employee must stay for many years to receive all of the ownership you make available to him.

There must also be a written agreement requiring the repurchase of the stock upon the employee's termination of employment for any reason. This is the "damage control instrument" and will obligate the employee to sell his stock back using an agreed-upon valuation formula.

Purchasing the stock with a cash bonus is another way a key employee can acquire stock from the corporation or from other key employees, including you. If the stock is purchased at less than fair market value, the employee will have taxable income on the difference between the fair market value of the stock and the price actually paid, and the company will have an offsetting deduction.

This concept is similar to the stock bonus plan, except that it often gives the key employee an option to select cash or stock. For example, each year a key employee may be given two percent of the net profits payable in cash or by stock of equivalent value. Again, the value of whatever the employee receives is taxable income to him and is an offsetting deduction for the company.

This method gives the employee a bit more flexibility than the standard stock bonus; if he needs cash in a particular year, it is available to him instead of stock. And because some employees, even key employees, will often have such a need for cash, offering the option of a cash bonus for superior performance is of overriding importance.

## Stock Options

Stock options can be separated into two basic types–qualified and non-qualified. The former is known as an incentive stock option (ISO), and like qualified retirement plans, it is a creature of the Tax Code. With both types the key employee is given the right to purchase stock at a given price. With the ISO, the price must be no less than the fair market value at the date the option is first granted. The option, which is granted for a specific time period not to exceed ten years and for no more than $100,000 worth of stock per year, is exercised when the employee pays money and receives stock in return.

The primary tax difference between the two types of stock options are the tax consequences, both to the company and to the employee. Typically, under a non-qualified stock option granted in a closely-held company, the difference between the amount paid by the employee when the option is exercised and the then-current fair market value of the stock is taxable as ordinary income to the employee and is deducted by the corporation. When an employee sells his stock he will recognize capital gain on the amount of appreciation of value from the date of exercise.

With an ISO there are ordinarily no tax consequences to either the employee or the corporation when the option is granted or exercised by the employee. Instead, if certain holding periods are observed, *all tax is deferred until the stock is sold* and then only upon the sale of stock does your key employee recognize capital gain on the difference between the sale price and price paid when the option was exercised. With an ISO, the employee is never taxed at his ordinary income tax rates if all of the requirements are met. Given today's difference between capital gains tax rates and the higher marginal income tax rates of individuals, as well as the timing difference on when taxes must first be paid, an ISO may be the more attractive plan to your key people.

As is the case whenever a corporation buys its own stock, there is no tax deduction to the company.

Consider the case of Ken Brown to observe how a typical incentive stock option plan works.

## A Case Study of a Typical Incentive Stock Option

*Let's suppose that the Acme Corporation offers Ken Brown, a key employee, an option to buy 100 shares of stock for $500 per* *share. The employee is not allowed to exercise the option unless Acme's cumulative profits exceed $500,000. The previous year's profits were $250,000. Once the company reaches $500,000, Brown has three years to exercise part or all of the option. The benchmark is reached two years later, and Brown is eligible to exercise the option a year later. However, he decides to wait until the last year of the option period because it does him no good to exercise his option before he needs to. By holding the option, he has been able to see the value of the shares of stock increase from $500 per share, under the formula originally used, to over $1,200 per share five years later.*

*If Brown leaves Acme at any time before he is entitled to exercise the stock option, he forfeits the option. If he leaves after he is entitled to buy the stock, but before he has actually done so, the plan provides that he is entitled to the "gain" on the stock–even though he did not actually purchase it. If he leaves after he has purchased the stock, the stock is automatically repurchased by the corporation.*

An incentive stock option plan can also be tied into a cash bonus plan in which the corporation gives the employee a bonus equal to the purchase price for the stock when the option is exercised. It works like this:

Suppose the total cost of Brown's option is $50,000. The company pays Brown a bonus of $50,000, for which it gets a tax deduction. Brown adds the $50,000 to his taxable income. Now Brown returns the $50,000 to his company in exchange for the stock. The company pays no tax on the sale of its stock. At this point the corporation has received an income tax deduction of $50,000, yet it is out no cash because it has received the $50,000 back tax-free for the sale of its stock. Brown gets the stock and is out only the tax cost of the bonus. From the employee's standpoint, this is a small cost indeed when the fair market value of the stock has increased substantially since the date of the offer.

As with the stock bonus plan, any stock option plan, whether qualified or non-qualified, should include a buy-back agreement (i.e., the "damage control instrument") that obligates the employee to sell his stock back to the company on the termination of his employment for a set price. Like any other redemption of stock, the company will repurchase the stock with after-tax dollars and will not receive a deduction for the payment of the employee's stock.

In sum, the stock option offers more flexibility than does the stock bonus, and thus more planning opportunity for the owner and key employee. *Stock options provide the added benefit of giving the key employee growth opportunities from the beginning without the need to pay money or even incur a current tax cost.* Further, until the option is exercised, he does not participate as a shareholder and has no shareholder rights.

Keep in mind that stock carries with it several characteristics. One, it reflects the **equity**–the value–of the company. As the company grows in value, the value of the stock grows proportionately. Two, stock ownership can mean **voting**–controlling the company. This latter factor can be eliminated by issuing nonvoting stock. Three, stock ownership means having general **shareholder rights**–the privilege of examining books and records and attending meetings. Fourth, (primarily due to the previous three factors) the key **employee's perception and sense of value** (and those of her fellow workers) of her role in the company will change–for good or ill.

## How to Motivate and Retain Key Employees Without Giving Up Stock Ownership

There are, of course, other ways to provide key employees with attractive incentives that don't involve the risk associated with stock ownership. These methods can even give rights to appreciation in stock without actually offering stock. At least 80 percent of the key employee incentive plans I prepare are cash-based rather than ownership-based.

There are four primary non-stock incentive plans: (1) the cash bonus plan, (2) the non-qualified deferred compensation plan; (3) the stock appreciation (SAR) or "Phantom Stock" Plan; and (4) a blended plan combining current cash bonuses with deferred benefits.

## The Cash Bonus Plan

With the cash bonus plan, the business owner simply promises to pay an amount of money, perhaps a flat amount or a percentage of the company's annual profits, if the key employee attains some measurable goal. The goal might be an increase in revenues or profitability within his department, or an overall increase in the company's profitability. To maximize the benefits of a cash bonus plan, the plan should be written, communicated in advance and, ideally, paid at least quarterly so that the reward paid is near in time to the beneficial performance.

The advantages of this plan are that it is easily understood, cash is always welcome and appreciated, and the bonus is generally awarded shortly after the goal is achieved. The only disadvantages to the owner are that it requires an actual outlay of cash and that it presents no "strings"–that is, the reward is given outright, rather than being paid at some future date and thereby tying your top employees to your company.

## The Non-qualified Deferred Compensation Plan

The non-qualified deferred compensation plan, if properly designed, *is the single best method of motivating and retaining your key employees.* For purposes of my discussion on non-qualified deferred compensation, I am focusing on **incentive-based** non-qualified deferred compensation. In other words, non-qualified deferred compensation plans that are designed to provide financial reward for key employees when predefined performance standards are met.

Remember, a properly designed plan must:

- Offer substantial and attractive financial benefits.
- Have specific methods of attaining financial reward for key employees.
- Increase the value of the company as the key employee attains his financial rewards.

- Lock your key employee to the company with "golden handcuffs" (vesting of benefits).
- Have meaningful and realistic objectives.
- Be communicated effectively.

Well, that doesn't exactly sound like a simple method of keeping and motivating your key people but, properly designed, it is in fact just that. What is non-qualified deferred compensation? How is it structured and designed?

Non-qualified deferred compensation is a promise to pay benefits in the future based on current or past services of a key or select group of key employees. As "non-qualified" plans, if the legal requirements are met, these plans don't have to meet the formal funding, reporting, discrimination and employee coverage requirements of "qualified" plans governed by the Employee Retirement Income Security Act ("ERISA"). With the exception of withholding for FICA taxes, in certain situations, benefits awarded to an employee under a non-qualified deferred compensation plan are not taxable until the date when such benefits are actually paid to the employee. The tax treatment of deferred compensation is reviewed in more detail in Chapter Five.

Non-qualified deferred compensation plans will typically include the following:

*Benefit Formula.* There are several types of benefit formulas, such as a defined benefit formula in which the company agrees to pay a definite amount at some point in the future, (for example, $25,000 per year for 15 years beginning at retirement) or a defined contribution approach in which the company promises to credit a specified amount to a bookkeeping account on a regular basis (for example, ten percent of the employee's annual compensation).

The defined benefit formula should rarely or never be used in closely held businesses because it creates an obligation on the company that it may not be able to fund if the company does not perform well. The defined contribution formula is seldom used because it is not tied to the performance of the company, and it does not provide an incentive for the key employee to do more.

A third approach, especially useful for motivating and retaining key employees, is the award of benefits based on an *incentive compensation formula*. Here, the business promises to award to the key employee an amount determined by an incentive formula. These awarded benefits are credited to a special ledger account on the company's books and are paid to the employee at a future date–usually retirement age or a stated period of time (usually 15-20 years hence). The amount credited to the account is based on attaining company performance standards. If the performance standards are selected carefully, *the business's liability to fund the plan exists only when the company is profitable.*

Use of an incentive compensation formula is a key to the effective use of nonqualified deferred compensation planning. It serves as a means of motivating the key employee to increase the profitability of your company. There are many different ways a compensation formula may be designed. You will see an example of an incentive formula below, and another example of an incentive formula when you review the Tom Wells case study described in the last part of this chapter. The essence of an incentive compensation formula, however, is to tie the award of benefits to the performance of the company and of the employee. Instead of a specified percentage of an employee's compensation, the awarded amounts should be derived from specific performance standards. The awarded amounts should be credited to a bookkeeping account on a regular basis.

One example of an incentive formula is to credit the employee's account each year with an amount equal to twenty percent of the company's net income in excess of $100,000. The only way the employee is awarded benefits is if the company makes money. The employee is then economically motivated to make the company as profitable as possible because he is awarded a **substantial** part of the company's income–20 percent of everything above $100,000. By tying the award to an objective and measurable performance standard, the employee knows **specifically** what has to happen to earn his benefit and, because he is a key employee he can influence or affect the company's operations to accomplish it.

In striving to reach his compensation objectives, the key employee contributes to making the company become more profitable. Because most valuation formulas rely on a capitalization (or multiple) of earnings as the primary means of determining business value, and, as was seen in Chapter Two, the greater the net profits the greater, *by some multiple,* is the value of the company.

***Vesting.*** Vesting is the proverbial "golden handcuff" that provides motivation for employees to stay with the company in order to become entitled to all of the benefits that have accrued to them under the benefit formula. Unlike qualified retirement plans, there is no limit on the length of any vesting schedule. If a plan has no vesting requirement, then your key employee has the right to 100 percent of whatever benefits he has accumulated whenever he quits.

"One-time vesting" is a simple schedule that, after a specified number of years of continuous employment, vests all rights to the deferred compensation in the employee. A key employee, for example, may be vested at the rate of ten percent per year in his deferred compensation account balance. After ten years of employment, the employee would be 100 percent vested as to all amounts in the plan when he terminates employment.

A second type of vesting is called "continual vesting." This is a single vesting schedule that is applied *separately to each year's contribution.* Since each year is treated separately–again, perhaps at ten percent annual vesting rate–the employee will never be completely vested in every year's contribution until the vesting requirement lapses, generally when the employee reaches retirement age. For example, with continual vesting based on the above continual vesting schedule (i.e., ten year/ten percent per year) if an employee quits after three years he would receive:

- thirty percent of the first year's deferral (because three years of vesting equals thirty percent);
- twenty percent of the second year's deferral (because that year has a new and separate ten year vesting schedule); and

- ten percent of the third year's deferral (again because that year has a new and separate ten year vesting schedule).

I've found continual vesting to be the best type of vesting because the yearly contribution can be vested over a relatively short period (for example, 20 percent per year for five years) while keeping "golden handcuffs" in place. The golden handcuffs remain because the key employee is never completely vested in more recent contributions.

*Forfeiture.* *Forfeiture provisions* allow an owner to terminate an employee's vested rights in benefits under the plan. This is another device for influencing your key employee's behavior. For instance, forfeiture can be used to reclaim some or all of an employee's vested benefits if he leaves your business and violates his employment agreement, which may include a covenant not to compete, a trade secret provision or a covenant forbidding him to take other employees. This gives your former employee, who also may know many of your trade secrets, an added incentive to honor the promises he made to you in the employment agreement.

*Payment Schedules.* The deferred compensation agreement should contain payment schedules, that is, provisions that determine when payments of vested amounts begin and how long they are to be continued after the employee leaves. I combine a payment schedule with forfeiture considerations to make sure a recently departed key employee cannot use any accumulated monies from the deferred compensation plan to compete against you. If he does compete, you simply stop or don't begin the payments.

*Funding Devices.* Care must be taken in choosing the method to fund a non-qualified deferred compensation liability and still maintain the plan's status of "non-qualified" and the tax-deferred status to the key employee. There are methods available to accumulate a pool of funds that the employer may use to pay deferred compensation *without subjecting the employee to current taxation.* These methods are commonly referred to as "informal" funding methods. Such an informal funding device also provides psychological security for the employee; he knows the monies will be there when he becomes eligible to receive them, and thus it is easier to convince him that the plan is of great benefit to him (which it is). Many plans can also be structured on an unfunded basis, although ordinarily I urge my clients to begin a safe investment plan, such as investing in permanent cash value life insurance products or mutual bond funds at the company level.

**Phantom Stock Plans**.

A useful variation of the standard nonqualified deferred compensation plan is the Phantom Stock plan. Tied to the company's performance, the Phantom Stock plan gives the key employee some of the benefits of stock ownership without requiring that he acquire actual stock ownership.

The idea behind the Phantom Stock plan is to give key employees something that looks like stock, grows in value like stock, and can be turned in for cash just like stock, but isn't stock. With a Phantom Stock plan, the key employee strives to make the company more valuable because it will make his interest in the Phantom Stock plan more valuable.

Typically, phantom shares corresponding to shares of stock–but not representing any actual ownership–are allocated to the participating employees and credited on the business's books and records. An account is set up and maintained for each key employee. Since key employees don't actually own the stock, they have no shareholder rights; however, each phantom share appreciates in value as the value of the stock increases. Any dividends paid on the stock–as well as other changes in the capital structure–are credited to the employee's account.

The employee's benefits are typically paid to him at the time he terminates his employment with the company. The employee is paid the per share equivalent value of each of the phantom shares vested in the employee. As with any other deferred compensation arrangement, depending on how the plan is designed, the employee receives his benefits, to the extent vested, in a lump sum or a series of payments over several years.

## Stock Appreciation Rights Plans.

Stock Appreciation Rights (SAR) plans are similar to Phantom Stock plans in that the value of benefits in the SAR plan is tied to the value of the corporation's stock. SAR units corresponding to shares of the corporation's stock, but again not representing any actual ownership, are awarded to the participating employee and credited to the employee's account. Unlike phantom stock, however, the employee under an SAR plan is *only entitled to receive appreciation* on a certain percentage of SAR units valued against the corporation's stock, not the entire principal value of the stock. Again, since key employees under an SAR plan do not own stock, they have no shareholder rights. An SAR plan can also be structured to give the employee the right to receive dividends when dividends are paid on the corporation's actual shares.

When the employee leaves the company, the units in his account are re-evaluated to reflect the current market price, or formula price of the stock. Depending on how the employer designs the plan, the employee receives his benefit *(to the extent vested)* in a lump sum at the time of departure or in a series of payments over several years. Thus, he benefits from stock appreciation even though none was ever issued to him because an SAR unit is equivalent to a share of stock. If the stock value increases by 40 percent, then the key employee's SAR unit increases by 40 percent.

Like other nonqualified deferred compensation plans, the chief elements of Phantom Stock plans and SAR plans are *vesting, forfeiture, payment schedules, and funding devices.* These elements are the same as those in regular deferred compensation plans, which also include benefit formulas. However, in the Phantom Stock plans and SAR plans, the benefit formula is not included because the valuation of the company's stock is, in a real sense, the benefit formula–instead of an annual benefit award, the employee's benefit is tied to the value of the company's stock.

## Comparing Nonqualified Deferred Compensation With Actual Ownership

Compared with actual stock ownership, nonqualified deferred compensation plans and Phantom Stock/SAR plans offer certain advantages.

For participating employees:
• No initial investment is required.
• Additional income may be deferred without current taxation.
• They eventually receive cash instead of a relatively worthless stock certificate.
• They can substantially increase the amount of money they receive by increasing the profits of the company.
• There is no income tax consequence until the cash benefit is received.

For employers:
• Benefits paid are tax-deductible.
• Employees are not granted rights to vote, inspect books, or attend meetings (or to complain about your company-owned Mercedes-Benz).
• Benefits accrue only during profitable years.
• Benefits may be tied to vesting requirements.

## When Non-stock Plans Work Best

Given the choice, almost all key employees would prefer cash to ownership.  Non-stock incentives work best in situations where:

• There are key employees within a family owned and operated business and where it is evident that the younger generation of that family will eventually run the company.
• The amount of ownership to be awarded will not be meaningful.

- The ownership to be conferred would offer no foreseeable benefit to the employee for either income or conversion to publicly traded stock at a future date.
- You do not want to expose the company (or yourself) to liability by conferring minority ownership on a valuable but problematic employee.
- The employee will understand and appreciate money more than stock. (A dollar is a dollar, but what is a share of stock really worth?)

In these situations something should be done to retain key employees. Naturally, this reminds me of a client–the Thomas Wells Construction Company.

*Tom Wells had started the company more than forty years before we met. It had grown to annual revenues of almost $30 million. Although Wells had done extensive family transition planning, he knew that as he stepped back from the business and allowed his son to take over its management and control he would need the active and intense involvement of his key personnel.*

*This group consisted of three construction foremen, the overall operations manager, and the chief financial officer. While Wells remained active, he knew he would be able to replace the loss of one or more of these key managers; however, Wells felt that his relatively inexperienced son needed time to gain further experience. Thus, it made sense to keep the current management team in place.*

*But what kind of incentive arrangement would be appropriate to keep them on the job? Issuing stock or stock options was not an alternative, since Wells intended that the business remain firmly in the hands of the family.*

*As we talked, I learned that Wells had historically given cash bonuses as a reward in profitable years. Given the nature of the construction business, it was not unusual for the company to make $500,000 one year and lose $200,000 the next. This history of cash bonuses seemed an appropriate concept to build upon, because everybody was already familiar with it.*

*We also knew that, as the business grew, additional key people would be hired. They, too, should be given an opportunity to participate in any incentive plan. The plan we devised followed the necessary elements of any well-designed incentive plan.*

*It offered a **substantial benefit**–25 percent of the after-tax profits on an annual basis was available to the group of key employees. Forty percent of this amount would be distributed outright to the participants under the incentive plan. The remaining 60 percent would go as a credit into the accounts of each of the five key employees.*

*As additional key employees were added to the plan, they would share in the overall 25 percent profit, which would be distributed among the participants as determined by a management committee of three people. The committee consisted of one member of the Wells family and two members of the key employee group.*

*There was a compelling **incentive** to remain a productive employee of the company. An eight-year continual vesting schedule was attached to the deferred benefit; it would take eight years for each key employee to become fully vested in each year's contribution. However, upon attaining age 58, the employees would be 100 percent vested in all amounts allocated to their benefit. All of this was contained in a well-designed **written plan**.*

*The key management also had some ability to control the amount of their deferred compensation because their performance directly affected the profitability of the company–another powerful incentive to consistently do well.*

*The plan was carefully **explained** to all members over a series of meetings attended by Tom Wells, his son, Tom's advisors, and all of the participants.*

*The plan has worked out well for all concerned.*

The Wells case study also illustrates a "blended plan"–a blend of current cash payment and deferred compensation, subject to vesting, all based on increasing the profitability of the company. Harken back to the basic elements of a well crafted employee incentive plan:

1.  The potential benefit is **substantial**.

2. There are **specific** guidelines on how to obtain the objective or benefit.

3. Attaining the key employees incentive objectives also furthers the owner's goal of **increasing the value of the company**.

4. The plan objectives are **meaningful** and **realistic**.

5. The incentive plan "**handcuffs**" the key employee to the business.

6. The benefits of the plan are periodically **communicated** to the key employees.

### Summary

Successful businesses have key employees. Providing your key employees with an incentive package that motivates them to continue to excel and to remain with you is in your best interest. These key employees not only will make your business more profitable, but will most likely be strong candidates to buy it should you choose to sell it. Your immediate task is to identify these key employees, find the right incentive package, and implement it.

If you are committed to leaving your business in style, you too, have key employees. Are you doing all you can do motivate and retain them?

Now is the time to sit down with your advisory team and take a hard look at your current employee benefit programs, especially those aimed at your key employees. Ask yourself the questions listed in the Employee Benefit Checklist. Make sure you include such programs as group health, disability, life, "cafeteria programs," qualified retirement plans, cash bonus plans, and any others.

### Appendix 4.1: Employee Benefits Checklist

❑   Do any of my business's plans favor a group of top employees? If so, how?

If not, can anything be done to increase their benefits without increasing the cost of benefits for all employees? For example, integrating the qualified retirement plans? (See Chapter Five for an explanation of this important concept.)

❑     Are existing employee incentive plans working?

❑     Who are the key employees? Why? _____

_____

_____

_____

Is their position key? Or are they the key?

❑     Am I interested in the possibility of key employees one day buying me out, in part or in whole?
       If so, do I have the type of key employees who are capable and motivated to one day run my company?
       Who are they? _____

_____

_____

_____

❑     What promises have I made to key employees regarding:
       1.  Stock ownership
       2.  Participation in management
       3.  Sharing in profits of the company?

❑     Are these plans consistent with my long-term retirement and financial goals? For example, if my key employees will not be buying me out, their incentives should be cash-based; if they are going to be the eventual owners, their benefits should be stock-based. In either case, is at least part of their incentive a golden handcuff that will motivate them to remain with my company?

❑ Do I have in place sufficient protection should a key employee leave?

1. Covenant not to compete? _____

2. Covenant not to take other employees at employment? _____

3. Trade secrecy protection covenant? _____

4. Forfeiture provisions on deferred compensation or stock repurchase agreements if covenants are violated? These covenants are best contained in an employment agreement supplemented by similar restrictions in the buy-sell agreement (if key employee is to receive ownership) or a nonqualified deferred compensation plan (if employee is to receive cash-based incentives).

❑ How are the incentive compensation packages reviewed and revised?
How are their benefits effectively communicated to all concerned?

❑ Do the incentive packages appropriately reward the employee in terms of being:

1. Financially attractive?_____

2. Founded on explicit performance standards that are measurable and realistic?_____

3. Determinable in specific dollar amounts?_____

4. Awarded at least annually?_____

If no incentive package is now in place, how would I design one using items 1 through 4 above?

❑ What obstacles are there in implementing a plan in terms of cost and the possibility of upsetting nonparticipating good employees?

❑   Would money spent now on company-wide benefits (e.g., a retirement plan) better serve my long-term goals by being reallocated to top employees?

❑   What is the best type of plan to motivate and retain my top employee(s)?
1.  Cash-based or stock-based? Which is better?
2.  If cash based:
    a.  What amount?
    b.  Based on what standards?
    c.  When should I give it?
    d.  How much should be deferred? Or subjected to golden handcuffs?
    e.  What type of vesting schedule?
3.  If stock-based, what terms and conditions should be placed on:
    a.  Stock bonus?
    b.  Stock or cash bonus option?
    c.  Stock option? If so, incentive stock option or nonqualified stock option?
4.  If stock-based:
    a.  How is stock to be valued?
    b.  How much stock is to be offered? Now and in the future?

❑   Finally, and most importantly, do my existing key employee incentive plans meet the following criteria:
1.  Are they specific?
2.  Are the benefits substantial?
3.  Are the plan objectives meaningful, realistic and well-communicated?
4.  Do they increase the value of the business when the employee attains his incentive goal?
5.  Do they handcuff the key employee to the business?

# 5

# A Dose of Castor Oil

*What you need to know about taxes–no more, no less*

As important as the subject is, there is no need for the business owner to be a tax expert. In fact, I can't think of any activity that will be less productive–and more taxing–than a self-imposed marathon over the labyrinthine course known as the Internal Revenue Code. There are others you can hire who have that expertise. Your time should be spent on things you know best–and enjoy most. After all, isn't that why you started your business?

Nevertheless, it is important that you have an understanding of the tax fundamentals that affect your business. You may find the subject a bit difficult, but try to stick with it; the knowledge you acquire will equip you to ask the right questions of your advisors and comprehend their answers. You'll be able to make the kind of tax decisions that will help you achieve your planning goals and objectives. If you're already up to speed on the IRS Code, you may want to skip this chapter. You can always come back to it later.

To begin, let's recognize that there are two types of income tax problems: you've either paid too little and the IRS is now after you, or you've paid too much.

In the former case, there's not much you can do. The IRS is generally unyielding, and the enforcement laws favor them exclusively. It is far more typical for the owners of closely held businesses to have overpaid. Up to a point, it may be possible to recapture some of that overpayment. The only sure way to minimize your tax bite, however, is by thorough, thoughtful, and proper planning based on a conceptual framework of the basic tax issues facing business owners.

The framework concerns rates, treatment, and timing. These issues must be addressed and favorably resolved in the business setting in which they arise. For example, the questions of how your business is organized and what tax-favored employee benefit plans you will put into effect will be answered by resolving these issues.

Let's review each.

### Tax Rates

You operate under one of four available options: (1) a corporation that has not elected to have any special tax treatment (also called a "C" corporation); (2) a Subchapter S corporation ("S" corporation) that has opted for special treatment under the Internal Revenue Code; (3) a partnership or Limited Liability Company; or (4) a sole proprietorship. Depending on which form of business organization you've chosen, your tax rates (as well as tax treatment and tax timing) may be different.

Here's why:

A "C" corporation has its own tax brackets that are different from those of its owners. For the first $50,000 of taxable income, the federal tax bite is 15 percent. The next bracket—$50,000 to $75,000—calls for a 25 percent rate; from $75,000 to $100,000 the rate is 34 percent and above $100,000 an additional five percent tax applies to phase out the benefits of the graduated rates. For corporations with taxable income in excess of $10 million, the tax rate is 35 percent. Personal service corporations, such as those in the field of medicine, law, and accounting, pay a uniform 35 percent. The taxable income of all other types of business entities such as "S" corporations, limited liability companies (LLC's) partnerships and sole proprietorships are taxed at the owners' income tax rate, generally an amount that does not exceed 39.6 percent.

As tax law changes, these rates change. At times the top bracket in a "C" corporation is higher than an individual's top rate; at other times it's lower. The tax rate on a "C" corporation's first bracket of taxable income has historically always been lower than an individual's top tax rate—usually at least 50 percent lower.

Another tax bracket differential can exist between individual taxpayers. For example, your tax rate on income might be significantly higher than your child's. Wherever there is a difference in tax rates between business entities and an individual or between individuals, a tax planning opportunity exists to shift the tax consequence to the taxpayer in the lowest tax bracket. The IRS is not unaware of this tax planning idea; but, surprisingly, many business owners are.

For instance, most business owners understand the need to retain earnings at the business level to fund expansion, but they don't understand how they can take advantage of the tax system to reduce the overall cost of expansion. To grow, businesses need to add equipment, increase inventory, and hire more employees. Further, as accounts receivable grow in size, a timing difference is created between the increased production and the receipt of payment for that increased production; that is, in a growing business billings increase while receipts lag.

Retained earnings provide the cash needed to fund these needs, but retained earnings are subject to income tax. Because a "C" corporation pays less in taxes on the first $75,000 of annual retained earnings than an individual (or "S" corporation, partnership, or proprietorship), "C" corporation status can be useful to growing businesses.

## Tax Treatment

When a business spends money, the result is one of three tax treatments:

1. The expenditure may be nondeductible, which means that it does not reduce the gross income of the business for tax purposes.

This type of expenditure is often called "after-tax spending". An example is the life insurance policy your company buys on your life because you are its "key" person. Premium payments are nondeductible and consequently must be paid from income earned by the business after it has paid taxes on that income.

2. Money spent to buy a capital asset–machinery, office equipment, vehicles–is another expenditure. These assets can be depreciated over a number of years based on IRS guidelines on the useful life of the asset. A car or truck used in the business, for example, may be depreciated over not less than five years. If the vehicle cost $15,000, the payment of $15,000 would not be deductible in the year of purchase, but its depreciation is deductible. In this case, the annual depreciation deduction is $3,000 (the $15,000 purchase price divided by the useful life of five years equals $3,000 per year depreciation). At the end of the depreciation period, the business will have deducted the full purchase price of the equipment.

The depreciation schedules are based on the assumption that the equipment is useless at the end of the depreciation period and the company will need to purchase new equipment. From a tax standpoint, it's clearly preferable to buy assets that can be depreciated over a period of time, rather than to purchase nondeductible assets.

3. Better yet is the tax treatment that permits a total deduction. The IRS allows businesses to deduct from their gross income all reasonable business expenses such as salaries, supplies and overhead expenses of rent, and short-term leases, among others.

## Tax Timing

Deferring the occurrence of taxation is critical. If you can delay the date the tax is imposed, you gain the use of those funds earmarked for the tax payment. There is great value—the time value of money—in this planning technique. For example, a ten percent annual rate of return doubles the value of an investment (in this case the amount of tax being deferred) every seven years. The greater the rate of return, the less time needed to double the investment. A sufficient deferral time and rate of return could mean the taxpayer keeps his cake (his money) and allows Uncle Sam to eat his (the taxes) too.

In a real sense, tax payment delay is as good as tax avoidance since you are given the opportunity to continue to use the dollars needed to pay the taxes. Thus a deferral of taxation is in a true sense tax avoidance.

As we shall see, deferral becomes an especially important planning concept in employee benefit planning—both yours and your employees'. Further, the higher the current tax rate, the greater the benefit of deferring.

Let's look at how these three tax concepts (tax rates, tax treatment and tax timing) work together.

Assume your "C" corporation has a net profit of $50,000 at year end. If you retain that profit in the corporation, the corporation pays $7,500 in tax. If, instead, you pay yourself a bonus of $50,000, the corporation has no taxable income because salaries are deductible. However, when you receive the bonus, you have another $50,000 in taxable income and will pay approximately $15,000 in tax.

On the other hand, if the corporation pays its net profit of $50,000 to its qualified retirement plan, it gets a deduction, has no taxable income, and therefore pays no tax. Since you haven't received the income, you don't pay tax on it. Therefore you have deferred the income tax until you receive your retirement benefit. This is an example of the tax planning you can do.

Another example of the interrelationship of these tax concepts is the selection of the proper business entity form.

A "C" corporation with its lower initial tax rates may be preferable to other types of business organizations if there will be an ongoing need to accumulate capital at the business level. The accumulation of capital always carries with it a tax treatment cost because it is nondeductible. Even when the capital accumulation will fund the purchase of depreciable equipment, the depreciation amount in the initial year will not be sufficient to pay for the tax cost of the initial accumulation.

On the other hand, when there is no need to accumulate capital, as may be the case with many service-oriented businesses, it's often preferable to avoid "C" corporation status. The reason for this is that an after-tax distribution from the "C" corporation to you is taxed to you on your individual return. Unless that money can be taken out in the form of a deductible expenditure to the corporation (usually a salary or bonus) this second tax will have to be paid without an offsetting deduction. This "double taxation" is a major argument against the "C" corporation status unless the corporation's need to accumulate capital is even stronger. *This double-tax also requires critical consideration when you wish to sell your business.* If you are considering a sale of your "C" corporation, the potential of a double-tax on the sales price for your entire business—hopefully millions of dollars—can be avoided by doing business as other than a "C" corporation. Thus, to avoid the risk of a second tax being levied against corporate monies, an "S" corporation is often appropriate.

The relationship between the top income tax bracket for individuals and the top income tax bracket for corporations is also reason to consider the use of an "S" corporation, especially when large amounts of money—more than $100,000—must be retained by the corporation annually.

The form of corporate organization selected for your business should be evaluated periodically in light of your business's capital accumulation needs, current tax law, and your anticipated exit date.

### Employee Benefit Planning

In the broadest sense, employee benefits are those the company bestows upon one or more of its employees. Benefits are either "qualified" or "nonqualified." "Qualified" benefits are those which qualify under the Internal Revenue Code for favorable tax treatment: **Full deductibility** is applied when the benefit obligation is paid or incurred by your company on behalf of the employees. "Non-qualified" benefits, on the other hand, receive no special treatment under the tax code. The benefits of non-qualified plans are then primarily non-tax in nature. Let's look at the differences.

## *Qualified Benefits*

"Qualified" employee benefits are those that are income tax deductible when paid by the business—benefits our good friends at the IRS have determined comply with the Internal Revenue Code.

A properly cynical business owner might ask, "Why would the IRS ever give a tax break to my business?" The answer is quite simple: to encourage businesses to provide the benefits Congress considers necessary for the public good but which the government doesn't want to fund. After all, if the private sector did not provide these benefits, the government might have to accept that responsibility.

To be ruled "qualified," the benefit must reach all or most of the employees in the company on a nondiscriminatory basis. This means the same type of benefit must be available to lower-paid as well as to highly compensated employees.

Let's remember, though, that *a primary objective of most business owners is often to gain much of the tax-deductible employee benefit for themselves while minimizing the cost of providing benefits to their employees.* This results in a constant tug-of-war between the government's desire to broaden the scope of qualified employee benefits to accomplish social goals through tax policy on one side, and the business owners' desire to provide benefits to selected employees (themselves or key employees) on the other.

Qualified employee benefits focus on an employee's retirement, health, and disability. By extending special tax treatment, Congress encourages businesses to provide these benefits to all its employees, including owners and other key employees.

The exact benefits available change almost yearly as Congress tinkers with the tax code, but generally they include group benefits such as: medical expense insurance, disability income, life insurance, dental insurance, salary continuation plans, cafeteria plans and other qualified retirement plans including 401(k) plans and defined benefit plans.

In most circumstances, nondiscrimination rules practically eliminate the possibility of excluding any employees from participating in qualified retirement plans.

Many of these group benefits can be provided to your employees through a cafeteria plan: health insurance, reimbursement of medical expenses not covered by health insurance, disability insurance, or child care assistance. As the business owner, you can limit your cost by providing a fixed amount of money, say $100 per month to each employee. If health insurance premiums increase, the cost is passed on to the employee. If the employee wants additional benefits, he or she must pay for those extra benefits, but extra payments, if done via the cafeteria plan, are deductible by the employee.

This offers employees considerable flexibility in designing their own benefit packages. It also allows your business to place a cap on the cost of the benefits you provide your employees. Suppose, for example, you decide to spend $100 per month for each employee. Your employee may take that money in cash (and pay the tax on it), or receive $100 worth of benefits under the cafeteria plan (all of which are tax-exempt to the employee).

Your financial or insurance advisor will earn his fee by performing a detailed analysis to determine if a cafeteria plan makes sense for your business. Only the qualified employee retirement plans, however, offer owners a significant tax planning opportunity.

### Advantages of Qualified Retirement Plans

The first advantage of qualified retirement plans is the ability to contribute $30,000 annually (adjusted for inflation) on a tax-deductible basis for your own benefit. As the trustee of the plan, you make all investment decisions. (Giving this power to most owners, however, can make even a cynical lawyer blanch!) As long as the contribution remains in the retirement plan, it earns money on a tax-free basis. When you eventually take money out of the plan for your retirement (after age 59 1/2) you pay an income tax at the then current tax rate. The plan then has the best tax treatment and tax timing available. Money is deductible to the business going in to the retirement plan, and all personal tax consequences to you are deferred until taken out.

Also, depending on state law, the monies set aside in the retirement plan are not attachable by your creditors, an important consideration for all owners for whom liability or malpractice insurance may be too costly or impossible to obtain.

One method of reducing overall employee costs is to subject the right to receive the monies set aside for an employee to "vesting." This means that unless an employee remains with the company for a specified number of years (generally, no more than six years), upon departure the employee forfeits part of the monies set aside for his or her benefit.

An effective means of reducing your employees' share of the contribution is to **integrate** the plan with social security. Integration allows the company to take into account its FICA contribution in making contributions to the plan. The result is to allow a greater percentage of contribution for salaries above the "taxable wage base."

Of course, the biggest advantage of qualified retirement plans is the income tax provision allowing the company to deduct money going in the plan and you, as the owner/participant, to defer income tax consequences on that contributed amount and all its subsequent earnings until you take the funds out. *This makes the qualified retirement plan the most significant form of tax deferral and tax avoidance device currently available to closely held business owners.*

An often advertised advantage of retirement plans is the effect on your employees. By subjecting their contributions to vesting, you can motivate them to remain with the company. I must say, however, that my experience with closely held businesses convinces me that employees—especially younger ones—rarely appreciate the amount of money allocated for their benefit until they quit and receive a tidy lump sum. Then they say, "Gosh, this is a lot of money. My employer really did a nice thing for me." By then, of course, it's too late, and the retirement plan has failed to instill a sense of loyalty. Much of this lack of appreciation is due to insufficient communication on the part of the plan administrator.

Periodic and frequent communication of employee benefits, however, can heighten your employees' awareness of the value of their retirement plans. As they get older, their appreciation increases dramatically.

Finally, remember the primary advantage of a retirement plan in your company is to provide **you** with a substantial retirement benefit. Without the tax advantages of the plan, it's often difficult for a business owner to save enough money outside of the business to provide for a comfortable retirement benefit.

## Disadvantages of Qualified Retirement Plans

The first disadvantage of the qualified retirement plan is the cost of the contributions that must be made for the other employees. Aside from the integration amount, the percentage of contribution must be the same for all employees as it is for you. You can exclude part-time employees and employees who are under age 21 or who have been with the company for less than one year, but everyone else must be included.

The reasonability of the employee cost is determined by looking at the amount of income tax you would have paid if you had taken the entire contribution amount as a bonus in the year of contribution. If the tax cost to you of taking the money now as compensation would be substantially more than the amount of plan contributions made for the other employees, then a qualified retirement plan can make a lot of sense.

Obviously, as the number of your employee/participants increases, the percentage of the contribution your business makes to the plan on your behalf will decrease. At some level the employee cost may be too great, unless the benefit to the company as a tool for motivating and retaining good employees offsets the cost of the plan.

In many of those situations, the most appropriate type of a retirement plan is the 401(k) plan, which is discussed later in this Chapter.

A second disadvantage of qualified retirement plans is the set-up cost followed by the ongoing maintenance and administration costs. Plan administration can be complex and easily fouled-up, and keeping plans current with changing laws can be overlooked by the business owner. That's why I recommend to my clients that they have three responsible individuals involved with their plans: a "plan preparer," a financial or insurance advisor, and an administrator.

One easy way to avoid problems keeping up with changes in the law is to use a prototype plan—one that has been pre-approved by the IRS. As the law changes, the **plan preparer** makes those changes to his master plan and obtains IRS approval of those changes, which then applies to your plan with minimal further cost to you for amending the plan. (This cost saving is one reason I recommend a prototype plan from a benefits company as opposed to those available from an insurance company or bank. The latter usually want part of your investment business within the plan as the price of allowing you to use their prototype.)

The second individual on the team should be a good **investment advisor.** It's helpful if the advisor is also experienced in plan design and operation. His careful attention to your plan can be a safeguard against compliance or administrative errors.

The third person involved should be an **administrator.** In smaller plans this is often your CPA; in large plans it's a "third party administrator" whose primary function is to administer retirement plans. Administration involves allocating the money to various plan accounts and preparing an informational return to the IRS on a periodic basis. The plan administrator also provides a statement each year to all employee/participants showing the amount of money in their accounts, the earnings achieved, and the current year's contribution from the employer to their accounts. One last item: keep yourself off of this team—you'll only expose yourself to needless risk. When these three professionals work together, all areas of plan compliance work and investments should be adequately covered.

Other types of qualified retirement plans may also be appropriate as your work force grows. Such plans include 401(k) plans and defined benefit plans.

The **401(k) plan** is a derivative of a profit sharing plan. It allows employees to contribute their own money to the plan on a tax-deferred basis.   Often the employer agrees to match a certain percentage of the employee contribution.  This employer match is the only cost to the employer of the plan other than the ongoing compliance costs.

Another type of retirement plan is known as a **defined benefit plan.**  Unlike a defined contribution plan, which sets limits on the amount the employer can contribute to the plan on behalf of each employee, a defined benefit plan specifies the amount available to an employee upon his retirement.  Annual contributions are then made so that the desired amount is available when the employee retires.

A defined benefit plan is now used only in special situations. Generally, to take advantage of the plan, the owner must be substantially older than his workers and willing to work five years after the plan is established, usually until his retirement.  In those special situations, however, it's possible to contribute considerably more than $30,000 a year on behalf of the employer/owner.

I've gone into a lot of detail on retirement plans simply because *they are the one remaining substantial tax benefit available to owners of closely held businesses*.  Therefore, you must understand how they work.  You also need to know that as your business and employee work force expand, qualified retirement plans may make less sense. The employee cost may outweigh all other advantages.  At that point, nonqualified deferred compensation may become more attractive.

## Nonqualified Benefits

Nonqualified benefits, such as those provided under deferred compensation plans, split dollar insurance plans, stock appreciation rights plans or phantom stock plans, and stock bonus plans do not receive favored income-tax treatment.  But these plans also do not have to comply with the burdensome and complex Internal Revenue Code and other regulations.

Group benefits such as medical expense insurance, disability income, life and dental insurance are often provided by employers to their employees for altruistic as well as self-serving purposes.  The IRS encourages business owners to provide these benefits by making the cost of providing these benefits a tax-deductible expense while excluding those payments as taxable income to employees. (Certain limits apply to the benefits of life insurance.)

In contrast to the twin tax advantages of qualified plans, employer contributions to a nonqualified benefit plan are either deductible to the employer or not included in income by the employee, but not both. The primary attractiveness of a nonqualified plan is that it escapes the close scrutiny, supervision and regulation of the IRS. As an owner, you are able to determine which of your employees shall enjoy the benefits and how much each should get.

Indeed, this ability to single out an individual or small group of key employees and to provide them benefits to the exclusion of all other employees, is the major reason to use nonqualified employee benefits. Since this type of plan requires either the business or the employee to bear some tax cost as funds are contributed to the plan, its usage must be carefully examined and its implications understood before it can be effectively employed.

A typical nonqualified plan may be a salary continuation plan, a *deferred compensation plan, a stock appreciation rights plan or a phantom stock plan* (the last three are explained in detail in Chapter Four).

**Salary continuation plans** are nonqualified plans and do not qualify for deductibility of funding contributions until the employee actually receives the benefit. These plans usually offer retirement benefits starting at age 65; they may continue for a specified number of years or as long as the retiree lives. Because no IRS approval is required and there are no nondiscrimination rules with which to comply, these plans are favorably viewed by business owners for their flexibility. However, in part because the corporation does not get a taxable deduction for any pre-funding of these plans, many plans remain unfunded and benefits are paid out of current operating funds.

As with all tax-driven business decisions, nonqualified benefits should be considered in light of the conceptual framework of **tax treatment, rate,** and **timing.**

The law does not require a business to fund a nonqualified benefit as it does in the case of qualified plans. As a result, there need not be a current cost or outlay of money by the business.

The tax code demands that the accumulation of funds for tax treatment, or simply for investment purposes, be a nondeductible event. Accordingly, the tax rate of the business becomes more important.

Nevertheless, the employees normally want some assurances that money will be there when they become entitled to benefits under the plan. Entitlement often occurs upon termination of employment because of retirement age, or because the employee or the business has achieved a certain long-term goal. Consequently, some method of informal "funding" often is necessary, however, to avoid the pitfalls associated with not funding a nonqualified plan. This informal "funding" is set up by the business with the understanding and agreement that the funds must be accessible to the business's general creditors. The business can take steps to further protect the benefit, such as agreeing not to use those funds or the earnings they generate as long as the business remains solvent, but the funds must always be available to the business's creditors.

To the extent there is funding, the tax rate is the business's tax rate. For this reason these plans usually work best for "C" corporations, because of the low income tax bracket on the first $50,000 of taxable income. However, if this money is already being used for other nondeductible business purposes, then any further accumulation of taxable income would be taxed at the next corporate bracket, which may be higher than an individual's rates.

Obviously, a nonqualified plan can be advantageous or detrimental when used as a benefit for owner/employees. Why be taxed at a high corporate rate when monies can be currently distributed to you in the form of compensation and deducted by the business? The answer is that non-qualified deferred compensation plans for owners are seldom, if ever, "funded." Instead, they are a tool to move income earned by the business out to the owner—after his departure from the company. As such, non-qualified deferred compensation plans for owners are important in exit strategies and are discussed in detail in Chapter Seven.

The tax bracket of the company should also be considered at the point when the benefits begin to be distributed out to the benefitted employee. At that time the benefits are taxable to the employee as compensation and consequently deductible by the company as wages.

There is one aspect of a nonqualified plan which confers a timing benefit. This is the timing difference between the date the employee is given the benefit (with that money accruing at the corporate level) and the date he receives it. Often those funds are invested in an asset that accumulates income without current income taxation, such as a life insurance policy or annuity. When this accumulation is paid out to a retiring employee, it is tax deductible; thus giving the business a tax deduction on untaxed monies.

If the investment is in the form of a life insurance policy, the death proceeds are usually made payable to the company. At the employee's death, before or after he has received all of the deferred compensation, the death proceeds are generally received income tax free by the company (subject to the alternative minimum tax if paid to a "C" corporation). And, when the company actually pays part or all of those proceeds as deferred compensation, it receives a deduction–proving that sometimes you do get something for nothing... or close to it.

## Summary

I reiterate that there's no need for you to become a tax expert. You can always hire experts. In a sense, you need to know just enough tax theory to be slightly dangerous—to develop a sense of when to bring in expertise, and **why**. Remember that the mistakes owners of closely held businesses make, typically involve overpayment of taxes, not underpayment. And overpayment is something that can often be avoided with a little help from an expert. Again, ask yourself these three questions to ensure you're on the right track:

1. If the transaction is nondeductible, is the taxpayer with the lowest tax **rate** paying for it?
2. What is the income tax **treatment** of the particular transaction?
3. What is the income tax **timing**?

You now know enough tax law to understand the tax fundamentals that affect your business. And you're dangerous!

# *Part II*

# EXIT STRATEGY:
# Transferring Ownership and Value

Now that you're on the right track to creating and preserving value for your business interest, you need to know how to transfer it in exchange for money. For at some point, you **will** transfer your ownership interest. Hopefully, it will be under favorable and voluntary circumstances, such as a transfer during your lifetime to your son or daughter, a co-owner, a key employee, or a third party. But the transfer may also be triggered by an unfavorable and involuntary event, such as death or total disability.

In order for you and your family to obtain the maximum value for your ownership interest, it is vital that you begin planning now to cover both voluntary and involuntary transfers of that interest. I can't emphasize enough the critical difference a moderate amount of planning will make to you—both in terms of creating a market and value for your interest, and as a means of ensuring that you receive full payment for it.

Surveys of business owners report that the vast majority of owners wish to transfer the business to family, co-owners or key employees. Yet most owners end up transferring the business to outside third parties. The reasons for this are obvious: Children, key employees and co-owners do not have any money and without planning no money will be available.

Without the financial security of receiving cash, most owners have no option but to sell the business to an outside third-party. This "Part II" will help you design a plan to exit the business by transferring it to the person of your choice. Certainly, there is no guarantee that this can be accomplished but, without planning, you will not even have a fighting chance. With planning, it becomes possible to meet not only your financial security goals but also your objective of transferring your business to the party of your choice.

# 6

# Leaving Your Business Is Easier Than Leaving a Lover

*The four basic ways–and how to pick the one that's best for you.*

*After many years of building a thriving medical instruments business, Royce Cassidy, age 55, wanted to sell his business and retire to a leisurely life.  But when he looked for possible buyers, he found no established market for his specialized business.  And when he looked within his company, there was no one to buy it from him because—like most small business owners—he was the only one in the company who knew how to attract new business and run the operation.  Only he possessed the entrepreneurial spirit and drive that had made his company successful.*

*Royce was looking straight into the mouth of an owner's worst retirement situation:  liquidation.*

*Royce has not identified who gets the business when he leaves it.  Until he does so, the planning process can not move forward.  Like all owners, Royce cannot leave the business in style without selecting successor ownership.  It is difficult to hand off the torch when there is no one else on the relay team and there will not be anyone there until you have carefully evaluated the advantages and disadvantages of transferring the business to each possible type of successor owner. Once that is done, the transfer process can continue.*

Selecting your successor is a fundamental objective that is decided early in the Exit Planning process, first identified in Chapter One, "When You're Too Busy Fighting Alligators." The purpose of this chapter is to make that decision an informed one.

Recall that almost all owners want to transfer the business to other family members, an employee or a co-owner. Only about five percent of owners want to sell to an outside third party.

Unfortunately for most owners, the persons they first identify as their successors do not usually end up as the ultimate owners. Much effort is wasted riding the wrong horse. This chapter aims to save you some effort by setting forth the advantages and disadvantages of transferring the business to each category of potential purchaser: family member(s), co-owners, employees and outside third parties. Use the information in this chapter to help assess what you want from the business and who can best give you what you want. Again, identifying your successor is a fundamental objective. The purpose of this chapter to make the choice an informed one.

That's just what I helped Jim DeBoer do.

*Jim started his manufacturing company over 25 years ago and took in Tom Metz as a ten percent minority owner ten years later, forming DMC Manufacturing Company. Now, at age 58, Jim wants to retire while maintaining his current lifestyle. He would like to sell his shares to Tom—if he can be guaranteed a good retirement income. To enable him to maintain his lifestyle, Jim feels he'll need $1 million but Tom, who is 41, doesn't have $25,000 in savings, let alone a cool million. Consequently, Jim thinks he should sell the business to an outside cash buyer.*

That was their problem when they came to me. Before I explain the plan I came up with to resolve their dilemma, it's important to lay some groundwork that applies to your business as well.

Remember a few years back (Okay, it's many years ago) when Paul Simon's hit song told us there were "fifty ways to leave your lover?" Well, here's good news: Basically, there are only four ways to leave your business. If you know these methods and decide in advance which one you prefer, then you can look forward to leaving your business under terms and conditions you choose. Without planning you are more likely to settle for terms and conditions beyond your control.

There are pluses and minuses to each choice. Knowing what they are will help you determine which method is most suitable for you. Take time to compare the relative merits and disadvantages of each departure option before making your decision.

## Option I:  Transfer of Ownership to Your Children

If you are a typical business owner, there is a 50 percent chance that you want to transfer the business to your children. If you are a typical owner, you will end up transferring the business to someone else. Fewer than one in three owners, wishing to transfer to a child, end up doing so.

Following the advice of this book will, of course, increase your odds. But it is still in your best interest to realize the difficulty of this transaction. You must prepare the business for the possibility, indeed the **likelihood**, that it will be conveyed to another type of buyer.

### *Advantages*

- Fulfills personal goal of keeping the business and family together.
- Provides financial well-being for younger family members unable to earn comparable income from outside employment.
- Allows you to stay active in business with your children.
- Allows you to control your departure date.

- Enables you to fix value by starting with the question, "How much do I need or want?" rather than being told, "This is how much I am willing to give you." This is especially useful in situations in which the business is worth less than the amount needed to live on–if the business were sold to a third party. When you keep the business in the family, you can sell for what you need to live on even if the business value does not justify that sum of money.

### *Disadvantages*

- Great potential exists to increase family friction, discord and feeling of unequal treatment among siblings. The normal objective of treating all children equally is difficult to achieve because one child will probably run or own the business at the perceived expense of the others.
- Financial security is normally diminished not enhanced; although with careful planning and implementation, financial security can often be achieved while transferring the business to the children.
- Because family is involved, your control may be weakened. You can lose effective control even though you still have voting control–due, of course, to the vagaries of family dynamics.
- The real risk of transferring the business–because of family ties–to someone who can't or won't run it properly, threatens your financial security and the existence of the business.

As you will read in Chapter 10, many of these disadvantages can be minimized or avoided through proper planning.

Because transferring ownership to children is one of the most desirable, most frequently used and riskiest ways to leave a business, the subject is reviewed in depth in Chapters 10 and 13. I think you will find those chapters interesting reading even if you will not be transferring your business to your children–provided, of course, you enjoy television soap operas.

## Option II:  Sale to Other Owners or Employees

One of the great advantages of having other owners in your business is that they can be your means to retirement.  Especially with smaller businesses, a common retirement planning technique is to have a younger individual buy into your business while you are still active.  Upon your retirement, the younger owner will purchase your remaining stock.

This can be advantageous because the younger person learns the business—its structure, employees, customers, operation, and management—under your tutelage.  More important for you, the younger person's capabilities (as well as his weaknesses) are known to you, so you have a pretty good idea of how your business will be run after you leave.  And most important of all, the business can be sold to a market you create and control.

### *Advantages*

- Owner can structure the deal ahead of time to suit his particular needs and objectives.
- Establishes a fund inside the business for the eventual purchase of owner's interest.
- Maintains a greater measure of control during the buyout.
- Pre-qualifies the buyer(s) through on-the-job training and observation.
- Continues the "culture" or mission of the business.
- Ensures that all of the employees who helped build the business won't lose their jobs and future with the company.
- A side benefit of planning an employee buyout is that the steps taken to build value and train future owners will make

the business more profitable, more stable, and better-managed–even if the owner decides to postpone his retirement. Thus, grooming the "heir apparent" allows an owner to slow down, to have options that will give the owner flexibility in case the unexpected happens, such as a sudden disability or inheriting a bundle from Aunt Emma. At the same time the owner has developed a stronger business, both from a financial and employee standpoint.

### *Disadvantages*

- No cash up front, unless the owner has pre-funded, and even then, he has probably pre-funded with money that was his anyway.
- Greater risk exists because the owner's buyout money comes from the future earnings of the business after he leaves it.
- In my experience, if the business is worth more than $2 million or so, it is very difficult for the employees to be able to afford it. The owner simply has too much money and financial independence at risk.
- Employees are often employees because they don't have an owner "mindset." They're not entrepreneurs and they don't respond well to the challenges and pressures of ownership.

The cash flow of the business, especially with smaller businesses, may not permit much pre-funding since the owners already take out all of the excess cash flow. Therefore, the risk to you as the owner can be quite significant because all available money will come out after you leave, leaving little cushion in the business. Although there are many ways to minimize this disadvantage, bear in mind there is still a significant **risk** in transferring control of the business when you leave it. I don't think you will want to come back into the business after you've tasted the good life and after your successor has run the business into the ground and made customers, cash flow, employees and the good reputation of the business all vanish.

## Option III:  Sale to a Third Party

In a retirement situation, a sale to a third party too often becomes a bargain sale—the only alternative to liquidation.  This option becomes necessary because you have failed to create a market for your stock through sale to your family, co-owners, or employees.  The problems—and opportunities—inherent in this situation are reviewed in greater detail in Chapters Eight and Nine, but a few observations are in order at this time.

### *Advantages*

- If the business is prepared for sale (and this is a big if!) you can get *cashed out*.  Many owners don't realize this.  But, unless you are truly a "Mom and Pop" business, you should get most or all of your money from the business at closing.  Therefore, the fundamental advantage of the third party sale is cash.  Now.  This ensures that you attain your fundamental objectives of financial security and, perhaps, avoid risk as well.
- A second primary objective, that of treating all children equally, is also easier to achieve, because eventually, you just divide the money among them on an equal basis without having to worry about who is going to run the business, etc.
- Often an unanticipated advantage in selling to a third party is the ability to frequently receive substantially more cash than your CPA or other business appraiser anticipated because the marketplace is "hot."

### *Disadvantages*

- Regardless of what the buyer says, the personality, the culture of your business will undergo a radical change.  The buyer would not buy the business unless convinced that the business can be improved through change.  Maintaining the culture of the business is normally best achieved by selling to someone other than an outside third party.

- If you do not receive the bulk of the purchase price in cash, at closing, your risk normally becomes immense. The best way to avoid this risk is to get all the money you will need at closing so that anything you carry is "gravy."

## Option IV: Liquidation

If there is no one to buy your business, you shut it down. In a liquidation the owners sell off their assets, collect outstanding accounts receivable, pay off their bills, and keep what's left, if anything, for themselves.

The primary reason liquidation is considered is that a business lacks sufficient income-producing capacity apart from the owner's direct efforts and apart from the value of the assets themselves. That is, if the business can produce only $75,000 per year and the assets themselves are worth $1 million, no one would pay more for the business than the value of the assets. In general, smaller businesses (those producing less than $75,000 of income to the owners) are unlikely to be sold to anyone other than, perhaps, a key employee.

Service businesses in particular are thought to have little value when the owner leaves the business. This certainly is true if liquidation occurs.

Since most service businesses have little "hard value" other than accounts receivable, liquidation produces the smallest return for the owner's lifelong commitment to his business. *In a service business with little accumulated assets, liquidation is preferable only to death as a means of getting money out of your business.* Smart owners guard against this. They plan ahead to ensure that they do not have to rely on this last ditch method to fund their retirement.

## Summary

Up to this point we've looked briefly at the four ways to leave your business. Each method contains not only related characteristics, but also substantial and often dramatic differences. Each departure method is reviewed in greater detail in the following chapters. Chapter Seven analyzes the sale of your business interest to co-owners or key employees. Chapter Eight and Nine review the sale to a third party. Also, in Chapter 10, you'll get a closer look at the method of transferring ownership to your children.

The following exercise will help you determine which qualities appeal to you most and which least fit your business. It also helps determine what needs to be in place before you leave the place.

### Appendix 6.1:  Four Ways to Leave Your Business Checklist

☐      1.  Transfer of business to children.

     a.  This method appeals to me because:

_____

_____

_____

     b.  This method might be appropriate for my business for the following reasons:

_____

_____

_____

     c.  This method would be appropriate only if the following conditions were present:

_____

_____

_____

    d.  This method is inappropriate for me and my business for these reasons:

_____

_____

_____

❑    2.  Sale to co-owners, key employees, or all employees.

    a.  This method appeals to me because:

_____

_____

_____

    b.  This method might be appropriate for my business for the following reasons:

_____

_____

_____

    c.  This method would be appropriate for my business only if the following conditions were present:

_____

_____

_____

    d.  This method is inappropriate for me and my business for these reasons:

_____

_____

_____

❑    3.  Sale to a third party.

    a.  This method appeals to me because:

_____

_____

_____

    b.  This method might be appropriate for my business
       for the following reasons:

_____

_____

_____

    c.  This method would be appropriate for my business
       only if the following conditions were present:

_____

_____

_____

    d.  This method is inappropriate for me and my business
       for these reasons:

_____

_____

_____

❑    4.  Liquidation.

This should be used only as a last resort.  Don't even
consider this.

# 7

# Getting Blood from a Turnip

*Structuring the business sale for co-owners or employees*

You've been thinking about it all year. This morning you woke up and, over a cup of coffee, told your spouse, *"I've made up my mind. I'm going to sell out. Then we're going to take that long, long vacation we've always talked about."*

But how do you proceed?

First, revive your spouse. Then look at the best way to *structure a retirement buyout* by asking and answering these fundamental questions:

- How do I minimize tax consequences to me, to the business and to the new owner on the transfer of my ownership?
- How do I structure the transaction to guarantee I receive all the monies due me?

These issues must all be resolved in the transfer of your business to children, to key employees or to a co-owner. The transfer techniques described in this chapter are used when transferring a business to anyone other than to an outside third party.

### Minimizing Tax Consequences

No one likes to pay more taxes than absolutely necessary. But in a sale of a business to "insiders," the tax issue is aggravated by the lack of excess cash to fund your buyout. Since a key employee or a co-owner (or your children, for that matter) will not have significant funds on their own to buy your interest–nor will any bank, hoping to maintain solvency, loan them money for buyout purposes–your dollars can be generated from only one source: The Business.

The business then must generate cash and you must receive it. The structure of this transaction determines how much money the IRS receives . . . and what is left for you. Realize, that however the transfer is designed, the business has to produce 100 percent of the cash flow. The insiders do not have a separate source of money to give to you.

Secondly, realize that the cash flow to pay to you will be generated *after you leave the business.* Cash flow earned before you leave is **yours** because you still own the business. It makes no sense to give part of **your** cash flow to insiders before you leave in order to pre-fund your buyout or to begin the buy out before you leave. Why would you fund your own buyout with your money? Of course, there can be good reason to begin this process before you leave, if you realize that the true purpose of pre-funding or partial sale is to place "golden handcuffs" on those employees you want to stay with the company **after** you leave.

Always keep in the forefront of your Exit Plan your needs to:

(1) Structure the sale to minimize taxes; and
(2) Secure the success of the buyout by securing your right to the cash flow of the business.

### Methods of Transfer.

Transferring the business to a key employee or co-owner will take one or more of the following paths:

• Sale of ownership interest

- Non-Qualified Deferred Compensation and similar methods
- Enhanced Qualified Retirement Plan contributions
- Employee Stock Ownership Plan (ESOP)

Now, let us examine each method from a tax standpoint–yours and the buyer's. After this examination, our focus will shift to securing the cash flow which has been maximized by choosing the best buy out method.

## Sale of Stock to Shareholders or Key Employees

If the retirement monies are proceeds from the sale of their businesses, the "retiring" owners will pay a capital gains tax on the difference between the price received for their stock and their basis in the stock. In selling your business interest to an insider, you will normally be selling stock as opposed to the assets of the business. Without getting too technical, basis is ordinarily the price the owner originally paid for the stock. Basis can also be affected by distributions made in respect to that stock, especially in S Corporations.

In the typical closely held business, the owner's basis is very low in comparison to the ultimate selling price. In that case, most of the purchase price paid is subject to capital gains taxes. If you, the owner, are to receive $1 million for your business interest, and we assume your basis is zero, you will be taxed on the entire $1 million gain received.

### Consequences to the Buyer.

Assume, on a $1 million sale that, after paying State and Federal capital gains taxes, the net to the owner is $750,000. An effective tax of 25 percent doesn't sound all that bad. And it isn't. The problem? That isn't the only tax. It's less than one-half the tax on the entire sale. The buyer–key employee, co-owner, or, for that matter, a child–must first receive money from the business, then pay a tax on it because it is compensation, then pay the remainder to you.

The process is like this:

1. Business earns one dollar
2. Business pays that one dollar to Key Employee, with Business getting deduction.
3. Key Employee pays tax at approximately 35 percent (State and Federal Income Tax, FICA, Medicaid Tax, etc.), leaving Key Employee with 65 cents.
4. Key Employee pays 65 cents to you as part payment for ownership.
5. Former owner pays 25 percent or 16 cents Capital Gains (Federal and State) Tax.
6. Net in Former Owner's pocket is 49 cents. And, depending on State income taxes and what Congress decides to do from time to time with the Capital Gains Tax and the Income Tax brackets/rates, the net to you as Former Owner can be even smaller.

Result: Few businesses can be successfully transferred when the IRS gets 50 percent or more of the available proceeds.

It only makes sense then, to *sell your ownership interest for the lowest price.* The lower the price paid for your stock, the less money is subject to the double whammy of income tax to buyer (key employee) and capital gains tax to seller (you). It doesn't seem right to strive for as little, rather than reap as much, for something you've worked so hard for. No doubt you're thinking–"I'd rather have a double tax, than to almost give my business away. At least I'll get something."

The key is *to get the income you want and need without subjecting the business cash flow–the golden goose–to the double tax.* If the cash flow is subject to a single tax there is more of the cash flow available to pay to you. You will not only get more money, you'll have a far greater likelihood of receiving it. The business will not need to earn as much money, or to allocate all of it to the buy out, thus increasing the chance of business survival. Finally, the key employee will be able to use a portion of the extra cash flow (unless you want all of it) for growth, investment within the business, etc.

The real question is: *To what extent* will the total monies you receive be from stock sale proceeds, and how much will be by tax favored methods? These tax favored methods transfer money–but not for the ownership interest itself–from the purchaser to you. These methods result in a tax deduction at the company level and a single tax at the owner level. Accordingly, they are used in conjunction with a sale of stock because of their tax advantages. The most common, and perhaps best of these tax favored methods is a non-qualified deferred compensation plan for the owner.

## Use of Deferred Compensation

If you had continued to receive compensation from the business after retirement in an amount equal to periodic installment payments of your desired purchase price, the tax consequences to you would be roughly the same–that is, an income tax, at about the same effective rate as the capital gains rate. Thus, usually there is little difference to you, from a tax standpoint, between the sale of the ownership interest and receipt of earned income–at least if FICA and related taxes are avoided.

The business, however, gets to deduct the deferred compensation payment to you. Thus, it needs to earn one dollar to pay you one dollar. If the business is acquiring your stock (a non-deductible capital acquisition) it must earn about $1.50 or more to pay you your one dollar.

For this type of plan to work, it must be in place well before (preferably years before) you begin to sell or transfer the business. Other types of direct, deductible payments from the business to the departing owner work equally well. These include:

- Lease payments at the **highest** defensible rate between you and the business. Consider increasing the leasing rate on the office or warehouse space you might currently be leasing to the business. Also, if your business uses a significant amount of equipment, begin buying the equipment personally (or better yet via a limited liability entity you own) and lease the equipment to the business. After the equipment is paid for, the rental payments continue–giving you a tax deductible method of receiving "value" for the business after you've left it. And it is secured and not subject to the claims of the business creditors.

- Consulting fees. Like non-qualified deferred compensation, consulting fees are tax deductible to the business and ordinary income to you. The big difference is that to receive a consulting fee, you have to consult. In other words, you must work. That may or may not fit into your plans.

- Royalty or licensing fees. Again, these require something you can license to the business–an idea, a copyright, a patent. Keep it outside the business to receive deductible payments.

The bottom line on all of these techniques, from deferred compensation to license payments is receiving money generated by the business that is taxed but once. It takes planning, it takes effort, it takes time to use these techniques effectively. *But you cut the tax consequences in half.*

A final technique that can be most effective at reducing value, minimizing taxes and lowering the risk that the transaction will boomerang: Take as much money out of the business **now** as the company can afford and which doesn't subject you to significantly greater taxes.

Many owners simply accumulate too much money in their companies. This creates a burden when it comes time to transfer the business if it is a regular corporation. A burden in the sense that you want the money, but getting it will be a taxable event to you. If it is too much money, the IRS may consider it "unreasonable compensation" and tax it at the company level as a dividend (thus denying a deduction to the company for the payment). Also, leaving unnecessary cash in the business subjects that money to the creditors and increases the value of the company.

## Using Increased Retirement Funding

You should already be aware of the tax advantages of retirement plans. If not, take a deep breath and reread the information on tax (or is it taxing?) in Chapter 5. Contributions to such a plan by the business are deductible, and the tax on income earned through the plan for your benefit is deferred until you withdraw the money from the plan. Ordinarily these plans cannot discriminate in your favor as the owner; any funding for your benefit would also have to benefit the other participating employees.

But through proper design of the plan, you can increase the amount of your benefit relative to the other co-owners or key employees who are also purchasing the stock. This will change the character—and therefore the tax treatment of payments to you, the retiring owner—but not the total amount of your payment.

In companies where you and the purchasers of your stock are the only significant participants in the retirement plan, it may be possible to have the purchasers (if they are highly compensated individuals) opt out of the retirement plan. At the same time, the funding formula can be increased so that a greater amount of retirement plan benefits accumulate for you, but not for the other, and presumably younger, participants. You will then receive a disproportionate amount of the company's cash flow as a retirement plan contribution.

In order to pay the plan's increased funding requirement for your benefit, the other co-owners or key employees may even reduce their current salaries. Thus, if there is enough time, the company can increase your current salary as well as its contributions on your behalf into the retirement plans. The sum of these monies will reduce the amount of money you will need to have paid to you by other means at your actual retirement.

## Using an ESOP

Recently one of our clients sold his stock in his closely held business.  The transaction benefited him, the business, and the employees.  Our client realized no taxable gain, the company earned a tax break, and the employees received a benefit plan that eventually will make them their own employers.  Something straight from Aesop's Fables?  Well, sort of.  It was an ESOP.

The ESOP is more than just another qualified retirement plan recognized by the Internal Revenue Code.  When considering the 1986 Tax Reform Act, the U.S. Senate recognized ESOPs as "a bold and innovative technique for strengthening the free private enterprise system."  As a result of this strong congressional support, ESOPs came through the tax reform process relatively unscathed.  In fact, some commentators believe that ESOPs are more attractive than ever.

So just what is an ESOP?

It's a qualified plan, an Employee Stock Option Plan, usually profit-sharing, adopted by an employer corporation which is designed to invest primarily in the employer's stock.  There are many ways for the ESOP to acquire and finance that stock, each a method having different business and tax advantages.  For example, the client described above sold his stock directly to the ESOP in order to achieve the results I mentioned.

The stock contained in the ESOP, or its value in cash, is distributed to participants of the ESOP upon termination of their employment.  As in other qualified plans, certain participation and vesting requirements will limit the available benefits.

In a closely held business, the ESOP provides a buyer for the owner's stock, a buyer who might not otherwise exist.  ESOPs can also be pivotal in the structure of a leveraged buyout of a company by co-owners, employees, or third parties.

The most touted ESOP incentive allows you to sell your stock to an ESOP and to *defer all gain* on that sale if you reinvest the proceeds in the stock of other publicly traded operating companies, such as General Motors.

To make it easier for ESOPs to purchase stock, the tax law allows a bank making a stock purchase loan to an ESOP to report as income only half of the interest it receives. Thus, ESOPs can secure below-market-rate loans.

### Summary of Transfer Methods

So much for laying the groundwork. As we've seen, a stock purchase is generally nondeductible to the buyer. The payment for the stock is ordinarily completely taxable to you after you have recovered your cost basis. Deferred compensation is fully deductible by the business and fully taxable to you. Retirement plan funding is fully deductible by the business and tax-deferred to you. Sale of stock via an ESOP results in deductibility by the corporation and long-term, perhaps, permanent, tax deferral to you and your family.

Thus, there is a sliding scale of income tax benefits. But like everything else in business, there is no free lunch–any tax-advantaged transaction carries with it certain obligations and increased complexity that may cause you to prefer a simple stock sale.

Now, let's get back to our case history.

*Remember Jim DeBoer and his junior partner, Tom Metz? If you recall, Jim wanted to retire with a half-million bucks, but his partner couldn't come close to buying him out. Tom knew that if DeBoer-Metz Corporation would purchase Jim's stock, Tom would own 100 percent of the outstanding stock. And there was cash flow at the corporate level to pay Jim $500,000–if it could be spread over a ten-year period. But there were complications.*

*If the company purchased Jim's stock for $500,000 payable over ten years, it would need to pay about $40,000 in interest annually during the initial years, plus an annual $50,000 principal payment. As a nondeductible item, the principal payment would require the company to use taxable income of $75,000, pay taxes of about $25,000 on that $75,000 to net the $50,000.*

*In addition to the $75,000, the company would also have to pay interest of $40,000 and would use another $50,000, pre-tax, in order to fund the ongoing capital needs of the business, such as equipment replacements, leasehold improvements, and other items. Therefore, the business would need to earn, **before tax**, $165,000.*

*Since Jim's salary had been $75,000 per year, including bonus, and the company systematically retained $50,000 for capital needs, there would be a shortfall of about $40,000 during the initial years, decreasing to less than $20,000 as the principal was paid down in later years. A cash flow shortfall like this is typical in "boot strap" acquisitions or leveraged buyout situations.*

*What to do? We looked at three possibilities in conjunction with a stock sale:*

1. *A retirement plan.*
2. *Deferred compensation plus an ESOP plan.*
3. *Deferred compensation without an ESOP plan.*

***First, we looked at using the company's existing retirement plan in terms of increasing the company's contributions to DeBoer while decreasing Metz's salary.*** *The company had been contributing about $20,000 per year to the company's retirement plan. By changing the type of retirement plan from a profit sharing plan to a defined benefit plan, decreasing Metz's salary slightly to partly allow for the increased amount of contributions, and having Metz elect not to participate in the new plan, the proposed total of compensation plus retirement plan contributions for each owner looked like this:*

*Metz:*      *$60,000, all compensation.*
*DeBoer:*    *$75,000 compensation plus*
            *$75,000 plan contribution.*

*Since we integrated the defined benefit plan (see explanation of "integration" in Chapter Four), and the other employees were all fairly young, only a small portion of the defined benefit annual contribution–about $10,000–was allocated to them.*

*Unfortunately, we didn't have the luxury of time. This type of retirement plan funding needs time while DeBoer is still an employee of the company. If we had three years, we probably could have funded about $300,000 for DeBoer. Combined with a stock sale for $200,000, he would have had his half million. But he wanted to retire much sooner than that.*

Nevertheless, this example illustrates the important point that there is still a considerable amount of flexibility in designing retirement plans to benefit primarily the departing shareholder under the following circumstances:

- The retiring shareholder is between 50 and 60 years old.
- The other co-owners are highly compensated and therefore can elect not to participate.
- There is enough time, five years or so, to fund the plan.
- The other employees who participate in the plan do not take a large proportion of the plan contribution, because they are few in number and, for the most part, considerably younger than the departing owner.
- The co-owners can reduce their current compensation enough to make cash available to meet the company's increased contribution requirement.

Next, we looked at *using an ESOP* as one method of getting money to DeBoer. Under this method, DeBoer would sell his stock valued at $300,000–an amount an appraiser thought equal to fair market value–to the ESOP. DeBoer would receive deferred compensation payments totaling $200,000 from the business.

*DeBoer would pay no taxes on the $300,000 received from ESOP if he reinvested the proceeds in qualifying securities–essentially stock and securities in companies that operate ongoing publicly traded businesses. He would pay taxes on the $300,000 when he sold the qualifying securities. He would have to pay income taxes on the deferred compensation as he received it.*

*The ESOP would obtain the $300,000 cash by borrowing from a bank at a reduced loan rate. Banks are generally eager to make ESOP loans because they need only pay income tax on one half of the interest income earned on the loan. The loan would be secured by the assets of the DeBoer/Metz Corporation, personally guaranteed by Metz, and paid off by annual contributions to the ESOP from the business over a seven-year period.*

*There are substantial advantages in using an ESOP for the selling shareholder. He gets a significant amount, if not all, of his selling price up front; and there is a potential deferral of the gain until he ultimately sells the reinvested securities. If he holds the securities until death, his estate can even avoid paying income taxes on the gain.*

*The remaining shareholders stand to benefit as well. The payoff of $300,000 to DeBoer is, in effect, tax-deductible by the company, since it pays the debt off through its tax-deductible contributions to the ESOP. Meanwhile, Metz remains firmly in control of the company since he already owns half of it and will elect himself trustee of the ESOP. Although the participants of the plan are entitled to vote on significant corporate decisions, Metz will manage the day-to-day operation of the company.*

*When an ESOP is involved, the primary disadvantage to Metz is that he would own not 100 percent of the stock, but only 50 percent. Only half of any future appreciation in value of the company would benefit him. Metz could increase his ownership interest by agreeing, or having the corporation agree, to buy some of DeBoer's stock instead of the ESOP buying all of it.*

*An additional disadvantage was that as the participants of the ESOP retire and request their retirement plan shares, the company (or Metz if he wants to increase his ownership percentage) will need to acquire the stock otherwise owned by the departing employees. That purchase is not tax-deductible and, in a sense, is paying for the stock for a second time–once through the original retirement plan contribution and a second time when the stock is reacquired.*

For these reasons DMC decided not to install an ESOP. (However, another owner may have found it ideal, especially if that owner wanted a large sum of money up front and the other co-owner or key employees was not in as significant a bargaining position as was Metz.)

In addition to a stock purchase, we finally settled on our third option: deferred compensation. Here's why:

*Instead of having the company pay $500,000 for Jim's stock, the accountants assured us that they could justify a value of $100,000 for his stock as its fair market value. The remaining $400,000 could be paid to Jim in the form of deferred compensation.*

*Since Jim's basis in the stock was only $25,000, his tax consequences would be basically the same–that is, he would have experienced a recovery of basis of $25,000 and all the remaining payments from the corporation, under either scenario, would be taxed at a similar income tax rate.*

*The corporation's initial cash flow needs under each scenario can be seen in Charts I and II:*

---

### Chart I.  $500,000 Stock sale only.

|  | Cash Needed Annually After Tax | Cash Needed Annually Before Tax |
|---|---|---|
| Installment payments: |  |  |
| Principal | $  50,000 | $  75,000 |
| Interest | 40,000 | 40,000 |
| Deferred compensation | 0 | 0 |
| Total | $  90,000 | $ 115,000 |

## Chart II.  $100,000 Stock sale and $400,000 deferred compensation.

|  | Cash Needed Annually After Tax | Cash Needed Annually Before Tax |
|---|---|---|
| Installment payments: |  |  |
| Principal | $  10,000 | $  12,000 |
| Interest | 8,000 | 8,000 |
| Deferred compensation | 72,000 | 72,000 |
| Total | $  90,000 | $  92,000 |

*The advantages of proper tax planning should be apparent in the above example. As illustrated, DeBoer receives roughly the same amount under either scenario.  The corporation, however, saves $250,000 (about a third of the total cost) over a ten-year period through such planning, because the funds are not going to Uncle Sam.  These additional monies can be kept either at the corporate level, distributed to the departing shareholder, or divided in some proportion between the corporation and the departing owner.*

At first glance it would seem that the departing shareholder would always want the entire savings passed on to him.  However, in any type of installment buy out, the individual who is leaving the company must be concerned with its future economic health and profitability–if he expects to receive his payout over time.  Therefore, easing the tax burden to the company is one way to help ensure future payments.  In our example the extra money was needed at the business level to make the deal work.

The lesson to be learned here is that *because of substantial tax advantages to the corporation and the lack of any offsetting tax disadvantage to the departing shareholder, deferred compensation is a vital element in tax planning, especially planning for retirement.* It's important to install a deferred compensation agreement long before your actual retirement so that the IRS has no justification to tie the agreement to the sale of your stock. Otherwise the IRS might argue that the deferred compensation is payment for the sale of stock.

And how about Royce Cassidy, whom we met in Chapter Six?

*He told me his company had earned $450,000 in taxable income the previous year, but the strain of running the business virtually single-handedly was too much. In seeking a buyer, he discovered to his surprise that he himself was the company's most valuable asset. Without his presence to oversee day-to-day operations, no one was interested in buying him out.*

*He soon realized that his best alternative was to remain on the job while he found, trained, and delegated responsibilities to key employees who could replace his technical and marketing skills. After twice picking the wrong person, he finally found two people he had confidence in. One was a skilled marketer; the other possessed a background in operations. Cassidy provided them with an incentive and ownership package that motivated them to stay with the company. He also gave his business added protection by insisting they agree to trade secret and non-compete provisions in their employment agreements.*

*A deferred compensation agreement for Royce was implemented and partial funding was accomplished by keeping the salaries of the two key employees lower than they otherwise would have been. This again gave the key employees a stake in the future. They would want to be around when Cassidy did leave, since they paid—indirectly—for the deferred compensation. It also gave Cassidy and the employees more confidence that the payment could be made upon his retirement.*

*The two key employees eventually will own the business, which is worth much more than they could ever hope to purchase with their own funds. At the same time, Cassidy will hop along into a comfortable retirement, albeit years later than he'd hoped, confident that he has the right people in place to replace him and some of the funding already done. Should one or the other of the employees falter, Cassidy has retained the ability to replace them through buy-back agreements.*

Cassidy eventually found a solution. It's too bad, though, that he took so long to recognize his problem. Ideally, his search for replacement ownership would have begun much earlier–soon after he started his company. That way the business would have had more time to test and build a management team, more time to make–and learn from–mistakes.

### Securing the buyout

The cardinal rule of all buyouts by co-owners, key employees or children is:

### Before control is transferred, all owner objectives must be met.

These owner objectives include:

- Financial security and independence
- Attainment of departure or retirement date
- Business continuity
- Other unique owner-based objectives, if any.

Keep in mind that this class of purchaser does not have cash to pay to you, at least not in substantial amounts. The question then is: How can meaningful ownership transfer be accomplished without premature loss of control?

For new owners to work long and hard you must dangle the carrots of ownership and control before them. But you can not afford to give them meaningful control before you have achieved your owner-based objectives. Thus, a natural tug-of-war pits you against the new owners: you are reluctant to give up control without receiving money, and the new owner is reluctant to make needed sacrifices and commitments without receiving meaningful ownership. This contest stymies many otherwise mutually beneficial transfers. Avoid this obstacle by using a process which has worked for many of my clients.

First, have the proposed new owners (whether your children, co-owner or key employee) *replace you in the business operations*. This doesn't necessarily mean that the proposed new owner, especially a child, is able to run the business. They may not be running the business now–your employees or co-owners run the business. But it does mean that **you** are not needed to run the business. It becomes the responsibility of the proposed new ownership to either run the business themselves (the likely case) or at least to find qualified key employees to help them operate the business.

Second, you, as owner, must *transfer the risk of financial loss to the proposed new ownership*. Usually this means that before you lose control through transfer of ownership interests, you no longer personally guarantee debt, bonding or any obligation related to the business such as leases, supply contracts and so on.

Third, *begin the ownership transfer process without losing control* by doing one or more of the following:

1.  *Sell a minority interest* in the business with the promise to sell the balance once your owner-based objectives are met, or the certainty of their being met is evident. Establish objective standards such as: receipt of purchase money, release of your personal liability exposure to third parties, pay off of third party debt by the business, and so on.

2.  Begin *transferring a majority of the equity* ownership through nonvoting stock or similar types of ownership interests while you maintain control through owning a majority of the voting interests. This allows you to transfer more than 50 percent of the equity without risking loss of ownership control.

3. Whenever transferring any type of ownership interest *always have a buy back agreement* which allows you to reacquire all of the transferred ownership upon the occurrence of certain events, such as: default in making payments to you as due, default in making payments to third party lenders of the business, a decrease in the net equity of the business, or whatever measurements or standards you deem vital to the best interests of the business.

Fourth, when control is transferred, all owner-based objectives have ideally been met. But if not, financial security can be enhanced through one or more of the following techniques:

1. *Pre-funding your departure through enhancing retirement plan benefits* to you. This concept was discussed earlier in this chapter.

2. A second pre-funding technique is to *establish a nonqualified deferred compensation plan* for you. Although this concept was discussed earlier in this chapter, the twist I now propose is that the purchasers at least partially fund your nonqualified deferred compensation plan before the buy out process begins. To accomplish this, they must be employees and must agree to have their compensation reduced prior to the beginning of the buy out process. That compensation reduction will be paid to you in the form of deferred compensation benefits.

   If the buy-put does not proceed, this salary reduction on the part of the proposed buyers will instead be paid out to them through establishment of a nonqualified deferred compensation plan created for *their benefit*. This is similar to the arrangement made by DeBoer and Metz described on page 128.

In other words, we create two nonqualified deferred compensation plans funded with deferred salaries (or bonuses) from the proposed purchaser. If the purchase does proceed, you receive the deferred monies and the key employees' nonqualified deferred compensation plan is terminated. On the other hand, as I mentioned, if your purchase does not go through, then the key employees receive the deferred compensation, to the extent vested, upon their termination of employment. Proceeding on this basis gives the key employee the security of knowing that his continued efforts to enhance the profitability of the company will result in a greater deferral under the nonqualified deferred compensation plan which in turn means a greater down payment is available when he eventually buys the business.

3. *Use an installment sale with substantial security* in the form of the *ownership* interests (stock or partnership interest), the *assets of the business, the personal guarantee of the purchaser and of his or her spouse.* (I like to get the personal guarantee of both husband and wife to prevent transfers of assets from one spouse to the other in the event of impending default under the installment sale obligation.) In smaller sales it might be possible to get the personal guarantee of other family members such as a wealthy parent.

4. *Receive cash up front through third party financing.* This concept is similar to the way many buy outs are structured to outside third parties, especially where purchase price is not great. Typically, the purchaser puts up about one-third of the value of the company. Third party financing, usually through a bank, is then obtained for approximately another third of the purchase price. The owner is expected to carry back, in a subordinate position to the bank, the final one-third of the purchase price.

If you elect this route, I give you the same advice I give to those owners selling to third parties: be sure that the two-thirds you receive up front is sufficient to meet all of your financial security objectives, because you may never see anything else. I also doubt you will get more than about one-third of the fair market value in the form of third party financing. If financing is readily attainable, then reexamine your purchase price–you may be selling too low.

5.  *Receive cash via a partial sale to a third party.* The third party may be an ESOP (See discussion earlier in this chapter), a passive investor, or Santa Claus. I mention this latter potential purchaser only because the likelihood of finding a qualified third party interested in buying a partial interest in a closely held business, where that third party investor is not going to be owning and operating the business, is about as likely as seeing Santa Claus.

6.  *Alternately, don't transfer a controlling interest in the business, ever.* Simply transfer enough of an ownership interest to entice and to attract the key employees (including your children?) as permanent co-owners. They will attain the controlling interest only upon your death through a pre-funded (with life insurance) buy-sell agreement. You will then receive the bulk of your "retirement income" necessary for financial security through ownership distributions from the business. These distributions will likely be in the form of partnership distributions or Subchapter S distributions on non-qualified deferred compensation.

## Summary

The central message of this chapter is simply this: In addition to death and taxes, there is the certainty that sooner or later you will depart from your business. How handsomely you reward yourself on that occasion depends on the retirement plan you put into motion today. The more time you give yourself, the greater range of options you will have.

We've explored several (but by no means all) ways to transfer ownership to your employees or co-owners. The particular method, or methods, you select depends on several factors. The first factor is time: When do you want to retire? Set a date now. At that time, do you want to retire completely or work on a *reduced schedule*?

If your retirement date is less than five years away, you probably haven't enough time to fund a defined benefit retirement plan or even to properly establish and fund a deferred compensation program. A leveraged ESOP buy out can work as well as a straightforward stock sale. However, you may want to give yourself more than three years, even with a stock sale or an ESOP buyout. If you can allow five years before you retire, then any method, and any combination of methods, can usually be made to work. Consider what's just been discussed by answering the questions in the following checklist.

### Appendix 7.1:  Transfer of Ownership Checklist

❑ Whom do you wish to sell to? _____

_____

_____

❑ Does the potential buyer, or buyers, have as much skill as you do? _____

_____

_____

❑ With your retirement, what gaps in the running of the business need to be filled?_____

_____

_____

❑ Will the new owner(s) have the skills to fill those gaps?

_____

_____

❑ If not, what is the best way of finding someone who has the required skills? _____

_____

_____

❑ When should the new owner(s) be brought on board?

_____

_____

❑ Will they need to own stock as well? _____

_____

_____

❑ How much is your business worth today?_____

_____

_____

❑ How much will the business likely be worth at your planned retirement date?_____

_____

_____

❑ How much money do you need from the business in total? And what form can this payment take? For example, lump sum? Per year? For how many years? _____

_____

_____

❑ How much money do you need to live on after retirement? What portion of that amount must come from the proceeds of the sale of your business? _____

_____

_____

These are all simple questions. They are questions most people never ask themselves. Yet, if you have no goal or objectives to reach for, how can you attain a satisfactory retirement? Review the goals you set in Chapter One and review them periodically. Revise as needed.

The answers to these questions may also help determine the form the buy out must take. For example, if you feel the need for a large amount of cash up front, deferred compensation is not the answer; perhaps a stock sale or an ESOP, either one financed with a bank loan, would be more appropriate.

On the other hand, if time is on your side because you've started the planning process early enough, all the actions we've just covered may work; it is your happy task to select the most appropriate. Finally, if none of the ideas discussed in this chapter are workable, you're probably faced with making the same decision as the bulk of business owners: the decision which is the subject of the next chapter.

# 8

# From Swampland to Alligator Farm

*Selling smart by using transaction advisors, structuring the sale, and minimizing taxes.*

Selling one's business to a stranger is often considered a "last resort"–just short of total liquidation. In my experience, however, this "last resort" is often the finest my clients have ever experienced. In fact, they often end up at the resort of their choice.

Surveys show most owners initially want to transfer their businesses to co-owners, employees, or family members. Yet, these same owners usually end up selling to outsiders. While the reasons for this are many, the most common are:

1. The business is too valuable to be purchased by anyone other than someone who has access to a considerable source of money.
2. There is no prospective buyer among the owner's children or employees who desires to, and is capable of, running the business.
3. The owner wants to receive a substantial amount of cash at the closing, an unlikely event if he or she sells to a co-owner, an employee or a family member.

Usually, a third party sale results from a combination of these factors.

As we discussed earlier, it is of the utmost importance that you assemble a strong management team that could someday assume ownership. In some smaller businesses that can't support a management infrastructure, that's just not feasible. But even if it is, you might at least consider a sale to a third party for several reasons:

- You want to receive most of your selling price up front.
- An additional cash infusion into the business is needed for it to remain viable after your departure.
- Your employees or co-owners are willing to purchase only part of your business.

Should any of these conditions exist, look seriously at a third party sale. Factors critical to a third party sale include: (1) determining the sale price of your business; (2) knowing how to find a buyer; (3) structuring the sales transaction from the seller's perspective; and (4) knowing how the sale process works.

This chapter discusses finding the buyer using transaction advisors and structuring the sale to minimize taxes. The next chapter concentrates on setting an achievable sale price and on describing the ins and outs of the sale process.

One final point. Many owners begin the transfer process with the thought that a sale to a key employee or co-owner or even to a family member is the path to maximum cash upon departure. This is very, very seldom the case. With proper preparation, advice and counsel the vast majority of business owners maximize the net dollars they receive by selling to a third party. Not only that, but most third party sales are cash sales; seldom are sellers forced to "carry" greater than 30 percent to 35 percent of the sales price. The bottom line:

*Selling to a third party maximizes the money in your pocket and minimizes your financial risk.*

## Finding the Buyer

Finding a buyer can be as difficult as finding a snip of hay in a mound of needles. True, some businesses are continually approached by potential purchasers. Usually these "eager buyers" are business brokers looking for a commission or unfunded buyers looking for a fire sale opportunity. Is it difficult to find a qualified buyer? There are two answers, each mostly accurate. Yes, it's almost impossible to find a qualified buyer if the business is not prepared for sale and if you try to find the buyer yourself. No, finding a qualified buyer is not only possible, it is inevitable–if the business is properly prepared and you use the following techniques to locate and qualify your purchaser.

### *Selling Your Business to Someone Familiar With It*

Criminologists say that most murderers know their victims. That's good news for people who have few enemies or travel in friendly circles. Similarly, you may already know the future owner of your business. The buyer is likely to be a fellow competitor, one of your suppliers, a major customer, or someone who has heard of your business through these sources.

Sometimes you will know these people well enough to tell them you are interested in selling. Often they will sense you are ready to leave your business by watching your level of interest in the day-to-day operations of the business. That's why it's critical that you always present your business operation in the best possible light to those competitors, suppliers and customers.

"Competitor" is not limited to those in your immediate trade area. Instead, a potential purchaser is often a fellow competitor who is active in your national trade or industry organization. It's much easier to be open with someone in a similar line of business in a different locality. They, or people they know, may be interested in expanding into your area. They will be familiar with your type of business. They may well have known you, or at least heard of you, years before any sale takes place.

Again, if you're interested in selling at a future date, but are not active in your national industry organization, think about joining. You may find the buyer of your business at that organization's next function.

In a similar vein, national suppliers are often interested in acquiring company-owned stores. Although their marketing plans seem to change direction with each management shift, national companies that franchise their retail operations or give territorial rights for the sale of their products are often interested in acquiring a sound local operation. Whether it's a restaurant franchise or a tire distributorship, large companies are especially interested in those operations whose loss or defection to a different supplier or manufacturer would adversely affect their revenues from your area.

National or regional businesses similar to yours may want your business as an entrée into your particular city or trade region. The name of the game as the century ends seems to be growth through acquisition and consolidation. Manufacturing companies, distribution companies and others are all seeking to expand their marketing and operational strengths by moving into new territories.

Make a list now of potential buyers. Add to the list as businesses approach you or as you see a "fit." These are businesses which will be contacted when you actively begin to sell the business. Use Appendix 11.2 "Designation of Business Advisors" to record names now.

Finally, large users of your services or products may decide that acquiring your business would be less expensive than either continuing to use your business on a contract basis or starting a similar subsidiary of their own. Obviously, this carries with it both a risk and a reward. You could lose all of your business if they start their own subsidiary based on confidential information they obtain while considering the purchase of your business. (We will discuss how to protect yourself from this event later in this chapter.) An alternative would be to sell your business to another financially strong company.

• The likelihood that a complex financial transaction will arise is minimal.

The broker's primary role is to find a buyer for your business. methods used include: 1) placing advertisements in the business unities section of the newspaper, 2) direct marketing to potential and 3) co-oping with other brokers. Good business brokers ly maintain a list of qualified buyers, and are well-connected brokers both locally and nationally. The experienced brokers nd just finding the buyer. They also facilitate negotiations, ate buyer "due diligence," work closely with your attorney throughout the process until closing and sometimes continue with you and the buyer after the sale to ensure a smooth n.

### ge Fees

brokers generally charge minimal fees for preparing the valuation. They receive the bulk of their compensation in of a commission. The broker's commission is generally a rcentage based upon the size of the deal and on local market an example, a broker may charge 12 percent for the first 0 percent for the second, 8 percent for the third, 6 percent rth, 4 percent for the fifth, and 2 percent for each million value thereafter. Discuss and negotiate the broker's fees agreement using your attorney and CPA *before you sign* Consider competitive bids to ensure that you are paying s.

### Bankers and Merger and Acquisition Consultants

ness is worth more than $5 million, has been in business of three years, is in a rapidly growing or consolidating s a proprietary technology, or is in an attractive geographic should consider using an investment banker, merger and consultant or a merchant banker. (See the discussion of nkers below.) If your business meets these criteria it

---

### Using Your Advisors

Our clients frequently ask us if we know of anyone who would be interested in buying their businesses. Conversely, we have clients who ask if we know of any businesses for sale. Normally we are of little use as "business brokers." Lawyers, CPAs, and bankers simply do not know enough businesses interested in selling or buying. It's not the business of these professionals to know that; they don't get paid to know that. Consequently, they don't know many potential buyers or sellers. If a business does manage to get sold via its advisors, it is a rarity. The effectiveness of this form of business marketing has yet to be demonstrated to my satisfaction.

If you're considering using outside individuals to help sell your business, I suggest you contact someone who specializes in the field.

If you're fortunate, a qualified purchaser will appear on your doorstep of his own volition. Your personal efforts to locate such a suitor will likely be disappointing. You simply haven't the contacts, experience, skill or time necessary to locate such a company. Your business can be ready and you can be ready, but you need a matchmaker. Enter the "Transaction Advisor."

### Using a Transaction Advisor

Let's look at the types of transaction advisors available, how they work, the fees they charge, what characteristics they should possess and the fee arrangements.

Most owners know very little, if anything, about the crucial role these advisors play in the sale of a business. Their only experience is the unsolicited letter or phone call from an unknown broker informing the owner that the broker has a qualified buyer for his businesses. Give these brokers no more credence than you give lawyers who advertise on billboards. Instead, over the next few pages learn what type of transaction advisor to use, how they assist–and even lead–the sales process, and (not that you care any more about this than how much legal fees you pay) how much they charge.

If you have reached the point where you are interested in selling your business, but are uncertain about whether your company might be salable to a third party, what its market value might be, if there are potential buyers for your business or who they might be, you are ready to seek the help of a professional advisor. Professional advisors skilled at the sale of privately held businesses are business brokers, investment bankers, mergers and acquisition consultants and merchant bankers. Selecting the most appropriate advisor begins with understanding what each of these advisors brings to the table and how they are compensated.

Let's look at how these issues affected my client, Richard Meyers.

*Over a several year period, I sensed that Rich Meyers was gradually losing interest in his lawn and tree service. It had become the largest such service in his community but he had lost his sense of challenge and adventure. In short, Rich was bored and I was not the least bit surprised when he came to me with a proposal from two of his key employees to buy out his interest.*

*There was only one problem: Rich wanted out now and the employees had no money. Rich, a husband and father of three teenage children, couldn't afford to sell out unless he was cashed out at the same time. Still he was unwilling to sell to a third party out of a sense of loyalty and commitment to his key personnel.*

*Consequently, Rich had attempted to find, through his industry association, a compatible buyer who would welcome his key personnel with open arms (and perhaps some stock options). Having no luck, he came to the court of last resort. The court where the hourly fee was king. He came to me. By now I sensed a quiet desperation on Rich's part, but also a rather firm resolution finally to sell the business.*

*This is what we did.*

*First, we contacted two business brokers. They requested the following information, initial information, by the way, that you must have available as you prepare to sell your business:*

- *The last three years' financial statements and business tax returns*

- *The current financial statement y*
- *Sales material or company broc*
  *nature of the business*

*Of course, your transaction advisor*
*need much more information as the sales p*
*business brokers requested this minimal*
*business information so they could make a*
*Rich's business.*

*Both advisors estimated the sale pr*
*to $2.6 million range. They further an*
*experience, that Rich would receive at l*
*price in cash and would need to carry ba*
*no more than $750,000. Rich, using the i*
*pages ahead in the section titled "Ch*
*selected his business broker and in six m*
*abnormal timeframe) closed on the sale*

## Business Brokers

The business brokerage community is c
brokerage community and the entry requ
Thus, many business brokers have littl
business experience.

Fortunately, there are some ver
can be extremely helpful to you in se
the successful business brokers h
experience and have formal training
This real world business experience
them an understanding of the comp
how to position your business to m
It is appropriate to use a bu

- The business is worth l
- The business would m
  who desires to own an

Sales r
opportu
buyers.
general
to other
go bey
coordin
and CPA
working
transitio

## Brokera

Business
business
the form
sliding pe
rates. As
million, 1
for the fou
dollars of
and listing
*anything.*
market rat

## Investmen

If your bus
a minimun
industry, ha
region you
acquisition
merchant b

If you have reached the point where you are interested in selling your business, but are uncertain about whether your company might be salable to a third party, what its market value might be, if there are potential buyers for your business or who they might be, you are ready to seek the help of a professional advisor. Professional advisors skilled at the sale of privately held businesses are business brokers, investment bankers, mergers and acquisition consultants and merchant bankers. Selecting the most appropriate advisor begins with understanding what each of these advisors brings to the table and how they are compensated.

Let's look at how these issues affected my client, Richard Meyers.

*Over a several year period, I sensed that Rich Meyers was gradually losing interest in his lawn and tree service. It had become the largest such service in his community but he had lost his sense of challenge and adventure. In short, Rich was bored and I was not the least bit surprised when he came to me with a proposal from two of his key employees to buy out his interest.*

*There was only one problem: Rich wanted out now and the employees had no money. Rich, a husband and father of three teenage children, couldn't afford to sell out unless he was cashed out at the same time. Still he was unwilling to sell to a third party out of a sense of loyalty and commitment to his key personnel.*

*Consequently, Rich had attempted to find, through his industry association, a compatible buyer who would welcome his key personnel with open arms (and perhaps some stock options). Having no luck, he came to the court of last resort. The court where the hourly fee was king. He came to me. By now I sensed a quiet desperation on Rich's part, but also a rather firm resolution finally to sell the business.*

*This is what we did.*

*First, we contacted two business brokers. They requested the following information, initial information, by the way, that you must have available as you prepare to sell your business:*

- *The last three years' financial statements and business tax returns*

### Using Your Advisors

Our clients frequently ask us if we know of anyone who would be interested in buying their businesses. Conversely, we have clients who ask if we know of any businesses for sale. Normally we are of little use as "business brokers." Lawyers, CPAs, and bankers simply do not know enough businesses interested in selling or buying. It's not the business of these professionals to know that; they don't get paid to know that. Consequently, they don't know many potential buyers or sellers. If a business does manage to get sold via its advisors, it is a rarity. The effectiveness of this form of business marketing has yet to be demonstrated to my satisfaction.

If you're considering using outside individuals to help sell your business, I suggest you contact someone who specializes in the field.

If you're fortunate, a qualified purchaser will appear on your doorstep of his own volition. Your personal efforts to locate such a suitor will likely be disappointing. You simply haven't the contacts, experience, skill or time necessary to locate such a company. Your business can be ready and you can be ready, but you need a matchmaker. Enter the "Transaction Advisor."

### Using a Transaction Advisor

Let's look at the types of transaction advisors available, how they work, the fees they charge, what characteristics they should possess and the fee arrangements.

Most owners know very little, if anything, about the crucial role these advisors play in the sale of a business. Their only experience is the unsolicited letter or phone call from an unknown broker informing the owner that the broker has a qualified buyer for his businesses. Give these brokers no more credence than you give lawyers who advertise on billboards. Instead, over the next few pages learn what type of transaction advisor to use, how they assist–and even lead–the sales process, and (not that you care any more about this than how much legal fees you pay) how much they charge.

- *The current financial statement year-to-date*
- *Sales material or company brochure which explains the nature of the business*

*Of course, your transaction advisor and other advisors will need much more information as the sales process continues, but the business brokers requested this minimal amount of financial and business information so they could make a preliminary valuation of Rich's business.*

*Both advisors estimated the sale price to be in the $2.3 million to $2.6 million range. They further anticipated, based on their experience, that Rich would receive at least two-thirds of the sale price in cash and would need to carry back, on a fully secured basis, no more than $750,000. Rich, using the information outlined several pages ahead in the section titled "Choosing the Right Advisor," selected his business broker and in six months (a fairly quick but not abnormal timeframe) closed on the sale of his business.*

### Business Brokers

The business brokerage community is closely related to the real estate brokerage community and the entry requirements are generally similar. Thus, many business brokers have little formal training and minimal business experience.

Fortunately, there are some very capable business brokers who can be extremely helpful to you in selling your business. Generally, the successful business brokers have many years of business experience and have formal training and professional designations. This real world business experience and professional training give them an understanding of the complexities of your business and of how to position your business to maximize its value to an outsider.

It is appropriate to use a business broker if:

- The business is worth less than $5 million;
- The business would most likely be sold to an individual who desires to own and operate a company; and

- The likelihood that a complex financial transaction will arise is minimal.

The broker's primary role is to find a buyer for your business. Sales methods used include: 1) placing advertisements in the business opportunities section of the newspaper, 2) direct marketing to potential buyers, and 3) co-oping with other brokers.  Good business brokers generally maintain a list of qualified buyers, and are well-connected to other brokers both locally and nationally.  The experienced brokers go beyond just finding the buyer.  They also facilitate negotiations, coordinate buyer "due diligence," work closely with your attorney and CPA throughout the process until closing and sometimes continue working with you and the buyer after the sale to ensure a smooth transition.

### Brokerage Fees

Business brokers generally charge minimal fees for preparing the business valuation.  They receive the bulk of their compensation in the form of a commission.  The broker's commission is generally a sliding percentage based upon the size of the deal and on local market rates.  As an example, a broker may charge 12 percent for the first million, 10 percent for the second, 8 percent for the third, 6 percent for the fourth, 4 percent for the fifth, and 2 percent for each million dollars of value thereafter.  Discuss and negotiate the broker's fees and listing agreement using your attorney and CPA *before you sign anything.*  Consider competitive bids to ensure that you are paying market rates.

### Investment Bankers and Merger and Acquisition Consultants

If your business is worth more than $5 million, has been in business a minimum of three years, is in a rapidly growing or consolidating industry, has a proprietary technology, or is in an attractive geographic region you should consider using an investment banker, merger and acquisition consultant or a merchant banker.  (See the discussion of merchant bankers below.)  If your business meets these criteria it may attract the interest of a regional, national or international buyer, or be a candidate for a transaction other than a straight sale. Generally, an investment banker or merger and acquisition consultant who specializes in your industry will be in the best position to advise you in this situation.

Often investment bankers and M&A consultants are thought of as people in fancy suits who put together multi-billion dollar mergers and acquisitions, live only in New York and don't have an interest in smaller privately held companies. While it is true that many of the best known New York-based investment banks do not have an interest in transactions valued at less than $100 million, there are many other high quality investment bankers and M&A consultants throughout the country who specialize in "smaller" transactions. In fact, many local and regional investment banks and specialized M&A consulting firms are headed by people who received their training at larger well-known firms then left to work in smaller, boutique firms. Typically, investment bankers and consultants are professional financial advisors experienced in the intricacies of corporate finance.

Investment bankers generally provide a variety of services to their clients including public and private financing, advice on mergers and acquisitions and a variety of other investment-related services. M&A consultants, on the other hand, generally specialize only in providing merger and acquisition services to a specific industry.

As in any profession, there are some very good investment bankers and consultants and then there are the others. *It is vital to ask for and contact references.* Your investment banker should have a reputation for objectivity and professionalism, as well as exceptional analytical and marketing skills. Your investment banker must also be connected to a large pool of potential buyers and must understand the dynamics of your industry. In addition, a good investment banker will have the resources necessary to identify and seek out the buyers who will be most interested in your business.

One of the key differences between an investment banker and a business broker is that *an investment banker will market your business to a targeted buyer profile*, whereas a broker will be less selective as to whom they market your business. Another key difference between a broker and an investment banker is that *an investment banker can provide alternatives* if your business is not quite ready to be sold. An investment banker can assist you in **raising** capital to further the growth of your business, *arrange a transaction* that enables you to withdraw cash from the company while still retaining control of the business, *coordinate an initial public offering*, or *facilitate the implementation of a wide variety of financing options.*

### *Fees.*

Investment bankers and M&A consultants are compensated in a variety of ways. Depending on the circumstances of your business, an investment banker or consultant can be paid on a commission basis, hourly fee, equity participation, or some combination thereof. It is accepted practice for investment bankers and M&A consultants to charge an up front or monthly retainer fee. This fee is generally not large enough to cover all costs, but is sufficient to enable them to *maintain their objectivity and to determine that their clients are committed to the process.* Investment bankers' and consultants' fees are always negotiated according to the circumstances of the transaction and the services to be rendered. That said, however, for a business valued at less than $5 million the commission will likely range from eight to ten percent. A business with a $5 million to $10 million value will be charged about five percent. For businesses with values greater than $10 million, the commission will generally be less than five percent, with the percentage declining as the value of the company increases. Again, you must consult your attorney and CPA when negotiating the terms of the transaction advisor's engagement letter.

### *Merchant Bankers.*

Merchant bankers operate much like investment bankers. Merchant bankers, however, generally have *equity capital to invest in the acquisition of businesses* that come to them for advice on selling.

They team with management and business owners to create shareholder value. Typically, a merchant banker will, for a fee, team with management to acquire a business. The merchant banker will then implement a plan designed to increase the value of the business over a period of years, expecting to sell the business in the future at a tidy profit.

Merchant bankers typically have three resources to offer to the management or owner of a business: *capital, financial expertise, and access to capital markets.* Usually, merchant bankers lack specific experience in a given business, but they understand how to increase the value of a business and can be very helpful in positioning a company for an initial public offering or subsequent merger or acquisition. The objective of a merchant banker is to structure a merger or acquisition so that, with minimal equity investment, the shareholders can increase the value of a business to the point where it can either be taken public or sold at a price greater than the initial purchase price. If a given business does not meet the investment criteria established by the merchant banker, then the merchant banker will act solely in the role of advisor and work with the owner to sell the business.

The advantage to working with a merchant banker is that you may avoid the need to market your business to third parties if the merchant banker desires to buy or invest in your business. The disadvantage is that you do not have the benefit of exposing your business to a number of competitive buyers to determine that you are receiving a fair value for your company. Finally, the fee merchant bankers charge for their services varies widely depending on their role in a given situation.

### Choosing the Right Advisor

The type of transaction advisor that is right for you depends on the size and nature of your business, as well as on the level of complexity of the potential sale. As with most important business decisions, I recommend that you consult with your CPA and attorney when considering the selection of a business broker or investment banker. Unlike the standard for other advisors (lawyers and CPA's) the worth of this transaction advisor is more easily measured and known. If your attorney or CPA doesn't know of the reputation of a particular transaction advisor, ask others experienced in the transaction process. They are likely to have extensive contacts in the brokerage or investment banking community. If your CPA or attorney does not have these contacts, that is a signal to you that he or she may not have much experience in the succession transaction process. You may need to retain an atorney or CPA who specializes in this area. Next, interview, with your CPA, several candidates using the questions provided at the end of this chapter (Appendix 8.3).

In addition to selecting the right type of advisor, you need to find an individual with whom you can work well, and with whom you are comfortable discussing the most confidential details of your business. Consider these five key attributes in selecting your transaction advisor.

- First, transaction advisors must adhere to the highest levels of *professional integrity* and put your interests ahead of their own so that you can trust them to give you honest, objective advice. You can determine this by speaking to references, preferably the owners or former owners from the advisor's last three completed transactions.
- Second, transaction advisors must have the exceptional *oral and written communication skills* necessary to present your company in the most favorable light and to conduct effective negotiations. Try to determine this by reviewing at least three memoranda prepared as part of prior sales.
- Third, transaction advisors must have a keen *understanding of numbers*, because every negotiation regarding price and transaction structure hinges on a fair and accurate discussion of your business's historical financial performance and future projections. If you aren't comfortable analyzing this skill, send your CPA to meet with the potential transaction advisor.

- Fourth, a transaction advisor should possess the *creativity* necessary to enable him to develop imaginative strategies for marketing your business and to find win-win solutions to problems that arise during negotiations with buyers. In evaluating the three prior characteristics, you will have some insight into the transaction advisor's creative capacity.
- Finally, successful transaction advisors are very *persistent and methodical* and will pursue the transaction process in an organized manner until all reasonable alternatives are exhausted. Again, review their references, check their reputations and trust your "read" on a prospective transaction advisor.

### *The Fee Agreement*

After you've selected your broker or investment banker you must negotiate that advisor's contract. For business brokers these are known as "listing agreements" and are very similar to real estate listing contracts. For investment bankers and M&A consultants, the contracts are referred to as "engagement letters." The listing agreement and engagement letter spell out what the advisor will do for you and under what circumstances he will receive his commission. It is important to understand these agreements fully and be aware that under certain circumstances an advisor can earn his commission even if you ultimately do not sell your business, or if you sell the business within a specified time period (usually two years) following the termination of the advisor's contract.

## Structuring the Sale

You can help ensure a successful sale by considering the following four questions: (1) What is it that I'm selling? (2) How am I going to be paid? (3) How can I minimize my income tax consequences? and (4) How can I eliminate income taxes at the business level? Let's examine each.

## *What Am I Selling?*

An early determination of exactly what it is you're selling is critical in determining the ultimate sale price, the tax consequences of the sale, and your involvement with the business once the sale has closed.

A third party buyer will generally prefer to buy assets rather than stock not only for tax reasons, but also to protect himself from the contingent or unknown liabilities of your business. When the business interest is sold as a whole in the form of a stock sale, the purchaser acquires all the assets and all the liabilities. Unlike the key employee or co-owner, the third party purchaser will not be as familiar with the business history and consequently will be more reluctant to buy stock. But the tax cost of selling assets may be high, in effect a double tax, as discussed below.

This issue–the sale of assets vs. stock–may be the subject of extensive negotiations. In an asset sale, the following categories of assets are normally sold in the company:

- The furniture, fixtures, equipment, and supplies used in the ongoing business.
- The inventory, if any.
- The current telephone number of the business (particularly important if you are a personal service business, or a retail business that advertises heavily).
- Customer lists and records (especially important where a large part of the value attributable to the business lies in these records–a general medical or dental practice, for example).
- Leasehold improvements.
- Accounts receivable.
- Real estate, if applicable.

You also sell the going concern value, or goodwill. This is often represented in the form of a consulting agreement, or deferred compensation agreement, as well as a covenant not to compete.

Often a prudent purchaser will insist that you remain active in the business for a period of time after the closing. This can be important to the buyer in order to maintain relationships with customers, suppliers, and employees, as well as to help train and educate the new owners in the details of the business.

If you're going to spend time in the business after selling it, make certain your responsibilities are precisely defined: the number of hours you'll work each week, for what number of weeks, and the amount of compensation you'll receive for your services.

It's also prudent to have your employment agreement contain a severance clause that allows you to end the relationship at any time in return for a "declining penalty" payment by you. In other words, if you find the new ownership to be impossible to work with (as many entrepreneurs do no matter how good the new ownership is) make sure you have a provision that permits you to terminate your employment without causing a default of the overall purchase agreement.

Frequently the new owners, if they feel a need to retain your services, will insist on structuring your employment agreement in such a way that a major portion of your proceeds from the sale of the business will be paid only if you remain with the company and if the company continues to perform to expectations. If performance declines, so does the purchase price.

Retaining the former owner as an employee becomes less important if the business to be sold already has a strong management team and organizational structure in place with a proven track record. Similarly, your services are less crucial if the major portion of the sale price is represented by the asset value as opposed to a sale based on the going concern value.

A few words about the sale of real estate are appropriate here. Business owners frequently own the real estate on which the business is conducted. Often they want to sell the property along with the business. The typical purchaser, however, doesn't have enough cash to buy both the business and the real estate. In that case, the seller might consider a long-term lease–perhaps with a future option to purchase–between the seller and the business, personally guaranteed by the buyer.

This makes the purchase more affordable to the buyer and, if something goes wrong during the buy out period, the real property can remain separate from any difficulties that may otherwise be encountered.

### How Am I To Be Paid?

One way of getting paid is to be cashed out in full. If that happens, you have located not a snip of hay but a bouquet of roses in a mountain of needles. If you are not so fortunate–sellers of closely held businesses seldom are–you will be required to carry back some of the purchase price, probably subordinated to bank financing.

At this point "deals" begin to vary considerably. As a general rule, some type of carry-back is necessary. Even when a bank would be willing to finance the entire purchase price, the buyer will often require you to carry back 15 percent to 30 percent or more, subordinated to all other debt.

This carry back provides the new owners with some cushion for the financing they needed to buy you out. At the same time, it ensures your continuing interest in the affairs of the business. This attitude on the buyer's part is more prevalent when a portion of the purchase price is represented by the going concern value. In short, to the extent the bank's loan is not covered by the hard assets of the business, you can expect to carry the balance. If you recall, when employees, co-owners, or family members are involved in the purchase, the amount of your "carry" is often more significant–usually 90 percent or more.

In a third party sale, however, your control will not be as great, and your knowledge of the ability and attitude of the purchaser probably will be limited. Consequently, you must minimize your risk by getting as much of the purchase price up front as possible.

In receiving payment of the sale price, consider the following:

- *The amount to be paid in cash at closing.*

- *The amount of the promissory note, the interest rate, and the payback period.* Consider a floating interest rate, one or two points over prime. That rate is usually at least as good as any rate the purchaser will likely find. The payback period should be kept as short as possible–determined by the purchaser's ability to afford the payments.
- *The amount and type of collateral that will be satisfactory to you.* A deed of trust or mortgage should be used to secure any real estate. A uniform commercial code security agreement and financing statement should be used to secure the furniture, fixtures, equipment and accounts receivable.
- *Outside collateral.* Real estate or other assets owned by the purchaser can be encumbered. Although the personal guarantee of the purchaser and his spouse is mandated in all but the rarest of situations, an outside guarantor should also be considered–a form of "F&F financing." ("F&F" stands for friends and family.) A personal guarantee is not worth a lot if the personal assets of the guarantor are nonexistent. I often recommend to clients who are selling their professional practices–medical or dental–that they secure the personal guarantee not only of the buying professional, but also of his parents.
- *The inclusion of a prepayment penalty.* This is especially important when part of your payment is deferred compensation. With Congress constantly tinkering with the Tax Code, no one can ever predict whether tax rates will increase or decrease markedly from one year to the next. The inclusion of a prepayment penalty prevents the seller from paying large amounts of deferred compensation to you in a particular year in order to take advantage of high income tax brackets–a deduction for the company, but taxable income for you.

### *How Can I Minimize My Income Tax Consequences?*

The tax consequences on a sale to a third party are generally no different than on a transfer to employees or co-owners. Similarly, if not planned well, the consequences are just as devastating as an unplanned transfer to family or key employees. That is, Uncle Sam can take a 50 percent (or greater) tax bite from the sales proceeds thus making the entire transaction unfeasible. (Chapter Seven discusses the differences between a sale of stock only, or the sale of stock combined with deferred compensation, consulting agreement, use of accelerated retirement plan contributions, and use of an ESOP to help pay for your business interest.)

Generally, a sale of corporate assets (other than from an "S" corporation, partnership or LLC) will involve a double tax consequence to the seller. First, the "C" corporation will recognize gain on the sale of the assets (and pay taxes) and then the owner will also recognize gain (and pay taxes) when he receives money from the corporation as a result of that sale.

Use of compensation arrangements, deferred compensation, consulting or noncompete agreements can remove some of the pain from the double tax bite. Nevertheless, a double tax on any amount of gain is costly. Have your CPA calculate the tax consequences both ways: the consequences of a straight stock sale and those of a sale of assets and liquidation of the company. Occasionally a sale of assets is not adverse. This is true when the basis of the assets within the company is high or when the basis of your ownership interest in the company approaches the total purchase price of the asset sale.

### *How Can I Eliminate Income Taxes at the Business Level?*

The answer to this questions lies in the form of entity you have chosen for your business. If your business form is anything other than a regular (or "C" corporation) there will be a single tax on the sale of your business. This tax occurs not at the business level;

rather, it occurs at the owner level. Consequently, all entities other than the regular corporation are known as "Pass Through" income tax entities and are the preferred form of doing business if you anticipate selling your business to an outside third party. However, as discussed in Chapter Five, a regular corporation is often a preferred entity form for the accumulation of taxable income at the business level since its tax rates are generally lower.

At this point you might be thinking, "Why not do business as a regular corporation in the business's earlier years and switch to a pass through entity, such as an S corporation, just before the sale of my business?" This is a good question. In fact, it is such a good question that the IRS has thought of it. Naturally, its response benefits only the U.S. Treasury.

In general, if you convert to an S corporation from a regular corporation and then sell the business within ten years, the business will be forced to recognize a second tax on the "built-in gain" which existed at the date you converted from a regular corporation to an S corporation. I know all of this sounds complicated and confusing. It is. For your purposes, simply realize that a pass through entity is preferable to a regular corporation and that there will be tax obstacles to overcome if you convert from a "C" corporation to an S corporation within ten years of a sale of the business.

Don't let this complexity discourage you from seeking good tax advice. There are still many ways to minimize or even avoid the double tax bite. I can only encourage you to take action as soon as possible and not wait until you finally decide to sell to an outside third party. The tax savings, I might add, can be most substantial. Using a Pass-through entity avoids an entire layer of income taxation. This can result in a tax savings of between 15 percent and 35 percent of the purchase price!

Of course, if your company is a regular corporation, one way of avoiding a double tax is to sell the stock of your business but not its assets. If you are successful in negotiating a sale of stock of your "C" corporation, the questions remains: *How can I eliminate the income tax or capital gains tax when I sell my stock?*

### How Can I Eliminate Taxes at the Personal Level?

If you are successful in negotiating the sale of stock of your "C" corporation, the question remains, "Is there a method of avoiding even the capital gains tax on the sale of my stock?"

Yes Virginia, there is a Santa Claus. It is known as the Charitable Remainder Trust, commonly called a "CRT." The proper use of a charitable remainder trust in a sale of your ownership interest can avoid the capital gains tax. The following case study, illustrates its use.

*I recently met with two new clients, Paul and Diane Smith. Paul indicated he was interested in selling his temporary help agency which had a value of $1 million and very little basis. His chief concern was the ability to maintain an income stream of at least $75,000 per year from the proceeds of the sale. He was confident that he could get that kind of return—and more—if he had $1 million. When his accountant broke the news to him, however, that capital gains taxes (state and federal) would take almost a third of the sale price, he became most concerned. He was not prepared to take the risks necessary to get $75,000 per year from $700,000.*

*His accountant told him that a charitable remainder trust (CRT) might help. I said, "It depends." (By now, I hope you don't expect a different answer!)*

The first step is to create the CRT and to transfer Paul's business interest to the CRT **before** he has a binding obligation to sell the business to a third party. A valuation of the business will be done and the business will be sold for fair market value. The proceeds from the sale will be invested and Paul and Diane will receive annual income distributions from the CRT during their lifetimes. Upon the death of the survivor of both Paul and Diane, the remaining funds in the CRT will go to the charity that they designate.

Let's first look at living with the limitations of a CRT.

First, a CRT is an **irrevocable** trust. Once signed, it cannot be changed.

Second, the tax advantages all stem from the fact that the **assets** placed in the trust will eventually (after Paul and Diane's deaths) be given to a charity, not to their children.

Third, while Paul and Diane may serve as the trustees of the trust, they cannot invest the trust assets in a new business; they must generally invest in the stock market. So, options to use the sale proceeds are somewhat limited. In fact, they're limited to getting a predetermined stream of money (usually a percentage of the assets in the trust).

On the other hand, a CRT can be a very good personal tax planning vehicle. You can obtain multiple benefits from creating and funding a CRT.

First, a portion of the value of a gift to the CRT will generate a *current income tax charitable deduction*. For example, if Paul and Diane transfer $1 million worth of assets into the trust, they will receive a charitable income tax deduction of $178,000. The amount of this deduction is based on: (a) the percentage payout of the CRT, (b) the length of the payout to Paul and Diane (using their life expectancies), and (c) federal assumed interest rates.

Second, appreciated assets donated to the CRT and then sold by it avoid *capital gains tax*. Thus, Paul and Diane will have the full use of the sale proceeds ($1 million–not $700,000) to invest and receive a $75,000 per year income stream.

Third, the proceeds from the sale of one's business can then be used to purchase a number of investments, thereby *diversifying one's investments*.

Fourth, one makes a substantial *gift to the charity of choice* at his or her death. This gift is excluded from one's estate for estate tax purposes.

Fifth, the income, if any, accumulated in the CRT will not be subject to income tax, if there is no unrelated business income.

To illustrate how beneficial using a CRT will be for Paul and Diane, let's look first at the alternative. If they sold the business for $1 million outside of the CRT, they would be subject to capital gains tax. Given the low basis in the property, that capital gains tax amount is about $300,000 leaving $700,000 to invest. If we assume an eight percent return rate, this provides $56,000 of annual income. If, at Paul and Diane's deaths the $700,000 remains in their estates, it will be subject to an estate tax of approximately $300,000. Paul and Diane's children will receive the after-tax balance of $400,000. Using this plan, the charity would receive nothing.

Hold on. What about Paul and Diane's kids? They've just seen their inheritance go from $400,000 (without a CRT) to $0 (using the CRT). If Paul and Diane want to replace the children's "lost inheritance," they could purchase a life insurance policy using some of the income generated from the CRT. The first premium payment on a $500,000 (which is probably more than the kids would get without using a CRT) second-to-die life insurance policy is $11,700. This premium amount must come from Paul and Diane's "out-of-pocket" cash (not from funds generated by the CRT). Subsequent premium payments may be made from CRT income. If this life insurance policy were owned in an Irrevocable Life Insurance Trust, it would not be subject to any estate taxes and the full $500,000 would pass to Paul and Diane's heirs.

By eliminating the "wastage" of capital gains taxes, the CRT allows you to use all of the sale proceeds to provide an income stream to you. This means you either leave the business sooner or leave it with more income. Either way–you leave your business in style.

## Summary

Selling your business is one of the most consequential steps you will ever take.  This process begins with understanding how qualified buyers are found, and whom to use to help you find them. Before the business is sold, you must plan ahead to anticipate how the sale is likely to be structured and to assess the resulting tax consequences.

This chapter gives you the tools and information to begin the sale process.  The next chapter completes the process.  You will learn how your business will be priced and how the sale process works.

### Appendix 8.1:  Potential Purchasers

1.    The following persons/organizations have approached me with an interest in buying the business:

_____

_____

_____

_____


2.    The following are businesses I can approach because I think they may have an interest in acquiring my business:

_____

_____

_____

_____


You may want to move these names to the "Designation of Business Advisors" at the end of Chapter 11.

## Appendix 8.2:  Checklist of Financial Information Requested by Transaction Advisor

1.     The last three years' financial statements and business tax returns

2.     The current financial statement year-to-date

3.     Sales material or company brochure which explains the nature of the business

## Appendix 8.3:  Questions for References of Prospective Transaction Advisors

1.     Did the transaction advisor adhere to the highest levels of professional integrity?  Can you think of an example of how he might have placed your interests ahead of his own?  Did you trust him?

2.     How effective were the transaction advisor's verbal communication skills?
How effective were her written communication skills?

3.     Was the transaction advisor comfortable working with "the numbers?"  Was he able to translate his financial analysis into a workable, understandable strategy?

4.     Did the transaction advisor display any creativity relating to marketing strategies?  Was she a problem solver?

5.     Was the transaction advisor persistent? Were you comfortable with his organizational skills?

6.     Did the transaction advisor proceed according to her plan? Did she deliver information in a timely fashion?

7.     Would you use this transaction advisor again?

# 9

# Making a Mountain Out of a Molehill

## *Selling to a third party*

Chapter Two examined the methods your CPA uses to place a value on your business. In this chapter we will discuss the methods that are used to determine the "price" at which your business will actually be sold. This chapter will also build upon our discussion of the use of transaction advisors and the process that is used to successfully sell a business.

Rather than give you this information second-hand, I have asked Joseph M. Durnford, CPA, CVA, my partner in the investment banking firm of JD Ford & Company, to pen this chapter. As a Certified Valuation Analyst, Certified Public Accountant, and experienced deal-maker, Joe is well-qualified to tackle these topics. He has performed hundreds of pre-sale valuations and has set defensible (and attainable) sale prices for businesses in a wide variety of industries. More importantly, Joe makes his living buying and selling companies on behalf of his clients, and understands how companies are actually sold and the prices buyers actually pay for them.

## Sale Price versus Value

Like most things in life, beauty is in the eye of the beholder, or in this case, value is in the eye of the buyer. This simple concept is often overlooked when the valuation methods discussed in Chapter Two are used. Why? Because the valuation formulas used by most CPA's and business appraisers assume the value of a business to be *as it is*, in the hands of its current owner operating as a stand alone enterprise. The factors that determine the price at which a business will actually be sold are:

- Future Performance. The buyer's expectation of the future performance of the business under his ownership affects the price he is willing to pay.
- Investment Return. A prospective buyer will compare the investment return he expects to achieve through the purchase of your business to alternative acquisitions.
- Individual Needs. Each buyer will place a different value on your business based upon his unique needs and objectives.
- Timing. The timing of the sale is critical because the market for business acquisitions changes based on a variety of economic factors.

How can you know what a third party buyer will pay for your business? Well, until you actually negotiate the sale, you won't know its true fair market value. Therefore, it is important to establish your personal financial objectives before you begin the sale process. Knowing the amount of money you need to maintain your lifestyle after the sale of the business is critical to determining whether a sale of the business is an appropriate course of action. To help you assess your financial needs, I suggest that you review the objectives you first established in Chapter One.

The next step is to assess the price you are likely to receive from a sale. To accomplish this task, I recommend that you meet with an investment banker or business broker who is familiar with what buyers are paying for businesses in your market. (The role of an investment banker or business broker is discussed in Chapter Eight.) An investment banker is trained to analyze your business from a buyer's perspective. In fact, because investment bankers often represent buyers in acquisitions, they know what is important to different buyers.

*The primary determinant of what a buyer will be willing to pay for your business is the future cash flow that he expects to realize from the business.* The anticipated cash flow determines the internal rate of return that the buyer will achieve from the acquisition of your business. Cash flow also determines how much debt can be used to purchase your business. Therefore, the greater the anticipated future cash flow the greater the value. But which cash flow are we valuing— the business as it is, or as it will be in the new owner's hands? The answer is: both. The actual sale price will be the point between what you think the cash flow is worth, and what the buyer is willing to pay for the future cash flow that he expects to receive.

Determining how valuable the cash flow is to you is the basis for many of the valuation methods discussed in Chapter Two. These methods look at historical earnings (cash flow) and apply a capitalization rate or market multiple to determine value. While this method is acceptable for general planning purposes, it does not go far enough to determine what an outside buyer would be willing to pay for your business.

Let's look then at the value of a business and its cash flow from the buyer's perspective. The buyer's perception of value will take into consideration a number of additional factors that are generally not considered when using the methods described in Chapter Two. Among these factors are:

- Timing of the sale and industry cycles
- Current condition of the merger and acquisition market
- Interest rates (cost of borrowing money)
- Availability of capital (ability to borrow money)
- Experienced management
- Existence of proprietary technology
- Financial synergies

- Geographic location
- Strategic fit with buyer's business objectives
- Perception of risk

The buyer's analysis of each factor will focus on the impact each factor may have on the future cash flow generated by the business.

### *Timing of the Sale and Industry Cycles*

Timing of the sale is an important variable in determining the value of the business from the buyer's perspective. Generally, most business owners want to sell their businesses at the top of the market. Business owners believe that by doing so they'll receive the highest price and, at the same time, relieve themselves of the burden of managing the business through a down cycle. Unfortunately, most buyers have become quite sophisticated in analyzing business cycles and are not willing to pay premium prices at the top of the market.

I have found that in order to maximize the value of your business in a sale to a third party it is better to sell while the business is on the way up. The reason for this is that buyers must believe that the future cash flow will continue to increase, thus giving them the opportunity to benefit from ownership. I refer to this as "leaving some cookies in the cookie jar for the next owner." In my opinion, *the single most important factor in closing a sale of a business is the buyer's belief that future cash flow will continue to grow thereby increasing the value of the business for them.*

### *Current Condition of the Merger and Acquisition Market*

The condition of the M&A market impacts the value of your business due to the principle of supply and demand. Basic economics tells us that when supply is limited and demand is high, prices increase. If you are selling your business at a time when the number of buyers exceeds the number of quality sellers, you are likely to receive more money than if the situation is reversed. Fortunately for the owners of high quality companies, the current M&A market is very strong because interest rates are relatively low, corporate profits have been increasing and the number of buyers far exceeds the number of high quality businesses for sale. As noted in the February 20, 1996 *Wall Street Journal* report, because the healthy M&A market has put upward pressure on prices, owners of privately held businesses received 13 percent more for their companies in 1995 as compared to 1994.

### Interest Rates

One of the primary factors that determines the health of the M&A market, and thus the price that a buyer is willing to pay for your business, is interest rates. The cost of borrowing money has a direct impact on the investment rate of return that a buyer expects to realize from your business. The buyer's expectation regarding future interest rates will also have an impact on his perception about the future performance of your business. Even if your business is not interest rate sensitive, a buyer will likely pay a lower price if interest rates increase. This is due to the impact rising interest rates have on the discount rate buyers apply to the projected future cash flow of the business. If your business is interest rate sensitive and interest rates increase, the value of your business may take a double whammy, because the buyer's expectation of future cash flow decreases at the same time the discount rate increases. Volatility in interest rates can cause your business to have one value when the sale process begins and quite another (be it higher or lower) by the time you close.

Let's take a moment to look at an example of how timing, interest rates and industry cycle can impact the sale price of your business.

*Ben and Jerry owned a construction materials distribution company. At the time they first considered selling their business, interest rates were declining and, as a result, the construction activity in their market was increasing. This was great for business and profits began to soar. At that particular time a business broker estimated* *the value of Ben and Jerry's business to be approximately $25 million plus. This value was based on the fact that the industry and market were expanding, cash flows were increasing, and a large number of industry players were interested in expanding into the area through acquisition. These strategic buyers were aggressively buying companies like Ben and Jerry's throughout the country because they believed that interest rates would remain low, and the construction market would remain healthy for three to five years. Unfortunately for Ben and Jerry, the business broker they hired to represent them was not a deal maker and did not do his job. So, after 18 months of searching for a buyer, Ben and Jerry came to me.*

*At the time I met Ben and Jerry their business was booming and they had a large backlog of orders. Interest rates, however, had begun to move up and rumors were circulating that the market was fast becoming over-built. Before taking Ben and Jerry's company back to market I estimated that the sales price would be approximately $22. 5 million. I based this estimate on a lower projection for future cash flows and a higher discount percentage due to increasing interest rates.*

*After two months of marketing the business, I had four strategic buyers bidding for the company. The offers ranged from $19 to $22 million. While we negotiated with these four buyers, interest rates continued to increase. Each time we negotiated for a higher value the buyers wanted to decrease their bids because: 1) they believed that the business was at the top of its cycle, 2) they had less confidence in the future of the company, and 3) the cost of the leveraged acquisition increased with each up-tick in interest rates. As the process wore on, three of the four buyers ultimately withdrew their bids because the "value" of the business was not worth what they had initially bid, and the "price" was too high. Ultimately, the buyer with the lowest initial offer remained interested, and the business was sold for approximately $20 million. The final sales price was $5 million less than Ben and Jerry could have received two years earlier when interest rates were lower and the perception of future growth was greater.*

### *Availability of Capital*

The availability of capital is another important factor in determining what your business may be worth on the open market. This fact should not surprise any of you who may have owned a business during the credit crunch of the late 1980s and early 1990s. In a nutshell, buyers cannot pay more for your business than they can obtain financing for, either from you or from a bank. If the credit markets are very tight, as they were in the late 80s, buyers have a difficult time borrowing money to pay for the acquisition of your business. Therefore, they need to reduce the purchase price so that the deal has less risk and looks better to the lender.

Similarly, in a tight lending market a buyer may not be able to obtain any outside financing and therefore be unable to buy your business unless you carry back a substantial portion of the purchase price. Since most business owners are reluctant to carry a promissory note for more than 30 percent of the purchase price, a tight lending environment thins the population of buyers which in turn reduces market value. The availability of capital is another reason why capital intensive businesses, like manufacturing and distribution, tend to sell for higher prices than do service or software companies. Capital intensive businesses have more collateral assets and therefore can borrow money to finance acquisitions more easily.

In the late 1990s, there is plenty of capital available to fund acquisitions that are properly structured and reasonably priced. This does not mean that obtaining acquisition capital is easy; it isn't. What it does mean is that the pool of capital available for acquisitions is large and expanding.

This pool of acquisition capital comes from a variety of sources. First, many strategic buyers have earned significant profits during the past few years and are investing these profits in strategic acquisitions. Second, interest rates are relatively low and the lending environment is highly competitive. The increased competition in lending stems from the willingness of many non-bank commercial finance companies to loan money at rates competitive with those charged by banks. These commercial finance companies are excellent sources for acquisition capital because they are less regulated and can make more aggressive loans. Surprisingly, many of the largest commercial finance companies are now willing to lend to relatively small acquisitions.

Third, there has been a large influx of equity into the market from institutions, wealthy entrepreneurs (known as "angel investors"), and highly compensated executives who have abandoned corporate America in search of businesses of their own. Finally, the record shattering public markets have created substantial wealth and liquidity for many companies. The highly valued stock market has created opportunities for public companies to purchase smaller businesses by utilizing their stock as currency, or by selling shares in the market and investing the cash in acquisitions.

An example of how the availability of capital (and its by-product high priced public stock) can drive up the value of a private company is demonstrated by my clients, Tammy and Tom.

*Tammy and Tom had the good fortune of owning a temporary staffing company at a time when the industry was growing rapidly and undergoing a consolidation. Over a ten year period Tammy and Tom had built their business from zero to approximately $5 million in sales. The company was very profitable and had an established niche in a highly desirable market.*

*Tammy and Tom had noticed that many temporary staffing companies had gone public and that the stock of those companies performed very well. So well in fact that Tammy and Tom wanted to get in on the action. They knew, however, that their company was not big enough to go public so they decided to sell. They hoped that a public company would buy the business and pay for it in rapidly appreciating stock.*

*When I was hired I didn't know much about the industry but I quickly learned that most privately-owned temporary staffing companies were valued in the market at a multiple of eight to nine times net after-tax earnings (five times pre-tax earnings). Contrast this to public companies that were valued at 30 to 50 times net after-tax earnings, with some rapidly growing companies valued at more than 100 times earnings. Because of the extremely high public company valuations, many of the industry players were trying to grow as quickly as possible by buying up small companies at a rapid rate. The public companies were paying cash, stock, or a combination of both to acquire good companies in desirable markets.*

In addition to the public companies, the stock market valuations had attracted the interest of many financial buyers and other private temporary staffing companies that hoped to acquire the critical mass necessary to qualify themselves for an initial public offering. The net result was that there was a significant demand for companies like Tammy and Tom's, and there was ample capital available to finance the acquisitions.

Ultimately, Tammy and Tom sold their business to a financial buyer, who was actively assembling a portfolio of temporary staffing companies and preparing to go public. Tammy and Tom received approximately ten times the previous year's net after-tax income ($2.5 million) for their business including cash and stock. When the buyer goes public, Tammy and Tom expect to hit another home run due to the increased value of the stock they retained. The reason the buyer was willing to pay ten times earnings was that he expected to receive a greater value when he took the company public. As you will see, this expected future value is factored into the buyer's discounted cash flow analysis and is used to determine the purchase price.

### Experienced Management

One of the most important non-financial factors in determining the sale price of your business is the quality and depth of management. This factor is typically considered by all three classifications of buyers (strategic, financial and individual) and can impact the purchase price significantly. A business that lacks management depth is typically worth less to a buyer than one that has a solid management team. The depth and competence of management greatly influence the risk associated with an acquisition. Buyers believe that an experienced, competent management team is more likely to sustain the business during down cycles and more likely to grow the business during up cycles in the economy or industry.

Financial buyers, those who invest primarily for a return on investment, generally are not interested in a company that lacks a good management team. Because financial buyers generally do not want to run a business themselves they need to rely on the existing management team. If the owner of the business is the only competent member of management and does not want to remain with the business after it is sold, then a financial buyer is not likely to be interested in buying that business.

Strategic buyers also want to buy companies with good management teams. Although strategic buyers may have significant industry knowledge and employ people who could run your company, they know good management is hard to find. Therefore, strategic buyers also look for and pay more for businesses that have solid management teams that can continue to run the operation. Recently, a strategic buyer who acquires companies across the country told me that companies with good management teams already in place deserve a "premium price." His reasoning was that good management in his industry was very difficult to find.

### Proprietary Technology

To illustrate how control of proprietary technology can make the value of a business far greater than the capitalization of historical earnings would indicate, let's examine my client Will Rogers.

*Will owned a small systems engineering firm that designed and installed cellular networks. Like many small service businesses, Will's company had a sporadic earnings history.* **The most recent** *three years' profits and cash flow had been declining and Will had been told by his CPA that the business did not have much value.*

*On the surface I would have agreed with Will's CPA. When I probed further, however, and asked why the company had lost money in the past three years I learned that Will had been investing heavily in the research and development of a new switching device. This device would revolutionize cellular and wireless switching networks technology and was particularly applicable in the development of wireless networks which were just beginning to emerge. Through further inquiry, I learned that this technology was patentable and Will was certain that it would greatly enhance the services his company could provide. Supporting Will's assertion was a multi-million dollar contract from an international wireless communication company.*

*To capitalize on the significant potential for the device, Will had to greatly increase the size of the company and invest at least $1 million into the company. Will's recent heart attack convinced him that life was too short to pursue this strategy and that he wanted to sell the business. He recognized that the switching device technology would be attractive to larger companies in his industry. In fact, Will had been approached by a major competitor interested in buying his business.*

*To maximize his company's value, Will, his accountant and I set out to develop a financial model that would project the future cash flow of the business including the impact of the new technology. This cash flow projection had to be reasonable and defensible so that it would be convincing in negotiating the sale price and terms. Appendix 9-1 is a summary of the model and how it was used to determine a sale price.*

### Financial synergies

When a strategic buyer performs an analysis to determine the value of your business he uses the discounted cash flow method. In preparing his analysis, he will usually consider the financial synergies that can be achieved after the sale. Financial synergies are those elusive cost savings or increased sales that can result when two companies become one. Financial synergies can occur after the strategic buyer's operations are combined with those of your business. Synergies can include reduction of costs, such as administrative overhead, distribution, product development and other cost savings. Synergies can also include increased revenue which may result after the sale or merger is complete. Revenues may increase as a result of the buyer's ability to sell your product to his existing customers—often a much larger market than you currently reach.

In determining what your business is worth, strategic buyers will project future cash flow taking into consideration both the increased revenue and reduced costs that may occur. Thus, the future cash flow to the strategic buyer may be significantly more than what the business can generate on a stand alone basis. From the strategic buyer's perspective, as the future cash flow increases so does the value of your business.

The potential for financial synergies is the primary reason that strategic buyers are able to pay more for your business than either financial buyers or related parties. The challenge for you, and for your transaction advisor in negotiating a sale to a strategic buyer, is to create a situation in which the strategic buyer is willing to pay you for some of the benefits that he brings to your business. I've found that the most effective method is to negotiate with more than one potential buyer so that the strategic buyer understands that he may have to out-bid a competing buyer to gain the benefits of the potential synergies. We will discuss how to create a competitive environment later in this chapter.

### Geographic location

Another factor that will influence the price a buyer is willing to pay is the geographic location of your business. Geographic location may be the part of the country where your business is located, or it may mean which street corner your business controls. The location of your business can influence a buyer to increase or decrease the purchase price depending on his perception of the value of your location.

The value of a location can be easily illustrated when you think about a gasoline station that controls the intersection of Main Street and the interstate highway. Because of its location, the gasoline station is likely to have a high degree of traffic and hence have greater revenue and cash flow than a similar gasoline station that resides on a back street ten miles from the nearest interstate. In this case, location determines cash flow which in turn determines value.

The geographic location of a business has a significant impact on what a buyer is willing to pay for a business, because it influences his perception of the future benefits to be realized. A good example of how geographic location influences the buyer's perception of value is my former clients Sam and Eric.

*Sam and Eric owned a residential real estate brokerage that they wanted to sell. They had purchased the business from the former owner, a financial investor, who relied on Sam and Eric to run the business. When Sam and Eric bought the business the real estate market in Denver was terrible and it seemed that it might never recover. The owner of the business did not have confidence that things would turn around so he sold the business to Sam and Eric for very little money.*

*Over the course of the next several years, Sam and Eric did a great job running the company and made money even in a tight market. Fortunately for Sam and Eric, the Denver economy recovered and their business became highly profitable. When it came time to sell, Denver's economy was booming, Denver International Airport had just opened, and Denver had become one of the most vibrant real estate markets in the country.*

In representing Sam and Eric I was able to find a strategic buyer from Dallas who had made millions selling real estate during the twenty-five years since the Dallas - Fort Worth Airport had opened. This strategic buyer predicted that Denver would experience the same type of growth that Dallas - Fort Worth had following the opening of a new airport. From the perspective of this strategic buyer, Denver was the most attractive geographic location in the country. Therefore, he was willing to pay a premium price to acquire control of Sam and Eric's company.

## Strategic fit

Strategic fit is an important factor in determining what your business is worth to a potential buyer. The better the fit between the buyer's objectives and what your business has to offer, the more valuable he will perceive your business to be. If a buyer has a strong desire to enter your industry or to expand into your market, then he will be willing to take greater risk to achieve his objectives. Conversely, if your business does not match the buyer's goals, the business will likely have zero value to that buyer.

As an example, let's return to my clients Tammy and Tom and their temporary staffing company. Tammy and Tom's business was growing rapidly, was highly profitable, was in a growth industry, and was located in one of the most desirable parts of the country. In representing them, I identified several strategic and financial buyers. One of the strategic buyers we met was initially very interested in buying the business but, after visiting the company, determined that Tammy and Tom operated their business in a different niche than the buyer's existing business. After much deliberation this buyer decided that he could not change Tammy and Tom's business to fit his way of doing business. Therefore, he concluded that the business had no value to his existing organization.

A more positive example of a strategic fit is my clients Mike and Doug, who owned a medical products company. This company manufactured a line of medical devices directed at a very unique niche in the medical field. Mike and Doug's company was small but very profitable. The problem that Mike and Doug had was that they did not have enormous amounts of money needed to continue to invest in new product development. Therefore, they wanted to sell their company to a strategic buyer who could benefit from their existing products, while at the same time had the resources to invest in new product development.

After four months of searching I found three buyers that fit the profile of the ideal strategic buyer. Each of the strategic buyers sold complementary products to the same customers. Mike and Doug's products were a natural addition to the buyer's product line, and the buyer had larger distribution and sales networks which could be used to increase sales. The company sold to the strategic buyer who needed them the most (i.e., paid the highest price). Since the acquisition, Mike and Doug continue to run the division, product sales have increased due to the efforts of the buyer's large sales force, and the company was recently issued a patent and FDA license for a newly developed product. This transaction was truly win-win because the strategic fit between the buyer and seller was excellent.

### Perception of Risk

All of the factors discussed above are inter-related and influence the buyer's perception of the risk associated with the purchase of your business. The greater the buyer's perception of risk the higher his expectation for reward. Thus, if a buyer perceives a high degree of risk associated with your business and is uncertain about the future cash flow that the business will generate, he will pay less for your business. Conversely, if a buyer has a high degree of confidence in the future of the business and the stability of the cash flow that the business will generate, he will be willing to pay more.

The perception of risk is the reason that large diversified companies are more valuable than small, one-man consulting practices. Basically, a large diversified company is perceived to have the ability to continue producing positive cash flow in the future and the ability to transfer that cash flow to a new owner. A small consulting practice may or may not have the ability to continue to generate cash flow in the future and that cash flow is not easily transferable to a new owner.

To maximize the value of your business and to obtain the highest possible price upon sale, you need to plan for and manage those factors that influence the perception of risk. This planning should begin the day you start your business, and continue until the business is sold. Factors that you can control include: developing a good management team, having excellent internal controls, obtaining audited financial statements to document your historical success, investing in new products or markets and paying attention to the external factors that influence value. These external factors include: interest rates, stock market prices for companies in your industry or the industries you serve, the availability of capital, economic forecasts for the locations where you conduct business and the level of merger and acquisition activity in your industry.

### Discounted Cash Flow (DCF) Analysis.

Up to this point we have determined that the buyer will focus on cash flow, and we have examined the impact that a number of variables have on cash flow. In real world situations, the projection of future cash flow of a business is the most important factor in computing a business's value. In negotiating a sale of a business, both seller and buyer will prepare a projection of future cash flow. The cash flow will then be valued using a discounted cash flow analysis. The negotiation of price will be centered on whose vision of the future is more believable (i.e. how much risk is involved in predicting the future). Appendix 9.1 provides a rudimentary example of a discounted cash flow analysis that was used to negotiate the sale of Will's engineering service business. The four key steps in preparing a discounted cash flow analysis are:

- Prepare future cash flow projection for one business cycle (generally assumed to be five years).
- Estimate the value of the business at the end of the projection period (terminal value).
- Determine the risk adjusted rate of return expected to be achieved (discount rate).

- Apply the discount rate to the projected cash flow including the terminal value (computing the value).

## Cash Flow Projections

Cash flow projections must be based upon sound business judgment and reasonable assumptions. The cash flow projections should take into account the industry cycle, product life cycles, market trends, capital investment needed, increased working capital requirements and the other factors discussed previously. Well thought-out and well prepared projections can increase the buyer's comfort level when evaluating the business. The buyer's increased comfort level can enhance the seller's position during negotiations. It is important to realize that no matter how good your projections are, buyers will make their own assumptions and prepare their own projections. Your job, and the job of your investment banker, is to help the buyer see the significant opportunities your business represents and help the buyer justify using favorable assumptions when preparing his own estimates of future cash flow.

## Terminal Value

A second component of the future cash flow that your business will generate is called the terminal value. Basically, terminal value is the amount of money that you, or the buyer would receive in an assumed sale of the business at the end of the period for which the cash flow projections were prepared. The estimate of what the business can be sold for at the end of the projection period is determined using either a capitalization of earnings approach or a market multiple approach as discussed in Chapter Two. The terminal value can also be determined using a liquidation approach if the business is assumed to have no going concern value at the end of the projection period. In the case of the temporary staffing company that was discussed earlier, the terminal value would have been the market value that the buyer expected to receive when taking the company public.

Computing the terminal value is important because the value of a business is based on the total future cash flows. Those total future cash flows must include what the business may be worth at the end of the projection period. In summary, future cash flow is equal to the sum of cash to be received during the projection period plus the value of the business at the end of the projection period.

### Determining the Discount Rate

After the future cash flow projections are complete the next step in the discounted cash flow analysis is to determine an appropriate discount rate. The discount rate is a factor used to determine the current value of a stream of income to be received in the future, assuming a minimum acceptable rate of return for the risk being taken. The discount rate takes into account the time value of money, as well as the relative risk that future cash flows may differ from projections. There are numerous ways to determine a discount rate, but sophisticated buyers generally use the after-tax Weighted Average Cost of Capital ("WACC") as the method of determining the minimum acceptable rate of return on an investment.

Basically, WACC is a calculation of the buyer's cost of debt and equity, weighted according to the percentage of each in the buyer's overall capital structure. WACC is determined using the fair market value of the buyer's debt and equity which, if you are not dealing with a public company, is often difficult to determine. For those of you who are interested, any good corporate finance textbook will contain a thorough discussion of how to calculate WACC. For those of you who are less inclined to spend your time reading finance textbooks, I suggest that you rely on your investment banker to make this calculation.

As a final note, you should know that each buyer will have its own WACC. Therefore, it is important that you, or your advisors understand each buyer's capital structure, because it will impact the price that the buyer will be willing to pay for your business.

### Computing the Value

The final step in the discounted cash flow analysis is to apply the discount rate to the projected cash flow and the terminal value. This last step in the discounted cash flow process is merely a mathematical calculation that any computerized spreadsheet can complete in seconds. By applying the discount rate to the projected cash flow and terminal value cash flow a buyer can determine the maximum price they would be willing to pay today to receive the cash that your business will generate in the future.

At this point your head may be spinning and you are saying to yourself, "I knew there was a reason that I didn't major in accounting or finance." Not to worry. The concepts and formulas outlined above are generally understood by those of us who specialize in buying and selling businesses. If you are not convinced that your business broker or transaction advisor thoroughly understands cash flow forecasting, DCF and WACC, then you should find another advisor. The main thing for you to remember about the discounted cash flow method of valuing a business is that sophisticated buyers (i.e. those with real money) are using this method to determine how much they will pay you for your business.

In summary, the market value of your business will be determined by what a buyer is actually willing to pay. The amount that the buyer is willing to pay will be based upon his perception about the future cash flow that the business will generate for him. Your job, and the job of your investment banker, is: (1) to communicate to potential buyers the positive opportunity that your business offers; (2) to demonstrate how your business fits a buyer's overall strategy, and (3) to prove that your business is a cash flow-producing machine. Your investment banker has another job: to bring to the table a number of qualified buyers and to understand what it is about your business that appeals to each buyer. If your investment banker is able to attract the right buyers and create a market for your company, you should have little doubt about the true market value of your business because you will have real offers to consider.

## The Sales Process

Now that you understand more about how market conditions and a buyer's perception of risk and future opportunity impact the sale price, let's discuss how the sale process works and how the process itself can influence the final sale price. Ideally, when it comes time to sell your business you want to be well prepared and you want to have as many potential buyers as possible vying for the opportunity to purchase your business. To accomplish this I recommend the following four stage process:

I.    Pre-Sale Planning
II.   Marketing the Business and Finding a Buyer
III.  Negotiating the Sale
IV.   Closing the Deal

## Stage I: Pre-Sale Planning

The first step in any successful sale of a business is the pre-sale planning. This stage involves preparing the business for sale, reviewing your personal financial objectives, organizing your team, and performing pre-sale financial and legal due diligence. Preparing the business for sale is the main theme for this book, and John Brown has done an excellent job describing what must be done in order for you to leave your business in style.

### *Review financial objectives.*

To illustrate the importance of reviewing your personal financial objectives, let's return to John's client Rich Meyers from Chapter Eight. The last we knew, Rich Meyers was being told by a business broker that his business would sell for as much as $2.5

million. Prior to meeting with the business broker, Rich met with his investment advisor and John to establish his family's financial security objectives. This is a vital step because it told Rich what he needed to get from his business to meet his true financial needs.

The review of his financial objectives prevented Rich's ego from saying, "I want $3 million for the business" when in fact he could meet his objectives for less than that amount. Likewise, this evaluation protected Rich from being pressured to list his business with the business broker if a sale would not generate sufficient funds to provide for the family's financial security and independence. The critical points to remember at this juncture are: 1) understand what your financial objectives are before attempting to sell your business; and 2) seek out a business broker or investment banker that will give you an honest assessment of the market value of your business. In other words, avoid zealous brokers and investment bankers who will tell you what you want to hear just to get a listing or engagement.

### Assemble your advisors.

As noted elsewhere in this book, it is very important when selling a business to seek out competent advisors. The advisors needed to properly plan and execute the sale of a business are: your CPA, estate planner, investment advisor, transaction lawyer and investment banker or business broker. These professionals should be hired based on their skill, reputation and experience successfully advising clients in the sale of a business. I generally recommend relying on your CPA to help you evaluate the skill and reputation of the other advisors, especially the investment banker or broker. (Hereafter I will generally refer to investment bankers, business brokers, merger and acquisition consultants, or merchant bankers as "transaction advisors.")

### Pre-sale due diligence (financial and legal).

After you have assembled your team of advisors they should work with you to perform pre-sale due diligence. This due diligence should be initiated by your transaction advisor and transaction attorney. The purpose of the pre-sale due diligence is to evaluate your company in the same manner that a buyer will. This is a critical step, because you want to discover potential pitfalls to a sale **before** you expose the business to buyers.

The transaction advisor should conduct the pre-sale financial due diligence as a preparatory step in positioning your company for sale. The transaction advisor should get to know your business by examining the company's books and records, visiting facilities, meeting with select employees and the other members of your transaction team (especially your CPA and attorney). This financial due diligence process will help the transaction advisor determine a reasonable range of value for your business and suggest a possible sale price. This due diligence will also provide your transaction advisor with the information necessary to prepare the memorandum that will be used to market your business. Due diligence also provides your transaction advisor with the a detailed understanding of your business necessary to represent you accurately during the sale process.

Your transaction attorney should conduct pre-sale legal due diligence to identify any potential legal issues that need to be resolved prior to a sale. The legal due diligence includes reviewing important contracts, updating shareholder agreements, minutes, articles and by-laws, employee benefit plans, and all other legal agreements that govern the operation of the business. Ideally, this "legal audit" will identify and correct any potential legal issues that may delay or block a sale.

One of the key benefits that you gain from the legal due diligence is an updated, clean set of legal records. Up-to-date records demonstrate to a buyer that you operate a clean ship. This will help to increase the buyer's confidence about the future success of the business, and reduce the perception of risk. You will recall that the buyer's perception of risk is one of the key elements in determining the selling price.

A final note on pre-sale due diligence. It is critical that you be candid with your advisors and take all of the skeletons out of the closet. It is much better to evaluate the impact of those skeletons before they are discovered by a buyer. With proper planning and disclosure, most skeletons can be effectively dealt with by your advisors. If the buyer discovers the skeletons, they can quickly become "deal-killers," particularly if you and your advisors are not prepared to handle them.

To help you prepare for pre-sale due diligence I suggest that you begin assembling the documents that the buyer will request as early as possible. Space does not permit reproducing the complete due diligence checklist that a transaction advisor or transaction attorney would use. If you would like to review the rather exhaustive checklist used by JD Ford & Company Ltd., L.L.P., simply complete the Request Form at the end of this book and I will send it to you free of charge.

## Stage II: Marketing the Business and Finding a Buyer

The most significant value that a transaction advisor brings to the table is the ability to excite the identified buyers about the opportunity your business offers thus making them eager to pay the highest price. Therefore, it is important to understand that the negotiation of price begins with how the business is marketed. The old saying "You never get a second chance to make a first impression" applies to the sale of a business.

### *Develop a Buyer Profile.*

The first thing to be said about finding a buyer is: don't assume that your transaction advisor is omniscient and knows all of the buyers who may have an interest in your business. It is true that transaction advisors have access to a larger pool of buyers than you or your other advisors will. However, the transaction advisor's pool of buyers will not include every possible buyer, particularly those whom you may have already identified.

Work closely your transaction advisor to develop a profile of the most likely buyer for the business. The buyer profile should begin with an assessment of the benefits your business offers. Think logically and creatively about who might be interested in purchasing those benefits. In this regard, selling a business is no different from selling anything else.

### *Making a good first impression.*

To make a good first impression your transaction advisor should prepare an information package or confidential memorandum describing your business. This document is critical to maximizing business value. It is usually the buyer's first impression of your business and sets the tone for the sale process. The level of detail and the presentation style of the memorandum vary greatly from one transaction advisor to another. Due to the importance of this document, ask to see examples of previously prepared information or confidential memoranda before you hire a transaction advisor.

The information memorandum should contain the following sections and communicate a compelling story as to why someone should want to buy your business.

- **Executive Summary**. This section of the memorandum briefly discusses the highlights of your business and captures the buyer's interest.
- **Reasons for Sale**. This includes a discussion of your reasons for selling the business. It is best to put your motives on the table up front, since it is usually one of the first questions buyers ask.
- **Key Investment Considerations**. This section is organized in bullet point fashion to highlight all of the key attributes of your business and emphasize the benefits of ownership. This is where the real sales pitch is made.

- **Main Body**. This portion contains a description of your business's history, organizational structure, management team, products, services, markets, customers, competitors, business risks, and future opportunities. The Main Body should also include management's discussion and analysis of the historical financial information. Most importantly, the body of the document should also contain summary historical financial statements **recast** for unusual items for the last three to five years. The recasting of financial statements is important to demonstrate the actual earnings capacity of your business. Recasting involves adding back excess owner's compensation and benefits, excessive rents paid to owners and other unusual items. Involve your outside CPA or internal accountant in this "recasting" project and be honest about what constitutes a reasonable add-back. You will lose credibility if you add back every expense up to, and including, the kitchen sink.
- **Exhibits**. This section should include any relevant supporting information, or material which makes your business attractive such as historical financial statements, product brochures, detailed resumes of key personnel, and support for any future financial projections that are included in the document.

### Finding the Buyer

After the confidential information memorandum has been completed and approved by you, your transaction advisor will begin the search for a buyer. The actual buyer search can take many forms, including: direct contact, direct mail, advertising in local media, or listing the company in computerized databases. The exact marketing program should be carefully planned by the transaction advisor and discussed with you. The need to maintain confidentiality should be one of the primary concerns in determining which marketing approach to use.

### The Controlled Auction

One of the most effective ways to market a business is through a process known as "the controlled auction." A controlled auction introduces the acquisition opportunity to a pre-selected list of qualified buyers and requires that they adhere to a strict set of bidding procedures if they are interested in buying the company. The controlled auction is designed to create a situation in which a number of equally informed buyers are interested in buying your business at that same time. This process, if executed properly, should lead to a choice of buyers all competing to buy your business. The controlled auction process is not appropriate in all circumstances, and may not be practical if your business is worth less than $2 million. However, it is my experience that this process works very well for most mid-size companies. I recommend that you discuss with your transaction advisor whether a controlled auction is appropriate for your business.

The first step in creating an auction is to pre-screen all potential buyers to ensure that they have the financial wherewithal and business skill necessary to complete the purchase. It is your transaction advisor's responsibility to make sure that you don't waste time with unqualified buyers.

Next, the transaction advisor will contact each previously identified buyer, preferably by telephone, and introduce them to the opportunity. This first contact should be carefully scripted, because if the initial contact fails to capture the buyer's attention, a highly qualified buyer may be inappropriately eliminated from the process. That's why I do recommend that you hire a transaction advisor who is tenacious and who does not easily take no for an answer.

### Executing the Confidentiality Agreement

After the initial contact is made and the buyer is interested in learning more about the opportunity, your transaction advisor should have the buyer sign a "Confidentiality and Non-circumvention Agreement. " The Confidentiality and Non-circumvention Agreement will protect you from the buyer disclosing confidential information about your business, or from disclosing to anyone that your business is for sale. To make sure that you receive the maximum protection possible, I suggest that you have your transaction attorney review the Confidentiality Agreement that your transaction advisor uses.

Upon executing a Confidentiality Agreement, the buyer is provided with a copy of the "Confidential Information Memorandum." When the buyer receives the Memorandum he will also receive a set of bidding instructions that clearly state how long he has to review the material and what information he must submit to you if he wishes to pursue a transaction.

Keep in mind that the Confidential Information Memorandum is a marketing document that serves as an invitation to bid for your company. Therefore, the buyers' initial responses will be in the form of non-binding expressions of interest. The expressions of interest will provide you with a range of values that buyers may be willing to pay, as well as why they are interested in buying your company. The initial expressions of interest are used to limit the list of potential buyers to those that are most serious and best qualified.

### Preliminary Due-Diligence

The next step is to allow the remaining potential buyers to visit the company and to meet with management. This process is known as "preliminary due diligence. " At this time the buyers will be making a more thorough analysis of the value of your business and deciding whether to continue to pursue an acquisition. It is important that your transaction advisor prepare you for these meetings to help you "sell" the benefits that your company offers to each buyer. Your transaction advisor should learn as much about the potential buyers as possible so that you will know which benefits interest each particular buyer.

## Stage III: Negotiating the Sale

Once the preliminary due diligence is complete you and your advisors will enter into serious negotiations with one or more of the potential buyers. Ideally, at this point three or four buyers remain so that a competitive bidding environment exists. It is at this stage of the game that your transaction advisor really earns his fee.

A skilled transaction advisor must be able to thoroughly discuss price and terms of a transaction with multiple buyers. Maintaining momentum during the bidding process and structuring a transaction that stretches buyers to their financial limits requires significant skill and finesse. Your transaction advisor must also be able to work closely with your other advisors to ensure that each transaction scenario is evaluated in light of its tax, legal and estate planning implications.

### *Letter of Intent*

Ultimately, the bidding process will end when you select one buyer with whom to close a transaction. Once you have chosen the potential buyer, you and your advisors (usually your transaction advisor and attorney) will negotiate the final business terms of the transaction. The terms of the transaction are generally detailed in a letter of intent which will include the:

- purchase price,
- form of payment,
- closing date,
- contingencies to closing (including financing and due diligence) and
- a variety of other factors.

It is important that your attorney review the letter of intent before you sign it because some letters of intent can bind you and can significantly limit your bargaining position as you negotiate the final purchase agreement. The letter of intent will generally provide for a period of exclusivity for the buyer to perform his due diligence and to arrange financing. During this period you will not be able to talk to other buyers. Therefore, it is important to be prepared to sell under the terms of the letter of intent and to be convinced that the buyer has the ability to finance and close the transaction **before** you sign it.

Letters of intent define the basis for agreement, without intending to be a legal commitment to follow through with an agreement. They can often be more of a problem than a solution; if the negotiations break down, one party may try to enforce the letter against the other.

If a legally binding agreement is called for, a written purchase agreement subject to certain contingencies may be drawn up. Such a contract is binding if certain contingencies are met, such as the ability of the buyer to obtain financing, the consent of your bank or franchisor to the sale, and the confirmation of the accuracy of representations you've made.

### Final Due Diligence

After the letter of intent is signed, the buyer performs a comprehensive investigation of your business. The purpose of the buyer's due diligence is to verify all of the facts that you and your advisors represented to him during the sales process, as well as to uncover anything that might not have been disclosed.

Your broker, as well as your attorney and CPA, should help you to prepare for the buyer's due diligence to make sure that all goes smoothly. During the due diligence period the final purchase agreements will be negotiated. Ideally, all of the documents are ready for closing shortly after the buyer has completed his due diligence.

Given this tight schedule, you must not wait for the buyer's team of lawyers to start pouring through your books and records. Their job is to ferret out every possible problem, every possible contingency. Every stone must be turned so that their client will encounter no unpleasant surprise after the business is transferred.

It is at this point that the sale process can bog down or reach an untimely demise. No one, especially an already skittish purchaser, enjoys unpleasant surprises. It is to your great advantage to make a preemptive strike by anticipating this high level of due diligence on the part of the purchaser.

One of the transaction attorneys with whom I work frequently is John Brown's law partner, Ned Minor. He does something I believe to be unique in the transaction world. Ned prepares due diligence notebooks and work papers before the request is made by a purchaser; in fact, before the purchaser is even identified by your transaction advisor.

Ned knows, from long experience, that a properly motivated seller and a properly prepared business will sell. Therefore, he begins, with the active assistance of the seller, the undertaking of the due diligence process. When a potential buyer is identified, everything is ready to go. This proactive approach prevents delays, gives your efforts and business a professional appearance and, most importantly, gives us a chance to discover and **to correct** problem areas before they come to the attention of the buyer.

### *Maintaining Confidentiality*

A word about **confidentiality**. Any serious potential purchaser will insist on seeing all of your recent financial records. If, after reviewing them, he is still interested, he will want to see *all of your other operating files*: contracts, employee manuals and procedures, customer lists, and more. In short, the potential purchaser will want to know as much about your business you do.

With that knowledge goes the very real risk that, should the deal fall through, the knowledge can be used against you, especially if the potential buyer is a competitor or would-be competitor. The knowledge he gains about your company could enable him to approach a similar business and make a precise, lower offer.

So how do you protect yourself? You reduce your exposure using confidentiality agreements, letters of intent and purchase contracts.

Confidentiality agreements prevent information from being used in any way other than to determine whether or not to purchase your business. Because protection of your business secrets should not be overlooked, it's equally important to exercise your own "due diligence" with respect to the potential buyer. Before releasing financial and other information, you have the right to determine the buyer's financial ability to purchase your business by requiring financial assurances from him, or by reviewing the buyer's financial statements.

You should make every reasonable effort to check the prospective purchaser's references for honesty and financial solvency. Often it's easier for your advisors to conduct this investigation than it is for you. It is always more comfortable to blame your lawyer for over-zealousness than it is to accept the responsibility yourself. And lawyers are accustomed to being cast as the "bad guys." Some of them rather enjoy it.

The use of a transaction advisor can also help maintain confidentiality. Through the transaction advisor, you may divulge full financial and other details while withholding the name and precise location of your business. This allows her to disseminate information to a broad range of potential purchasers (who have been pre-screened as to financial capability) without jeopardizing the confidentiality of your business.

### Definitive Purchase Agreement

Your attorney should draft the purchase contract, taking into account all the elements described earlier as well as the determination of how the sale price is going to be paid.

Notice that I said "your" attorney, not the buyer's attorney, should prepare this contract. Don't think that you'll save legal fees by allowing the other side to prepare the contract. Invariably, when the buyer's lawyer draws up the agreement, it is tailored to the wishes of the purchaser and his attorney. You're better off putting all of your requests in the initial document, allowing the buyer to delete or insert specific provisions as the negotiation process progresses.

Yet, having said that, the buyer's legal counsel usually ends up preparing the purchase agreement. After all, we know you are a bit apprehensive. Imagine for a moment the buyer's feelings: he's paying millions of dollars for something he probably knew little about just a few short weeks ago.

### Representations and Warranties

The definitive purchase agreement will require that you make certain representations and warranties to the buyer. These items always survive the closing of the sale. Usually, you'll be required to give the purchaser warranties and representations when the purchase agreement is first signed. Naturally, you and your advisors will seek to limit the warranties you give. The warranties and representations are not just legal boiler plate. They have real meaning and very real consequences. For example, a common representation is:

> **Compliance With Laws**. The Seller has conducted its business in compliance with, and all of the Assets comply with all applicable laws, rules, regulations and applicable orders (including, without limitation, relating to anti-competitive practices, contracts, discrimination, employment, health, safety and zoning). The Seller has not received any notification of any asserted present or past failure by it to comply with such laws, rules, regulations or orders. The Seller has delivered to the Buyer copies of all reports, if any, of the Seller required under the Federal Occupational Safety and Health Act of 1970, as amended, and under all other applicable health and safety laws and regulations. The deficiencies, if any, noted on such reports or any deficiencies noted by inspection through the Closing Date have been corrected by the Seller.

The buyer will want to be protected by having this statement absolute. As the seller, you would rather not make the statement at all. Both parties should be willing to compromise. Keep in mind that these warranties and representations survive the closing. If, upon subsequent experience, they are shown to be breached, you, as seller, are in default of the entire agreement. Your retirement years could be your retirement months. Review your warranties and representations well before any purchase occurs. By knowing what to expect, you'll be better prepared to respond.

It's also likely that there will be additional warranties and representations required of you that are unique to your business. For example, if you are a medical doctor, you may be asked to guarantee the number of active patient files.

The buyer will ask for pages of warranties and representations. Review each of them with your advisors. Again, if you would like examples, request them from Minor & Brown, P. C. using the Request Form at the end of this book.

### Stage IV: Closing the Deal

After the buyer has completed final due diligence and the terms of the definitive agreement have been settled, a closing will occur. Usually, the closing is nothing more than a formality, as all of the hard work will be completed prior to that point. The closing is important and must be conducted in a professional manner so that all of the necessary paperwork is completed. I recommend that your transaction attorney be responsible for the closing. This will give you control over the closing time, place and location, as well as a sense of comfort that your attorney is in charge of the process.

Closing the deal will require adjustments to the purchase price. Count on it. These are typically standard changes of little consequence to either you or the buyer. They involve things like insurance premiums, rent and security deposits, utility company deposits, employee benefits, payroll and payroll taxes, and personal property taxes due for the year of closing.

Closing is important for another reason: you get paid!

### *Your Role in the Sale Process*

First and foremost, control your personality. Don't try to drive too hard a bargain. Be cordial and businesslike and, above all, be patient. Several rounds of negotiations are normal; you should not expect to sit down at the negotiating table and hammer out all the details of the sale in a few hours.

For most of us, selling our businesses is like selling a part of ourselves. The business, the customers, the staff, the vendors have become like family. The business is a home away from home.

Combined with a justified "fear of losing the known" is the equally justified "fear of the unknown"—life after the sale. And now, some stranger (the buyer you've sought) is in your business trying to uncover every piece of dirty laundry.

Most owners are sitting on knife edge throughout the sale process and when that process begins to move like a roller coaster, that knife edge can be painful. Part of your transaction advisor's and attorney's role is to keep you on track and to ease some of that pain.

### *Your Duties During the Transition Period*

After the closing has occurred, you may or may not continue as an employee of or consultant to the new owner. However, it's common to expect some continued involvement in the business even in situations in which you are cashed out. This means introducing the new owner to all key players: suppliers, customers, employees, bankers, and others.

## Summary

There are many elements involved in the successful sale of your company to a third party. The seeds of that sale are almost always sown long before the sale occurs. Creating value for your ownership interest is the first step. The second is determining the sale price in accordance with the process described in this Chapter. The sale process for your business begins the day you acquire it and does not end until the day you receive final payment.

The process of selling a business is generally very complex and can be very time-consuming. Also, every company is different and the issues that arise vary from one business sale to another. Therefore, it is critical that you involve the services of professionals who have the experience to guide you through the process. Your advisor should be someone you trust, and who you believe has the skills and contacts necessary to complete the sale of your business.

## Appendix 9.1:  Discounted Cash Flow Model

| | HISTORICAL | | PROJECTED | | | | | | | TERMINAL VALUE |
|---|---|---|---|---|---|---|---|---|---|---|
| | 1994 | 1995 | 1996 | 1997 | 1998 | 1999 | 2000 | 2001 | 2002 | |
| Net Revenue | 425,000 | 490,000 | 655,000 | 997,500 | 1,326,000 | 3,500,000 | 6,750,000 | 10,250,000 | 12,500,000 | |
| Cost of Sales | 148,750 | 171,500 | 229,250 | 349,125 | 556,920 | 1,505,000 | 2,970,000 | 4,356,250 | 5,125,000 | |
| Gross Profit | 276,250 | 318,500 | 425,750 | 648,375 | 769,080 | 1,995,000 | 3,780,000 | 5,893,750 | 7,375,000 | |
| Operating Expenses (including depreciation and interest) | 140,250 | 161,700 | 327,500 | 748,125 | 464,100 | 1,225,000 | 2,362,500 | 3,587,500 | 4,375,000 | |
| Earnings Before Income Taxes | 136,000 | 156,800 | 98,250 | (99,750) | 304,980 | 770,000 | 1,417,500 | 2,306,250 | 3,000,000 | |
| Income Tax Expense | 0 | 0 | 0 | 0 | 109,793 | 277,200 | 510,300 | 830,250 | 1,080,000 | |
| Net After Tax Income | 136,000 | 156,800 | 98,250 | (99,750) | 195,187 | 492,800 | 907,200 | 1,476,000 | 1,920,000 | |
| Adjustments to determine Cash Flow: | | | | | | | | | | |
| Depreciation | 21,038 | 24,255 | 49,125 | 74,813 | 46,410 | 122,500 | 236,250 | 358,750 | 437,500 | |
| Change in Working Capital | (10,625) | (12,250) | (16,375) | (24,938) | (33,150) | (175,000) | (168,750) | (256,250) | (312,500) | |
| Capital Expenditures | (25,500) | (29,400) | (29,300) | (59,850) | (1,000,000) | (250,000) | (150,000) | (100,000) | (100,000) | |
| Net Free Cash Flow | 120,913 | 139,405 | 91,700 | (109,725) | (791,553) | 190,300 | 824,700 | 1,478,500 | 1,945,000 | 9,725,000 |
| Present Value Discount Factor (WACC=18%) | | | | | 0.848 | 0.718 | 0.609 | 0.516 | 0.437 | 0.370 |
| | | | | | (670,841) | 136,673 | 501,912 | 762,610 | 850,160 | 3,692,140 |

Discounted Cash Flow Value Future Earnings + Terminal Value .................................................................. $5,182,655

Less Projected Balance of Long-term Debt at Terminal Date ..................................................................... ($650,000)

Present Value of the future cash flow of the Business (Value of the Business) .............................................. $4,532,655

## Appendix 9.2:  Abridged Due Diligence Checklist

1.      Legal Considerations

2.      Corporate Organization

3.      Financial Statements and Reports

4.      Tax Returns

5.      Agreements, Commitments and Understandings (Verbal and Written)

6.      Consents, Authorizations and Approvals Required to Complete the Transaction

7.      Employment

8.      Insurance

9.      Litigation

10.     Leases

11.     Identify and describe Permits, Registrations, Licenses, Authorizations material to the conduct of the Company's business required by Federal, State, Local governmental agencies, bureaus or boards.

12.     Accounts

13.     Accounts Receivable

14. Prepaid Accounts

15. Inventory

16. Fixed Assets (machinery, equipment, tooling, leasehold improvements including office, research and development and warehousing).

17. Real Estate

18. Intellectual Property

19. Accounts Payable

20. Long-term Liabilities and commitments (other than notes payable and inventory commitments exceeding 6 months).

21. Accounting

22. Manufacturing

23. Marketing and Sales

24. Research and Development

25. Environmental

26. Brokers and Finders

27. Management Resumes

# *10*

# Dad Always Liked You Best:  Part I

*How to leave the business to your kids and live to tell about it*

Lao Tzu, the ancient Chinese philosopher, may not have been a closely-held business owner, but he had it right, 2500 years ago, when he said that "A journey of a thousand miles must begin with a single step."

All family business owners face such a journey . . . a journey which begins with the decision to transfer the business to children and ends only when the final ownership interest is transferred.

Transferring your business to anyone, let alone to your children, is fraught with the perils of the unknown, the unexpected, the unplanned.  Most owners contemplate and may even take a few faltering steps, but few finish.  Recent surveys confirm that the goal of successful business transfer is seldom reached:  two-thirds of all family business owners wish to pass the business to children, less than one in three succeeds.

Why such an abysmal record?  Why are so many journeys, begun with the best of intentions, doomed to failure?

Many reasons are traditionally given:

- Estate taxes confiscate up to 55 percent of the business value, an asset both illiquid and difficult to value.

Nevertheless, the IRS requires payment within nine months after date of death. And, of course, it uses its own method to determine the fair market value of your business–a value certain to exceed your estimates–in order to maximize the take.

- Children lack the ability and often the commitment to run the business.
- Owners feel unable to leave the business until they are guaranteed financial independence.
- Family-based issues prevent agreement on the successor owner.

All of these reasons are partially to blame for the dismal failure of business owners to transfer businesses successfully to their children. All are valid yet they mask the core issue. Taxes, unprepared and uncooperative children, and the need for financial security are real, but seldom insurmountable obstacles.

*The real reason why business owners fail to transfer their businesses to their children is that they do not know what to do and don't know how to do it.*

Neither do their advisors.

As I travel across the United States speaking to a variety of professional groups, I am struck by one pervasive fact: no one–neither owners nor their advisors–has an organized coherent approach to transferring the family business to a younger generation. And I'm not just referring here to a lack of legal expertise or tax analysis skills. I mean that there is no unified approach to business transition planning. In fact, there is often no approach at all–much less a unified or coherent one.

This chapter will show you how to approach the family business transition process in a manageable, step-by-step manner as well as how to carry it to its successful conclusion. This is a business transition planning process that has worked for hundreds of business owner clients and can work for you. In short: you'll learn what to do and how to do it.

The place for you to begin is at the beginning and then proceed
logically with the planning process until it reaches its conclusion–
the final transfer of the business to the children.   Transferring a
business to your children is not simple; it cannot be done overnight.
Because there is much to do, it is best accomplished by dividing the
process into small tasks, each task can then be understood, undertaken
and completed.  Without this type of plan, a successful family business
transition is a near impossibility.

## STEP ONE:  ESTABLISH A PROCESS.

Where do we begin?  The first step on your journey is to gain
an overview of the steps necessary to transfer your business
successfully.  Prudent business owners will not begin planning for a
business transfer in a vacuum.  No responsible owner–no responsible
parent–facing a life-altering decision, will leap headlong into the
unknown.  Business owners, like you, need to know where they are,
where they need to go, how to get there, and whom to take with
them.  Once they understand the whole process, they can modify,
adapt, or change direction as they move through the transition process,
never losing sight of the ultimate destination.

Looking at the features of the entire process helps you to begin
sketching the outlines of a map showing where your journey begins,
the difficulties you may encounter along the way and the best routes
to complete your transfer–successfully.

Begin by addressing and answering nine questions:  questions
that take the rest of this chapter to answer and the rest of your business
life to resolve and implement.  The answer to each question is a step
on your journey.  The nine questions and the sequence in which they
need to be addressed are:

**STEP ONE:**       How do I establish the planning process?

**STEP TWO:**       What are my goals?  What do I need to accomplish
before the business is completely transferred to
the children?

**STEP THREE:**    What barriers stand in my way?

**STEP FOUR:**    What planning techniques are available to avoid or overcome these barriers? Alternatively, how can I avoid taxes, heart attacks, disruptive in-laws, lawyers, and other road blocks to a successful transfer?

After you are familiar with the general planning concepts outlined above, we can focus on specific transfer situations:

**STEP FIVE:**    How can I transfer the business and be guaranteed financial security?

**STEP SIX:**    How can I transfer the business and avoid paying deadly estate taxes?

**STEP SEVEN:**    How can I transfer the business to children when they cannot run it?

The final hurdle is to determine which child or children should own the business:

**STEP EIGHT:**    How do I transfer the business to the kids when not all of them are active in the business **and** be fair to the inactive children?

**STEP NINE:**    How do I transfer the business when all my children are active?

To better understand how establishing a process works in a "real-life" situation, let's look at the situation in which Joel Camp, owner of JRC Manufacturing, found himself.

*Joel knew that the time had come to begin the transfer of JRC to his children. He had started the company over 30 years ago, had poured his energy, talent and money into it and was proud of its success. Joel took the initiative and called me for an appointment to discuss his transition ideas. I knew Joel to be a real take-charge, "can do" person but as I listened, I wondered.*

*"I want to keep the business in the family and I know I need to begin the transfer to my children, but there are so many questions and I know none of the answers."*

- *"How can I continue to receive income from the business after I leave it?"*
- *"My kids don't have any money, so how can they buy the business from me?"*
- *"Is it really true the government will take half of my business if I give it away during my lifetime or at my death?"*
- *"Should I give the business just to my daughter, Amy, who works in the business, or should I also give equal ownership to my son, Todd, a cardiologist in Elkhart Lake, Wisconsin?"*
- *"Amy's not able to run the business without me–so how can I ever get away?"*
- *"If something happens to me, the business will also die– is there any way to prevent that?"*
- *"What do I do, how do I do it, and how do I get started?"*

Joel Camp is typical of most successful business owners. Lots of questions, lots of concerns, few concrete plans. He knows something has to be done if he is ever to ease away from the business. He knows something has to be done in case he becomes permanently disabled or if he dies. He knows something has to be done to keep everybody happy–Amy, Todd, his wife. He just doesn't know what to do, whom to turn to, or when to begin whatever it is that has to be begun.

This decisive, successful business owner has no clue of what to do. Joel not only has no map but he has no ship, no crew and no home port.

These are the feelings that typically overwhelm a business owner and derail transfer efforts before they even begin. Joel is to be congratulated for seeking assistance. Joel understands **he** needs to do something. He knows he is ultimately responsible for orchestrating a successful transfer of his business to his children.

It was also clear after listening to Joel that his motives for keeping the business in the family are also typical of most owners:

- For Joel, the business is his *alter ego*; his employees, his customers and his friends make the business much more than a place to work or an asset to own.
- Joel wishes to *remain involved* with the business–at a reduced level–and believes that a family transfer is the only option that will allow his continued involvement.
- Joel wants *continued contact with his children.*
- Joel wants his children to enjoy the same *opportunity* for financial success and stability that he has had–an opportunity in this rapidly changing uncertain world–that they may not otherwise have.
- Joel believes that the business provides *continuity for family life.* It is part of the fabric of the Camp family.
- Joel sees that the business is not just a source of income– it's **the** source of income and his family's only hope for true financial security. That income is best realized not from a quick sale, but from a long-term continuous cash flow from the business.

Joel knows he needs a system of discovering, organizing and addressing each major transfer issue. His failure to develop a system has stymied every thought, every effort, every action. Just as he would never begin a hunting trip through the Alaskan wilderness without an up-to-date trail map, he can not begin the process of transferring his business without knowing where to go and how to get there. Without a map, decisions necessary at the outset are never made, and the transfer never starts.

The problem for Joel and for all business owners is that no owner can create that map by himself.  No business owner, Joel included, has sufficient experience dealing with family business succession issues.  Joel can't map territory he's never seen.  The map–the planning process–begins in Step Two.

### STEP TWO:  FIX DEPARTURE OBJECTIVES.

Joel must first ask himself:  *"What are my objectives in leaving the business?"*  A more innocuous question was never asked, but, as with Joel, your response sets the course for everything to follow.  You may have specific objectives, but they surely include the following:

- **When** do I want to leave the business?
  Leaving for some means just stepping back and allowing someone else to run it.  For others it means getting out entirely.  Or it may be selling or giving away part or all of your ownership interest.
- How much **money** do I want when I do leave?
  This is not necessarily a lump sum amount, but rather an income stream for you and your dependents after your employment (and, with that, your normal salary) ends.
- Which child (or children) should run and **own** the business?
- How are all the children to be treated **fairly**?
- How will I keep or create family **harmony** while transferring the business?

Each of these major issues-timing, income, ownership, fairness and family harmony-must be addressed before moving on to the next step.  This Step requires original, fresh thinking from you.  After all, these are **your** goals.  In the end, you'll have your goals well-defined.  In a real sense, the rest of the Steps are all about how to achieve your exit goals.

Remember Seneca's advice: "When a man does not know which harbor he is heading for, no wind is the right wind." Establish a home port. The checklist (Appendix 10.1) at the end of this chapter will give you a start.

## STEP THREE:  UNDERSTAND PROBLEMS AND OBSTACLES.

As difficult as formulating objectives may be, the next step in the planning process appears even more formidable: *"What obstacles stand in the way of attaining my objectives?"* Look at it this way, if it were easy to meet your objectives, you would have done it by now. You wouldn't be reading this book. (And Joel wouldn't feel the need to meet with me at $250 per hour.)

Most owners view their years of effort to make the business financially successful as the "years of struggle." Now that the business has finally made it, it's fair to think the struggle is over, the war has been won. Well, you have won–but you have won only a battle. To paraphrase Winston Churchill, "It may not be the end, or even the beginning of the end. But it is the end of the beginning." The war is only won when you've secured the fruits of that first battle and passed them intact to you and to your family for all time.

Unfortunately, success breeds its own set of problems. The reality of a successfully operated business is that everyone wants a piece of it. But you, and Joel Camp, need a preview of the predators who might want to feed on your success–and how big their appetites might be.

To compound the problem, uninvited guests seldom feed alone. These problems often come in crowds. Here are four that deserve Joel's, and your, immediate attention:

- **Taxation**. Rates reach a high of 55 percent to 65 percent on the transfer of ownership–during lifetime if transferred to children by sale or gift; at death if transferred to children by your will.

- **Litigants** seeking the "big hit."
- **Former In-Laws**–the spouses your children marry and then divorce.
- **The Grim Reaper**–always a surprise guest–who may arrive before the business is transferred to the children.

The IRS, litigants and their lawyers, ex-in-laws, an untimely demise–each alone threatens the very existence of your business.  In combination, their effect is deadly.

Don't despair.  Specific techniques to overcome or avoid each obstacle are described in the remaining steps.  As you, or Joel, begin analyzing which transfer techniques work best, it's best to evaluate the strengths of the most valuable weapons in our arsenal.

## STEP FOUR:  PLAN TO OVERCOME COMMON OBSTACLES

*"Is there a way to avoid these problems of taxation, creditor attack, family disputes and premature death?"*

Picture for a moment the business transfer process as a child's board game.  You roll the dice and, sooner or later, your marker falls on a square marked "Lose One Turn," "Go Back Two Spaces" or "Go To Jail."  In the real world of business transfer, however, the "squares" carry far greater penalty–you give the IRS half of your net worth or allow creditors to take everything you own.  And it's not play money now.  Part of the fascination of board games is that inevitably everyone lands on one of these squares.  Every player can lose all his chips or start all over again.  The challenge in the real world is to remove that inevitability from play.  If **you** design the game, you can remove the penalty squares.  In short:  Make your own rules.

The only way you will ever get a chance to play by your rules is to act now.  Delay and you allow the IRS or creditors or even family members to make the rules.  Guess who loses?

To start playing your game by your rules you have to make the first move: the same first move we discussed in Chapter Two, Business Valuation.

Start by asking "What is your business worth?" When asked, Joel assumed it was important to maximize the value of the business in order to maximize what he could get from the business when he leaves it. There is nothing illogical with this assumption, but nothing could be farther from the truth.

A low value is desirable because it minimizes gift and estate taxes. It's also important when transferring the business to children during your lifetime. Without careful planning, the I.R.S. will likely take two-thirds of the available cash flow upon a sale of your interest to the children. The lower the sale price, the lower the total amount of taxes. *A low value is critical because no family business can support a huge tax drain on its cash flow.* Finally, decreasing the appearance of wealth decreases your attractiveness to potential litigants and limits what they can get if successful.

As I explained to Joel and for reasons you'll appreciate (and the I.R.S. doesn't), the best approach is usually to establish the **lowest defensible value** for your ownership interest. The issue of *how much money you want from the business* (a basic objective) normally has little to do with *how much the business is worth.*

Valuation is by no means the only weapon you'll use to keep these predators at bay–subsequent steps describe specific remedies for specific problems. But across the spectrum a low valuation sheds its beneficial light across every dark shadow.

As I've emphasized throughout this book, valuation (and value-limiting techniques) is the gateway through which all transfers must pass. Every transfer needs to be valued. So why not value the transferred interest in the most beneficial–yet legal–manner possible? Business valuation, because it seems mysterious and does require technical expertise, is too often brushed aside. Understanding and taking advantage of recognized valuation minimizing techniques often separates those owners who preserve their businesses for their families from those forced to sell out.

How can a business be valued low?  Review the value minimization techniques discussed in Chapter Two beginning on page 25.

Finally, proper business valuation is essential for equitable distribution of your estate to all of your children.  It's one thing to minimize the value of a business in order to minimize transfer tax costs as the business is transferred between parent and the business-active child.  It's another to treat fairly the children not receiving the *bargain basement*-valued stock.  What equivalencies should they, in fairness, receive?  Many are the issues in business valuation.

A significant part of this Step is establishing a structure which minimizes the transfer tax cost–whether income or gift or estate tax cost.  Ideas to explore include:

- creating multiple entities
- multiple ownership interests within a single entity
- generation skipping transfers, and
- trusts with spendthrift protection provisions.

Make a list of all these techniques and discuss them with your advisory team.

Let's turn now to the second phase of your transition planning–how to accomplish your objectives given the typical financial, tax and family constraints.

## STEP FIVE:  ACHIEVE FINANCIAL SECURITY

*"How can I transfer the business to the children when I still need income from the business?"*

One of Joel's chief concerns was money.  How was his income going to continue if he transferred JRC Manufacturing to his daughter?  She could hardly afford to buy the business because (like your children), she has no money (and she is unable to borrow any–at least from a reputable lender).  The only source of cash, for both father and daughter, is the future revenue stream of the business.

That being the case, *the primary thrust of Joel's planning must be to extract maximum income from the business at the least tax cost.* Doing so can not be dependent on Joel's continued employment, as he doesn't plan to work long past Amy's succession.

Getting the most money from your business in a tax-advantaged way is only the first step. It is equally vital that future payment of the cash you need from the business be **secure** upon your departure. If the projected stream of income diminishes, you must be ready and able to step in immediately and to take every measure appropriate to continue the cash flow to you and your dependents.

Specific techniques designed to create, maintain, and secure the income stream while transferring the business are the basis for Step Five. See Chapter Seven regarding transferring the business to key employees or co-owners.

### How to Retain Control and Protect Your Interest

You've made up your mind that you will transfer ownership to a son or daughter. But you're not ready to turn over total control of the company. In fact, you want to make sure you can undo any damage that may result from the transfer.

There are a number of ways to go about this. As a general rule, I suggest you do not transfer voting control to your children until you are ready to give them the entire business. Because of family loyalty (and blindness), it is often tempting to bring children in as owners too early. If you retain control initially, you can see if your decision was well-founded or whether you need to step back in to protect family harmony, not to mention to preserve the business that is probably funding your retirement.

The lesson to be learned is not to give up control until you are absolutely certain you have transferred that power to the right offspring—the one most capable of accepting that responsibility. When that isn't done or isn't done soon enough, your business and your retirement are in jeopardy.

What happens when your children want to not only run but also control the business before you are sure they are ready? You can sell it to them and take back a note, but you will lose control. Or you can use a technique I call "Oldco/Newco."

Under this planning technique the existing business (Oldco) remains under the parents' control and ownership. A new company (Newco) is formed, owned by the child or children who will run the new business. Oldco leases its equipment, office, warehouse or other facilities, and perhaps even employees to Newco, launching its business. If the new company fails, Oldco and its investment is not at risk; if Newco succeeds, it eventually buys the equipment, facilities, and other goodwill from Oldco. This plan worked nicely with Lambert Explosives Manufacturing Company (Lamco).

*The owner of Lamco was ready to slow down and turn the business over to his youngest child, Sherry. However, Lambert knew one serious error on her part could figuratively send the business, most of it involving government contract work, up in smoke.*

*We had Sherry set up a new, woman-owned enterprise. This status gave her an advantage in bidding for government contracts. She successfully obtained contracts and leased the manufacturing facilities and equipment from Lamco at a fair market value rental rate. This enabled the senior Lambert to retire in comfort and security.*

Over the years I've used this technique successfully with construction companies, tire distributorships, and other types of companies where capital investment was extensive.

## STEP SIX: AVOID ESTATE TAXES

*"How can I transfer the business intact to my children when estate taxes will take 50 percent or more?"*

I approached this Step head-on with Joel: "Joel, there is one step in the planning process you can't forget about. If we deal with it now, the problem can disappear. If you wait too long, it can destroy your business and impoverish your family. You need to plan to avoid the most confiscatory tax in our tax code–the Death Tax."

Like most owners, Joel saw estate taxation as a distant threat, nothing requiring his attention until he was much older. Unfortunately, through sad experience, estate planners know the importance of preparing for every owner's untimely death. You can decide when to transfer the business to children. You can decide when to retire. You can decide when to get out of the business. But none of us decides when death is going to snatch us away. No matter your age, it is necessary to confront the unpleasant consequences of an early death now.

Remember the board game analogy? While it is impossible for Joel to eliminate the square that takes him out of the game for good, it is possible for him to remove the financial disaster his death will cause for both family and business.

The estate tax millstone does not just hang round the neck of families whose loved ones die unexpectedly. This particular stone can drown even those families whose breadwinners live long and prosperous lives–but who wait too long to transfer their businesses.

Many planning professionals believe estate taxation prevents more businesses from being transferred than any other cause. When you consider that estate tax rates are not less than 37 percent and quickly reach 55 percent and that payment is due nine months after death, it is easy to understand that conclusion.

Just how much does the estate tax hurt? Joel's net worth for estate tax purposes is $3 million–the business consisting of about half. Without planning, estate taxes will take over $1 million after he and his wife die. If Joel dies without proper planning, the Camp family (and others like them) faces several significant problems:

1.  Paying the estate tax when it is due. (It is highly unlikely that without careful planning, an estate will have sufficient cash);
2.  Dealing with the unexpectedly high value placed on the business by the IRS. Reduction of a high valuation may necessitate significant negotiation with or litigation against the government (a time and dollar consuming effort with gloomy prospects for success);

3. Dividing the estate "equally." Most owners want to leave their businesses to children who are active in the business and an equal amount of other assets in the estate to inactive children. However, if estate taxes, to use Joel's example, take $1 million and the business-active child (Amy) gets the business intact (worth $1.5 million) only $500,000–less than 20 percent of the original estate–goes to her brother (and that's not fair even if he is a doctor!).

Few businesses can survive this level of unanticipated taxation and few owners want to pass on their businesses if, as a result, some children are treated unfairly. Thorough planning, then, is imperative and must be undertaken immediately–not solely because I think you are going to die tomorrow–because I know how many years of planning and implementation it takes to successfully meet the tax challenge.

Unfortunately, many owners shy away from this type of planning because they are misinformed. For example, they believe that:

- The IRS will agree with their estimate of the business's worth.
- The only way to pay estate taxes is to buy a lot of life insurance–and they hate paying insurance premiums.
- They will transfer the business to the kids long before they die.
- Nothing significant can be done to minimize the estate tax bite.

All of these beliefs foster passivity. Remain inactive and you become one of the IRS's strongest allies.

If, however, you take action, estate taxes are less likely to prevent an effective transfer than any of the other major obstacles standing in your path. Chapter 13, "Dad Always Liked You Best: Part II" deals with this in greater detail.

## STEP SEVEN:  LEAVING THE BUSINESS BEFORE KIDS ARE READY

*"How can I transfer the business to children when they cannot run it?"*

It was evident that Joel was acutely aware of this issue when he commented, "There is one other thing I am concerned about.  I'm ready to leave now, but Amy is just not ready to take over the business.  How can I transfer the business to her when she can't run it?  At least not now."

One of Joel's ultimate objectives is to transfer the business to Amy; yet, he is convinced that she is simply too young, too untested, and hasn't worked long enough in the business to know if this is to be her lifetime career.  Given these doubts, how can Joel transfer his business to Amy?

It may seem obvious that you shouldn't transfer the ownership of the business until the children are ready to be responsible owners.  Less obvious is the fact that *waiting too long creates significant tax problems, delays your own transition planning, and frustrates children looking to you for a commitment of ownership.*  On the other hand, transferring the business to children who lack dedication to the business, or who prove incapable of running it, creates an equally unappealing scenario.  Joel's situation is typical of most owners: difficult problems with no easy answers.

Fortunately for Joel and for you, experience has taught this author that there is a very clear course of action.  This course requires that you:

- First and foremost, create consensus within the family for the transition plan.  This involves harmonizing family issues and goals with business issues and goals.
- Consider giving children operational control well before voting control.
- Plan and document to get back whatever you give or sell to the children if the worst case scenario becomes reality.

This requires a business continuity agreement described in the next chapter.
- Keep ultimate control until your other transfer goals–most importantly, financial security–are achieved.
- Take preemptive measures, whenever gifting business interests to children, to keep the business in the family should your child divorce. Ownership interests such as stock, should be placed in trust or be subject to a marital agreement.
- Make contingency plans involving others (key employees, and sons- or daughters-in-law for example) if transferring the business to a particular child doesn't work out. Don't place all your eggs in one basket. Review Chapters Eight and Nine on third party sales carefully and keep this option **open**.
- Create a process that encourages the children to assume the mantle of responsibility by adopting performance standards that must be met before pay increases or stock transfers commence.
- Involve others in running the business while you are still active and after you have stepped back. This might include a key employee, an outside board of advisors, a board of directors or any combination thereof. Business consultants with psychological or sociological training can be most useful at this stage.
- Consider selling parts of the business to others who have the money or the necessary commitment to the business.
- Develop and maintain communication channels with all family members.

## STEP EIGHT: TRANSFER YOUR BUSINESS TO THE RIGHT CHILD

*"How do I transfer the business when not all my children are active in it?"*

*I can always recognize those business owners who have dedicated their lives to business planning–those who know the easy*

*way to transfer the business to the younger generation.*
      *They have but one child.*

For those of you with more than one child (thus demonstrating your failure to anticipate the trials and tribulations of transferring a business) I am sure you can empathize with Joel as he wondered how to give his business to both his children, when only one sought an active role and ownership.

Like most owners, Joel thought it best to give equal amounts of the business, and everything else for that matter, to each child. While this seems to be the easiest solution, it is generally unworkable, both from the perspective of the business active child and the non-active child or children.

The business active child will resent having a co-owner for a number of reasons:

- Amy's efforts to increase the value of the business, if successful, should reward Amy–not her brother.
- Just like you, your entrepreneurial "chip off the old block" wants to operate the business as her own. Joel couldn't imagine that she'd want to share ownership with anyone else, especially her brother.
- When there are other owners, simply giving a controlling vote to the active child is not enough. That child has a fiduciary duty of due care and loyalty to the other shareholders. That means that the active shareholder's actions such as personal bonuses, personal salary increases, and business "perks," all must be reasonable and comparable to what a non-shareholder performing the same duties for the company might reasonably expect. I doubt you would like **your** compensation and perks subject to that same scrutiny.
- You probably gave all children an **equal opportunity** to participate in the business and become owners yet not all seized the opportunity. Why force your most ambitious, risk-oriented child–the one who chose to succeed you–to share the rewards?

Many owners understand why the business-active child must control the business. Yet, this solution raises as many questions as it answers. Passing operational control to the business active child is not enough. Ownership, too, must pass. The best way to transfer the business when you have children who will remain inactive is to transfer all of the business to the business-active children and none of the business to the inactive children. Once this decision is made, much of your effort will be directed to providing the non-active children with a fair share of your estate.

Let's turn to the non-active child for a moment. That child would greatly prefer assets of comparable value to a business he or she has no personal interest in. Again, the reasons for this preference go back to how family businesses are operated:

- The non-active child will now own an illiquid, unmarketable security just like you own, only he'll receive no income or other benefits as a result of that ownership.

- The non-active child will have a valuable asset, yet be powerless to sell it–except to the business-active child, who will, in all likelihood, not have money to purchase it and whose idea of fair market value is likely to differ dramatically from that of the non-active child.

- The non-active child will be unable to make any decisions regarding the future course of the business.

Most of the time, the decision to leave the business to both active and inactive children results in family discord, which in turn causes the business to suffer, if not dissolve. If you decide to split your business in this way, you have probably signed its death warrant.

I hope I've made myself clear: there are almost always better ways of transferring the business than to sell to all of the children. Exception: When the business is large enough to be considered an investment–when it is mature, stable, run by non-family managers as well as one or more children, when there is enough income to handsomely reward the business active child and provide an income stream to other children who are simply investors.

## STEP NINE:  TRANSFER THE BUSINESS TO MORE THAN ONE ACTIVE CHILD

*"How do I transfer the business to all of the children active in the business?"*

This transfer scenario is only for the brave.  At first glance, the easiest route seems to be to transfer all of the business to all of the children, especially when they're all active in the business.  Once again, the obvious solution is not the best.

Look at your situation this way: you are asking children who couldn't share a 98-cent toy when they were young to begin sharing the ownership, management and control of a successful business enterprise.  Add to that the sometimes not so subtle influence of in-laws and you have a recipe for disaster that makes the journalists for *Forbes* and *The Wall Street Journal* smell a story.  Witness a story about the Dart Family: "When heirs fall out." (subtitled "Hell hath no fury like an heir spurned.  If you are fortunate enough to own a successful family business, don't put off planning for your exit.") (Forbes, December 6, 1993 pg. 140-143).

Transferring the business to multiple children is a bit like having brain surgery.  It is important that the surgery–or the transfer–be smoothly and cleanly accomplished, but the ultimate measure of success is whether the patient recovers.  It is this aspect–the long term survival of the business and the family–that is most overlooked.

When attempting to transfer a business to more than one child you must structure the transaction so that it endures longer than you do.  Consider carefully the issues of operational control, management, voting control, and dispute resolution and establish a framework well before you leave.  Delve into the murky, emotional, subjective, and interpersonal issues inherent to the multiple child transfer.  Consider the counsel of human resource experts when executing a multi-child transfer. Good luck.

## Summary

In this chapter, Joel Camp has illustrated the issues facing the business family as they embark upon that most difficult, but most fruitful of all journeys–the final journey to create financial security and a family legacy.

The Joel Camp example outlines the nine-step process used to uncover, explore, and resolve the issues that lie waiting for you, your business, and your children. I suggest that you complete the checklist at the end of this chapter and read other chapters on:

Business Valuation: Chapter 2
Transfers to co-owners or employees: Chapter 7
Third party sales: Chapters 8 and 9
Business continuity: Chapter 11
Estate Planning: Chapter 13.

Publisher's Note:
This chapter contains the central concepts of family business transfers. Business Enterprise Press expects to publish a 250 page book on this subject in 1998. That book expands each of these steps into a complete chapter. So you can see, you've just scratched the surface for transferring the business to your children. But there is enough here to begin the transition process in earnest. Begin by working with the attached checklist. If you'd like a more complete workbook, contact Business Enterprise Press via the Request Form at the end of this book or by calling toll free 1-888-206-3009.

## Appendix 10.1:  Checklist for Owners Considering a Family Transfer

1.    The date I want to leave the business is_____ .
      Remember, leaving for some means just stepping back and
      allowing others to run it.  For others it means getting out
      entirely.  Or it may be selling or giving away part or all of
      your ownership interest.

2.    I want to have $_____ accumulated (or $_____
      per year of after-tax income) when I do leave.  I understand
      that this is not necessarily a lump sum amount, but rather an
      income stream for me and my dependents after my
      employment (and with that, my normal salary) ends.

3.    I have decided that the child(ren) who should run and own
      the business is/are: _____

      _____ .

4.    My children will be treated fairly by adopting the following
      plans: _____

      _____

      _____ .

5.    I will keep or create family **harmony** while transferring the
      business by adopting the following strategies:

      _____

      _____

      _____

      _____

# *11*

# Planning for the Unforeseen

*The business continuity agreement: the most important document in your business*

The business continuity agreement is the single most important document that you, as the owner of a closely held business, will sign. To understand why this is so, we must first review what the business continuity agreement does.

The business continuity agreement (also called a buy-and-sell agreement) *controls the transfer of ownership* in a business when certain events occur. Typically these events include the death of an owner and a sale and transfer of stock from one owner to another or to an outside party.

In addition to controlling these events, you should also consider having the agreement include transfers to take effect upon an owner's permanent and total disability, termination of employment, retirement, bankruptcy, divorce, and–importantly–a business dispute among the owners.

At each of these events, the business continuity agreement may require the business or the remaining owners to purchase the departing owner's stock; or it may give an option to the business or the remaining owners to buy that ownership interest. Lastly, it may give the departing owner the option to require the company to buy his ownership interest.

The agreement should also *establish the value* of the stock, set the terms and conditions of the buyout, and give additional protection to all owners.

In short, the business continuity agreement, in addition to other protection, tells you to whom you can sell, at what price and terms, and under what restrictions you can (or must) sell your stock. These restrictions will be explored in the rest of this chapter.

This chapter often uses the term "shareholder" instead of "owner." The terms are interchangeable–the same planning principles and tax treatment can apply whether your business is a corporation, partnership or limited liability company. The major exception is regular or "C" corporations. Since that type of entity has its own tax structure, the rules will differ.

## Advantages and Disadvantages

Lawyers, being lawyers, are reluctant to discuss the advantages of any action without also discussing the disadvantages. This healthy characteristic helps us keep our clients out of trouble. With buy-and-sell agreements, however, disadvantages are hard to find if the document is well-drafted and kept updated for changes in ownership, value and other circumstances.

With that in mind, let's first look at the advantages.

### Advantages

- *Ownership in the business can be transferred only in accordance with the agreement.* This benefits both the owner wishing to transfer stock and the other owner or owners wanting to acquire the stock. In the first instance, the buy and sell agreement can assure a selling shareholder, or his estate, of a purchaser for fair value and upon terms and conditions that are mutually acceptable. For the remaining owners the agreement means that any transfers of ownership must be made, or at least offered, to them. This eliminates the threat that an outside party or a co-owner's spouse or children will become owners of the business, thereby diminishing management, control and value.

- *Valuation is set not only for purposes of a sale but also for estate tax valuation purposes.* Privately owned businesses are notoriously difficult to value. Your idea of your business's value at your death may be much lower than the IRS's. If you haven't fixed the value of your business, the IRS is free to use a variety of valuation techniques in an attempt to maximize value so it can impose the highest estate tax liability on your estate. A properly drafted buy-and-sell agreement can fix that value except, and this is a big exception, for businesses transferred among family members.

- *The terms and conditions of any transfer of stock, including interest rate, length of buy out period, and security, can be fixed.* In addition, where possible, the transfer can be funded. The agreement provides a clear picture to a departing shareholder of how much money he will receive, and how often. Likewise, the remaining shareholders know in advance the extent and duration of their buyout obligations. This allows both parties to plan their respective futures.

- *Buy-and-sell agreements establish and protect rights among shareholders that do not otherwise exist in the company.* Through a buy-and-sell agreement, a minority shareholder may attain more control over his or her destiny than is normally provided through voting rights. These safeguards include placing limits on the sale or purchase of the stock of the majority owner(s), establishing valuation for all owners' stock, giving minority owners the right to sell their stock if certain events occur, and other important items.

An example of the type of right that a buy and sell can establish is providing the owner of a minority interest the right to serve on the board of directors. Obviously, this can be an important right because a minority shareholder might not otherwise be able to garner sufficient votes to be elected to the board.

A second example is requiring the corporation and remaining shareholders to do their best to obtain the release of the departing shareholder from any personally guaranteed indebtedness as well as to release any personal collateral used for a corporate debt when the owner of that collateral sells his interest in the company.

- An *intangible benefit lies in the process of designing the buy-and-sell agreement.* All too often when there are joint owners of a business, they do not sit down together to discuss business issues. In order to draft a buy-and-sell agreement, however, a meeting of all owners is essential. In doing so, they address major questions affecting their relationship such as: What happens if one of the owners dies? What happens if the owners don't get along? What happens if one wants to retire before the other? Obtaining answers to these important questions requires owners to discuss their ideas about the future of the business.

I will always remember one of my client companies in which the two owners, equal partners, had a poor relationship. They were certain each had opposing views on the future of the business–in terms of both growth and their respective desires to remain in the business. And they each had their own ideas about their own importance to the business.

In meetings with their advisory team, they soon learned there were many reasons for their business's success. Although one owner was the "money man" and the other more active in the business, they learned both were equally concerned with the long-term future of the company. This recognition allowed us to draft a complete buy-and-sell agreement for their mutual benefit.

The process took almost a year. During that time the owners met periodically with their advisors to review business goals and aspirations. Increasingly, they found themselves in agreement–not just in matters contained in the buy-and-sell agreement but also with respect to operational ideas. Those bases of agreement soon broadened into a consensus on how the business should proceed if one of them were no longer with it.

As a result of this process their business today is more vibrant, more directed. The owners are more committed than ever. And, not coincidentally, profitability and value have increased steadily.

- *A buy-and-sell agreement establishes a market for an owner's stock at an agreed-upon price.* Without an agreement there's no market for stock in a closely held business unless you're a controlling owner. Otherwise, if you've not made firm arrangements for the sale of your stock, the buy-and-sell agreement is the only means of disposing of your ownership interest at a fair price. The agreement can obligate others to purchase your stock thus creating a market, at an agreed-upon price. It can also provide a market if you must sell your stock due to unforeseen events such as death or disability.

As is evident from the discussion above, there are many advantages to a buy-and-sell agreement. But there are also disadvantages. Here are the most common:

### Disadvantages

- *Legal fees can be a stumbling block.* An agreement may easily cost $800 to $5,000 or more, although most buy-and-sell agreements that are relatively straightforward, but still comprehensive and thorough, are much closer to the low end of this scale.
- *Drafting a complete buy-and-sell agreement is difficult.* It's virtually impossible to anticipate every contingency. This is especially true when the attorney first begins to

represent the business. After awhile, when the buy-and-sell agreement has been reviewed at several fiscal year-end meetings, revisions will normally occur. As a result, the business continuity agreement can be tailored to the particulars of the business and the individual goals of the owners.

- *The buy-and-sell agreement must be kept up to date.* Because a buy-and-sell agreement is a long-term contract, its provisions must be reviewed with your advisors at every fiscal year-end meeting. Like other living organisms, a closely held business continually grows or contracts. The dynamics of ownership, valuation, and events that could trigger a buyout require constant monitoring, updating, and adaptation. The cost in time and money is usually not significant, but the practice must be habitual.

## The Typical Buy-and Sell Agreement

The pattern of a typical business continuity agreement and the most important provisions of the agreement are discussed below in the order they would normally appear in buy-and-sell agreements. An outline of the business continuity agreement is included in Appendix 11.1.

### Mandatory vs. Option Buyouts

Before looking at the different types of events that can trigger a stock transfer, consider what type of purchase or sale obligation, if any, you want to impose on the transaction.

For example, if a shareholder terminates his employment, the buy-and-sell agreement could require that shareholder to sell–and require his company to buy–his stock. Alternatively, it could also require the company or remaining shareholders to purchase the stock of a departing shareholder only at the option of that shareholder. The buy-and-sell agreement could also give the company or remaining shareholder an option to purchase the stock of a departing shareholder if the company or shareholder chooses to do so.

In addition to establishing how each transfer event will obligate the company or remaining or departing shareholders, the obligation decision interacts with valuation and payment issues. For example, if a shareholder is fired, the company may want the option, but not the obligation, to purchase his stock–possibly at a value that is less than the fired shareholder might have received had he worked until retirement.

## Who Should Buy?

Yet another consideration in the buy-and-sell agreement is who should buy the selling shareholder's stock: the company or the other owners? This issue is resolved by asking:

1. Which entity has the most cash available to pay for the stock? The company or the individual owners?
2. At what level do the most favorable tax consequences occur?

Generally, when the buy out of a departing shareholder's stock is not funded by some form of insurance, the corporation is more likely to have cash available to fund an installment buyout. Also, the tax consequences may not be as severe when the company pays.

Of course, when the remaining shareholder sells his stock during his lifetime, taxes will generally be paid on the amount of gain. The gain is the same whether the remaining shareholders purchase the departing shareholder's stock (this is called a cross-purchase buy out) or whether the corporation buys the selling owner's stock (this is called a stock redemption). Still, at least with a regular corporation, there is a substantial tax advantage in using a cross-purchase arrangement. The advantage lies with the remaining shareholders when it comes time to sell their stock as illustrated in the example of George Kilpatrick and Barbara Joy, described in the following section.

Because, as a business owner, you should always be planning for the eventual sale of your business, you cannot afford to ignore this crucial difference between a cross-purchase and a redemption.

## The Death Buyout

A business continuity agreement almost always contains provisions for the purchase of an owner's interest upon his death; but there are certain exceptions to this general principle. One exception occurs when the business interest is strictly investment-oriented.

For example, if the business owner has been a passive investor–receiving large distributions from the business each year– he may want his heirs to continue receiving those distributions after his death. In that instance, the agreement can be drafted to allow remaining owners to control the future of the business while the heirs are assured a continued return on their investment.

Another exception occurs when, for estate and personal reasons, it may be appropriate to allow the transfer of a deceased shareholder's interest to family members, rather than to the remaining shareholders. This concept is more fully explored in Chapter 13.

These rare exceptions aside, in most situations a shareholder's death should create an explicit obligation on the part of his estate to sell his stock, either to the corporation or to the remaining shareholders. There should also be an explicit obligation on the part of the corporation or of the remaining shareholders to purchase that stock.

The purpose of creating these mandatory obligations is straightforward. Very few owners want to be in business with their co-owner's spouse or children–for obvious reasons. Most closely held businesses require the owners to actively participate in the business enterprise. Few spouses or children can fill the shoes of the deceased owner, and the remaining owner or owners usually are unwilling to continue the effort that is required to make the business successful if much of the benefit will accrue to a passive owner.

In some respects ownership means little in a closely held business unless the owner is in a position to use that ownership to earn his livelihood. A decedent's spouse or children are unlikely to be in that position. Upon an owner's death, his heirs are not likely to demand a fair market value for their stock. By requiring the remaining shareholders to purchase the deceased owner's stock, the decedent makes certain that his family will receive the value–in hard cash–set forth in the agreement. Without a buy-and-sell agreement, this conversion of what is generally the largest, but most illiquid, asset of the estate may not occur. The advantages of such an agreement are illustrated in the case of George Kilpatrick and Barbara Joy.

### The Killjoy Caper

*In 1983, George Kilpatrick and Barbara Joy started up a company called–what else?–Killjoy Manufacturing, Inc. Each paid $1,000 for one-half of the stock, giving each a $1,000 basis in their stock.*

*George and Barbara came to my firm for a buy-and-sell agreement at the suggestion of their insurance agent. Their company was now worth a million dollars, and the insurance agent wanted it to buy two $500,000 life insurance policies–one on each owner's life. The premium on both policies would total $20,000 per year, about $10,000 for each. The agent explained that the premiums, while not tax-deductible, are more affordable to the corporation (a "C" corporation) because it is in a lower tax bracket than the owners and it has more cash available than they have. As already discussed, this type of a buyout–in which the corporation purchases the decedent's stock–is known as a stock redemption. If the corporation is a regular or "C" corporation, there are adverse consequences to such stock redemptions as the surviving shareholder was about to learn.*

*Under this proposed plan, at George's death, the corporation would use the insurance proceeds to buy his stock, leaving Barbara the sole owner of all the outstanding stock in the business. Her basis* *remains at $1,000. If, after a period of time, she decides to sell Killjoy to a friendly competitor, a national corporation, or anyone else–and if Killjoy has not appreciated in value–her gain would be $999,000. A tax of $250,000 or more would be due. And due to a quirk in the tax law, that was just the beginning.*

*Receipt of the life insurance proceeds at the corporate level would be subject to an alternative minimum tax. This results in an effective tax of 15 percent. If any entity other than a "C" corporation receives insurance proceeds on a policy it owns, there are no income taxes.*

*Instead I recommended a cross-purchase agreement. Barbara, the surviving shareholder, would purchase George's stock after his death, using $500,000 of income-tax-free proceeds from the insurance that she, not the company, would buy on George's life.*

*For George's estate the result is the same under either scenario: The estate receives $500,000 income tax free.*

*But for Barbara the results are very different. If the second plan (the cross purchase) is followed, she is not subject to a 15 percent ($75,000) tax on the receipt of the life insurance. And, when she sells the stock for $1 million her gain is only $500,000; her tax on that gain is only $125,000. To obtain this favorable tax result, all she had to do was buy the stock instead of having the corporation buy it. This meant that she needed to own the insurance policy so that she would receive the life insurance proceeds, income tax free. As the insurance agent pointed out, because of her higher tax rate, it would cost Barbara more to buy the policy than it would the company; however, given the substantial tax savings down the road, it seemed to make sense to have her bear that expense. Fortunately, there is a way for Barbara to have the tax benefit of the cross purchase using tax-free insurance proceeds while avoiding, in large part, the tax cost of paying for that insurance. The answer is a split dollar agreement.*

*A split dollar insurance agreement divides the ownership and the corresponding premium payments between the corporation and the individual. In Barbara's case the agreement required the corporation to pay about 90 percent of the premium payment on the policy on George's life in return for the right to receive the cash value buildup in the policy. Thus, at George's death, the business would receive essentially a return of all the premium payments and Barbara would receive the remaining death proceeds.*

*The reason for the split dollar insurance agreement is to make certain that the bulk of the income tax consequences on the payment of the insurance premium remain at the corporate level. Yet, the insurance proceeds could be payable to Barbara to allow her to achieve an increased basis in the company upon George's death.*

This example shows the importance of a coordinated planning approach to your business. Through proper planning an income tax savings of $125,000 to Barbara and $75,000 to Killjoy Manufacturing was created without any inconvenience, complications, or disadvantage to anyone–except, perhaps, the IRS.

There's another potential problem you must avoid with buy-and-sell agreements. I often review a buy-and-sell agreement for a new client only to find that the valuation for death purposes is unrealistically high. Invariably this happens because it is so easy to buy a lot of life insurance to fund the purchase of the decedent's stock–a mistake that can lead to serious consequences.

Unfortunately, most buy-and-sell agreements are not reviewed often enough. Sometimes the underlying life insurance policies lapse and the owner subsequently dies, leaving no insurance owned by the corporation or other shareholders. In that situation the underlying obligation remains–to purchase at an inflated value–but there is no funding available. And when the valuation is large–several hundred thousand dollars or more for a decedent's stock–overvaluing the stock may lead to estate taxes that are otherwise avoidable.

In short, overvaluing for death purposes is just plain sloppy. It happens because the owner reasons, "Well, life insurance is cheap, and it doesn't really make a difference how much my company is worth. If I die, my wife will get the money." This line of reasoning allows the business owner to avoid the critical thinking so necessary to determine the true value of his business. And until he determines that true value, how can he expect to measure increases in that value?

The issues surrounding valuation, including methods of properly valuing your business, are discussed in detail in Chapter Two. For our purposes here, the point is simply this:

The same effort to arrive at a fair value for your business interest must be made for buy-and-sell purposes. In addition to events that can be funded with insurance, such as death and disability, the buy-and-sell agreement normally includes events for which funding is not available: involuntary transfers, business dispute buyouts, sales to third parties and retirement or termination of employment.

In these cases, a low but defensible value can be even more critical because the company will have to fund the buyout purely out of cash flow. If the value is too high or the terms too severe, these buy outs can destroy the company. Keep in mind the central tenet of all lifetime owner buyouts (other than third party sales): *your buyer does not have the cash to buy you out.* You need to get your money from the business at as low a net tax to the business **and** to you as possible. This means you actually want to receive a minimal price for your ownership interest (because of double taxes) and maximum cash flow directly from the business (because this is taxed once).

## When Disability Strikes

Most closely held business owners are active in their businesses. Should they become disabled, the company will endure substantial hardships, both economic and operational. More importantly, in the absence of a buy-and-sell agreement, the disabled owner's income stream from the company may also evaporate. This problem confronted Steve Hughes, one of three equal shareholders in a growing advertising agency.

*At age 38, Steve suddenly had a stroke. As with many stroke victims, his recovery was incomplete. Physically, he was the picture of health (his golf game even improved!); but he totally lost his ability to speak and read. Doctors told him he would never be able to return to work.*

*Hughes's firm had a buy-and-sell agreement, but it covered only a buyout at death and an option for the company to buy his stock if he were to try to sell it to a third party. Trying to find and sell closely held stock to a third party is a difficult proposition anytime; his disability made it impossible. Even if his fellow shareholders had wanted to continue his salary, they did not have the resources to do so indefinitely.*

*As a result, the company and Hughes were left in a classic dilemma: the company or rather the remaining shareholders wanted to purchase Hughes's stock so that its future appreciation in value, due now to their efforts alone, would be fully available to them. Conversely, as Hughes's family soon realized, the owners of closely held stock rarely receive current benefits in the form of dividends. The profits of a closely held corporation are either accumulated by the company or distributed to the active shareholders in the form of salaries, bonuses and other perks.*

*In short, Hughes's family would not get what it needed most–cash–to replace the salary he was no longer earning, while his partners faced the prospect that their efforts to increase the value of the business would reward Hughes as much as themselves. This dilemma could be solved only by a buyout of Hughes's stock. His family then could receive a fair value for his business interest when they otherwise would receive nothing until the company was eventually sold or liquidated. Meanwhile, ownership would be left with those responsible for the company's success.*

The Hughes buyout faced three difficult problems, each of which could be eliminated by a properly drafted and funded buy-and-sell agreement that would:

1. Agree upon the value.
2. Fund the buyout.
3. Agree on the payment terms of the buyout.

## *Value*

The disability of a key owner may, and probably will, reduce revenue (at least for awhile) and increase expenses because of the need to hire replacement personnel. At the very time when the disabled (or deceased or departed in good health for that matter) owner has left, the business feels the financial strain from the departure of that productive employee. A meeting of the minds as to business value is even more difficult. The family tends to look at historical value, the remaining shareholders at the uncertain future value.

## *Funding*

However, if properly planned, the company can prepare to pay that fair value by purchasing *disability buy out insurance*. The buy-and-sell agreement, in combination with the disability buyout policy, provides the means to achieve both the disabled shareholder's goal of receiving money for his ownership interest, and the company's and remaining shareholders' goals of maintaining active ownership.

Don't confuse the terms *disability buyout insurance* and *disability income replacement insurance*. The latter can help replace lost income in the event of disability. Disability income insurance normally pays a percentage of the disabled employee/owner's regular monthly salary directly to him until he overcomes his disability or attains a certain age, such as 65. *Disability buy out insurance* is paid to the business (or the other owner) in a lump sum or series of payments over several years. The company (or other owner) then pays that money to the disabled owner to buy back his stock. Disability buyout insurance intended to fund a buy-and-sell agreement should be acquired in addition to the owner's personal disability income insurance.

## *Payment*

The buy-and-sell agreement also addresses payment terms. Since disability buyout insurance will normally not cover more than 80 percent of the buy out price, a "balance owing" usually results. This means the owner and shareholders must agree on the payment terms for the remaining amount owed. Typically these terms are the interest rate, the length of the buy out period (usually three to seven years), and the security to be given to ensure payment for the balance owing.

When these key elements are negotiated in advance–before any of the shareholders become disabled–fair and equitable decisions can be made. In the Steve Hughes case, it was too late. His family eventually felt compelled to sell his stock for book value–a low return for a service company. It was that or nothing. Besides, it was all that his former partners felt they could afford to pay.

## *Other Events*

So far we've covered the easy events–death and disability–that trigger a transfer of ownership. Easy because the purchase of the departing owner's stock can be funded with insurance. The buy-and-sell agreement should also cover other types of voluntary or involuntary transfers (such as a shareholder's bankruptcy or divorce).

In the event of involuntary transfers the shareholder could be forced to transfer his ownership interest–in the case of bankruptcy, to the bankruptcy trustee or creditor; in the case of divorce–to the former spouse. The buy-and-sell agreement should simply give the business the opportunity to acquire the shareholder's stock in the event of an involuntary transfer. Perhaps the only thing worse than having your ex-spouse own a part of your business is having someone else's ex-spouse own a part of your business!

In addition to those involuntary transfers–death, disability, bankruptcy, divorce–the business continuity agreement should also cover events generally within the control of one or more of the shareholders. For example, where there are two equal owners, one of whom is president, an agreement can provide that the president can't fire the other owner.

A second termination situation arises where there are three equal shareholders, two of whom would generally have the power to fire the third. In that event they might want the ability to purchase the terminated owner's stock. The fired owner may want the ability to sell his stock back to the company. Or all the owners may simply want the agreement to require a mandatory purchase of stock in the event of a termination of employment of a shareholder for any reason, whether he quits or is fired.

Again, when these situations occur–as they often do–the scene is acrimonious and hostile. Litigation is always threatened or initiated. This is when a buy-and-sell agreement–one that has determined a fair market value for the business and the buyout terms and conditions, and has been agreed upon by all parties–can truly be a godsend.

### *Third Party Offers*

Every buy-and-sell agreement should cover restrictions on transferring stock to nonowners. Without this provision the agreement is toothless; an owner would be able to transfer his stock to anyone, at any time, thereby avoiding the agreement's primary purpose of restricting ownership to the current owners.

If an ownership interest is to be offered to an outsider, the agreement normally requires the owner to first offer his interest to the company, then to the remaining co-owners–at the same price and terms offered by the would-be buyer.

Often the agreements require that the purchase price offered the remaining owners be the lower of the value set forth in the agreement or the price offered by the would-be purchaser. This assures the remaining owners that they need pay no more than the value fixed in the agreement.

### *"The Texas Shootout" Provision*

When there are two or more non-controlling (usually equal) owners, neither may be able to fire or get rid of the other(s) in the absence of a provision in the buy-and-sell agreement.

It is when these owners become locked in a bitter dispute with respect to the future course of the business enterprise that the buy-and-sell agreement can become most valuable. It is the means to resolve the dispute by forcing one or more disgruntled owners to sell their stock and get out of the business. This is how it works.

The agreement stipulates that either shareholder may offer to purchase the other shareholder's interest. The second shareholder **must** then either accept the offer and sell his stock **or** purchase the first owner's interest for the same price, terms, and conditions spelled out in the offer. In other words, the second shareholder has two choices: He must either **accept** the offer and *sell his stock* or turn the tables and *buy the offering shareholder's stock.*

At the conclusion of this buyout procedure, there will be only one shareholder. I call this method "The Texas shoot-out provision." It's a painful remedy undertaken only when there is no alternative that the parties can agree on. I like to have this provision in a buy-and-sell agreement; it tends to encourage owners who are not getting along with each other to agree to a buyout of one party or the other. If they don't, the foot-dragging partner cannot prevent the eventual buyout of his stock.

The Texas shootout provision could offer one other alternative. It could allow either party–if both parties can't get along–to dissolve the business, pay off its debts, distribute the assets, and start all over.

### *The Sole Owner*

The buy-and-sell agreement can be even more important for a sole owner. Should you die or become totally disabled, there is no natural "market" for your stock. This absence can be especially critical in personal service companies where there is little value other than the "going concern value" (as discussed in Chapter Two). But don't despair. Business continuity agreements can sometimes be designed for situations in which there is only one owner.

In sole owner situations it's necessary to locate another owner of a business, usually similar to yours, who would also like to provide some type of continuity for his or her business. For example, I've prepared agreements for a group of independently practicing oral surgeons. If one of them should die, become disabled, or retire, the remaining surgeons have the obligation to purchase the departing surgeon's practice.

In a case of sole business owners, I've also drafted in their buy-and-sell agreements a total, temporary disability provision that requires the other parties of the agreement to help maintain the business or practice of the temporarily disabled individual until he recovers. If the sole owner is a surgeon, for example, who suffered a broken hand, the other surgeons must cover his practice and work a specified number of hours per week at a specified rate of pay. This is cheap insurance, indeed, to protect and preserve the value of the disabled surgeon's practice.

In lieu of finding another business to be a party to the buy-and-sell agreement, you'll need to turn to your key employees. This type of buyout provides a good incentive, because you become committed to ultimately selling the business to them, either at your retirement, disability, or death. The problem is that they ordinarily have no money with which to purchase the business. Unless you're careful, you will end up funding your own buyout by paying the key employee additional money to purchase insurance on your life.

For most sole owners, however, a business continuity agreement won't work if that owner suddenly dies or becomes disabled because there is no one to succeed as an owner. I had this happen to a client of mine, let's call him Clint Gerrity.

*Clint was the successful and hard-working owner of two businesses. Like most entrepreneurs, he tended to make all the decisions himself. At age 43, he knew he was far too young to be concerned with his death or disability and how that might impact his family or business. And then one day, as he bent over to unbuckle his ski boot, he dropped dead.*

*As tragic as that was to his family (not to mention Clint), the avoidable tragedy was his failure to make any plans whatsoever for the business. No one knew what Clint's wishes were with respect to continuing or selling the businesses. No one (within his family especially) knew the overall business financial condition, administrative status or operational concerns. The key employees knew only one thing for sure–the businesses would not long survive Clint's death. So, they promptly found new employment; thus hastening the inevitable shutdown of these once vital businesses.*

If you do nothing else, as a sole owner you have a duty to your family and to your business to answer and to communicate to them the following answers to the following questions:

1.  Who can be given the responsibility to continue and supervise:
    (a) business operations?
    (b) financial decision
    (c) internal administration?

2.  How will these people be compensated for their time and, most importantly, for their commitment to continue working until the company is transferred or liquidated? Consider key person insurance on your life to fund this need at the company level. Use the money to offer the key employees a "stay bonus," a cash bonus receivable by them if they stay and see the company through its transition.

3. Should the business, at your death or permanent incapacity
   be:
   (a) sold to an outside third party?
   (b) sold to employee(s), and if so, to whom?
   (c) transferred to family members?
   (d) continued?
   (e) liquidated?

4. Who should be consulted in the transfer process described
   above? _____

   _____

   _____

5. If the business is to be sold, list the names and contact of
   businesses which have expressed an interest in acquiring
   your business. _____

   _____

   _____

I suggest that you write down the answers to these questions now.
Discuss this issue with your family before placing your answers
alongside your other estate planing documents. Use Appendix 11.2
to expedite this process.

## Summary

The buy-and-sell agreement should cover certain events that trigger a transfer of stock: death, disability, involuntary transfer, termination of employment and irreconcilable business disputes.

The agreement should also cover the terms and conditions of a buy out that is not totally funded by some form of insurance–the term of the buyout, the interest rate on the unpaid balance, and the security to be given to the selling shareholder.

These provisions might be different for each event. For example, since most death buy outs are at least partially funded by life insurance, the unpaid balance is likely to be much smaller and thus paid off in a shorter time frame than in the case of the unfunded lifetime transfer.

As you can see, there are literally hundreds of decisions that must be made in the buy-and-sell agreement. All these decisions may seem legalistic and overly technical. But I can assure you that should an event causing a stock transfer arise, the decisions you make now will be the most important "minutia" of your business life.

A buy-and-sell agreement is the most important business document you will ever create. It is a mechanism that maintains control over the business by the active shareholders. For the departing shareholder, it guarantees a fair value, a ready market for stock, and equitable terms and conditions of any buyout of his stock. No other document will do this.

### How Do You Design The Agreement?

The following checklist highlights seven events that could trigger a transfer of stock under a buy-and-sell agreement. It's possible your buy-and-sell agreement will not need to include all of these events. However, you should analyze the issues listed under each event. Familiarize yourself with these issues and work with your advisors to design and implement this most important agreement.

## Appendix 11.1:  Events That Could Trigger a Stock Transfer Under a Buy-Sell Agreement

❑   I.   Death.

  A. Buyout (select one).

   1. Mandatory purchase and mandatory sale (the typical case)
   2. Optional purchase to business or remaining shareholders

  B. Terms and Conditions.

   1. Cash funded with life insurance
   2. Percentage of down payment
   3. Length of installment note
   4. Interest rate of installment note

❑   II.   Disability.

  A. Buyout (select one).

   1. Mandatory
   2. Optional to business or remaining shareholders
   3. Optional to disabled shareholder (or selling shareholder)

  B. Terms and Conditions.

   1. Cash to be funded with disability buyout insurance
   2. Percentage of down payment
   3. Length of installment note
   4. Interest rate of installment note

❏   III.   Transfer to Third Party.

        A. Buyout First Right of Refusal to remaining shareholders.

        B. Terms and Conditions.

            1. Percentage of down payment
            2. Length of installment note
            3. Interest rate of installment note
            4. Price to be paid: price offered by third party or value stated in agreement? or lower of the two?

❏   IV.   Termination of Employment.

        A. Buyout (select one).

            1. Mandatory
            2. Optional to business or remaining shareholders
            3. Optional to terminating employee/shareholder

        B. Terms and Conditions.

            1. Percentage of down payment
            2. Length of installment note
            3. Interest rate of installment note
            4. Price
            5. Covenant Not to Compete

❏   V.   Retirement.

        A. Buyout (select one).

            1. Mandatory
            2. Optional to business or remaining shareholders
            3. Optional to deceased retiring shareholder

B.  Terms and Conditions.

    1.  Percentage of down payment
    2.  Length of installment note
    3.  Interest rate of installment note
    4.  Price
    5.  Covenant Not to Compete

❑  VI.  Involuntary Transfer Due to Bankruptcy or Divorce.

A.  Buyout.
    Optional to business or remaining shareholders

B.  Terms and Conditions

    1.  Percentage of down payment
    2.  Length of installment note
    3.  Interest rate of installment note
    4.  Price

❑  VII.  Business Disputes.

A.  Buyout (select one)

    1.  Mandatory-the Texas Shootout.
    2.  Option to sell or liquidate by any shareholder

B.  Terms and Conditions.

    1.  Percentage of down payment
    2.  Length of installment note
    3.  Interest rate of installment note
    4.  Covenants not to compete
    5.  Price

## Appendix 11.2: Designation of Business Advisors

1.    Who can be given the responsibility to continue and supervise:

(a) business operations? _____

_____

(b) financial decisions? _____

_____

(c) internal administration? _____

_____

How will these people be compensated for their time and, most importantly, for their commitment to continue working until the company is transferred or liquidated? Consider key person insurance on your life to fund a "stay bonus" at the company level.

2.    Should the business, at your death or permanent incapacity, be:

(a) sold to an outside third party? _____

_____

(b) sold to employee(s), and if so, to whom? _____

_____

(c) transferred to family members? _____

_____

(d) continued?_____

_____

(e) liquidated?_____

_____

3.    Who should be consulted in the transfer process described above?

_____

_____

_____

4.    If the business is to be sold, list the names and contact of businesses which have expressed an interest in acquiring your business.

|  Name of Business  |  Name of Contact  |
| --- | --- |
| | |
| | |
| | |
| | |

# *Part III*

# Planning for the Owner at the Individual Level

Until now the emphasis has been on how to help you plan your business so that you will be able to leave it under the most favorable circumstances. The business itself has been the focus of our attention. Now it's time to look at integrating your business planning with your personal financial goals. By paying careful attention to your personal financial planning and estate planning, you'll be able to keep in check Uncle Sam's influence on your retirement objectives, enabling you to retire comfortably.

# *12*

# Meeting Uncle Sam on a Level Paying Field

### *Financial and personal tax planning for the business owner*

As a business owner, you have a need for personal financial planning.  You have financial goals, but like most people, you're unsure how to go about achieving them.  The time and energy you spend starting up and running a successful business or professional practice probably prevents you from giving this subject the thought and planning it requires.  Moreover, your business may provide you with many of the rewards you seek while you are active in the business, so you tend to ignore what it can do for you when you leave it.

Chapter One described a different definition of success in business—one that measures success in terms of the benefits your business will provide when you leave it.  One of those benefits is the attainment of your financial goals.  That's why a financial plan is so important.

This plan becomes the link that integrates your owner-based business objectives with your personal financial and estate planning objectives.

In Chapter One, I suggest that most business owners look to their businesses for the bulk of their assets.  They need to find a way to use these assets to meet their own financial needs and those of their families.  As part of your advisory team, the financial advisor will help formulate a plan to do this.

One of the benefits of having a financial advisor on your team–
this applies to all your advisors–is the opportunity to obtain fresh,
objective insights into your business planning. Business owners are
frequently lone rangers. Caught up in the press of day-to-day crises,
they begin to lose perspective. Often they have no firm idea of new
planning developments that may affect them–until it's too late to do
anything about them. Your financial advisor can bring to the table
knowledge and experience you don't have. When complemented by
the knowledge and experience of your accountant and attorney, his
or her input provides you with a formidable array of services and
support.

### How A Financial Advisor Works

Typically a planner follows a six-step process.

1. **Determining Objectives**. Usually, a financial advisor
   will begin this process by first establishing a starting point.
   After listing your assets, liabilities, projected income, and
   other information needed to prepare your net worth
   statement, the advisor will help you to define your
   objectives: what you want or need to attain financial
   security. Hopefully, this will be stated as an after-tax
   monthly income figure adjusted for inflation for your and
   your spouse's lifetimes.

2. **Making Assumptions**. With your input, the advisor will
   make certain assumptions regarding a variety of issues.
   Among them are: the date you wish to retire, the future
   income-producing capacity of your business, the
   performance of your existing assets, inflation rates, college
   tuition costs, expected income needs upon retirement, etc.

3. **Evaluating the Current Situation**. Based upon the
   information gathered in the two previous steps, and on
   information provided by your CPA, the advisor injects
   reality into your plans and assumptions regarding your
   financial future.

4. **Making Observations**. It is at this point that the advisor clarifies the timing and financial requirements for your objectives. If, for example, you had assumed that you needed $1 million from the sale of your business to enable you to retire in style, your advisor may inform you that based upon realistic assumptions, you'll need $1.5 million. Not only that, you may need to work five years longer in the business to reach that goal or, you may need to sell to a third party rather than to that trusted key employee. (Let's hope that the news is better in your case!)

5. **Making Recommendations**. Your advisor will examine ways to improve the performance of your financial resources. A good financial advisor will make specific recommendations about the mix of investments you should make and how they fit into your overall estate plan. There are only two suggestions I can make: One, diversify, diversify, diversify. Two, don't invest in anything I've ever invested in. That's a sure-fire way to spot a loser.

6. **Implementing the Plan**. With your agreement, the advisor identifies specific investment vehicles and coordinates selected financial services and products needed to make your plan operational. The advisor must monitor the plan periodically and suggest adjustments when necessary.

Whenever I discuss financial planning, I immediately recall one of my clients, a senior partner in a cardiology practice.

### *The Case of the Spendthrift Surgeon*

*Dr. Harold Avery appeared to have everything going for him. Because his practice was eminently successful and widely-respected, he and his wife enjoyed an enviable lifestyle. They lived in the most fashionable area of town, and each drove a new Mercedes Benz. When their youngest child had just been graduated from college and was planning to attend graduate school the next year, Dr. Avery came to me with a simple request. He felt it was time to complete a task he had neglected; it was time to draw up a will.*

*Long ago I stopped being surprised by the number of business owners who had failed to prepare a will. Incredibly, more than half of them die intestate–without a will. In Dr. Avery's case, this problem was irrelevant. I soon discovered he had a more pressing problem:*

*The good doctor was 63 years old–and he was broke!*

*I couldn't help but compare his situation with that of another physician/client, Dr. Felton. Dr. Felton had already contributed enough money to his retirement plan at age 45 so that the income requirements of his planned retirement at 60 would be met. Felton's biggest "problem" was adjusting his plan so that he could retire at age 50 if he chose to do so.*

*In contrast, here was Harold Avery at age 63–with no retirement in sight!*

I've purposely selected physicians in discussing the role of financial planning for business owners because physicians have traditionally looked to personal wealth accumulation for their income needs, rather than to the proceeds from the sale of their practices.

Let's use Dr. Felton's situation to see how he approached his decision-making and how you can profit from his experience. Dr. Avery is the archetypical "non-planner." The difference between Avery's and Felton's financial outlooks is, in a word, **planning**– financial planning, to be precise.

Despite a long and successful practice, Dr. Avery had done no financial planning. He had retained financial advisors only to buy the year's hottest tax shelter–an investment that frequently backfired, produced no economic benefit, and was usually challenged by the IRS.

Dr. Avery was a victim of the "TMSTF" syndrome: too-much-success-too-fast. The money had come so easily that he'd succumbed to the temptation of conspicuous spending and lifestyle. Some business owners can handle this nicely; others fail because they think they've tapped an inexhaustible vein of gold and they don't establish adequate reserves.

The best way to avoid the trap of taking excessive cash out of the business to "live it up" is to create a plan that forces the business owner to confront his needs–now and in his retirement.

That's what Dr. Felton did. In fact, he started using a financial advisor when he started his practice. The advisor, in turn, introduced him to a good CPA and an adequate business attorney–me.

We approached Dr. Felton's plan as a process that included six steps or phases: (1) determining objectives, (2) making assumptions, (3) evaluating the current situation, (4) making observations, (5) making recommendations and (6) implementing the plan. In so doing, we adjusted his plan to allow for his retirement at age 50.

## Phase I:  Determining Objectives

Planning is a process that must have goals as ends.  These goals, or objectives, are both short- and long-term.  They are never to be viewed as immutable; rather, you must review and adjust them continually in the presence of your advisors as part of a full-fledged, joint planning effort.

We divided Dr. Felton's objectives into three categories: living, disability, and death.  For our purposes, let's focus on living objectives. Meeting the disability income objective was simply a matter of providing income protection, amounting to $15,000 per month, in the event he became disabled.

Dr. Felton's living objectives included the desire to have an annual inflation-adjusted, after-tax income stream of $150,000 at retirement.  His investments, primarily inside of his qualified retirement plan, will (with normal growth) allow him to reach his income objective at his originally projected retirement date of age 60.  But now the good doctor decided to move up his departure date by ten years–to age 50.  This necessitated that he reap real value from his practice when he leaves it.

Thus, his adjusted departure objective requires him to expand and increase the profitability of his practice so that he can bring in a second physician as an employee and eventually establish a group practice. By evaluating and revising his objectives, Dr. Felton knew he needed to receive $450,000 from the practice after he left it. With this objective closely quantified, it became a straightforward task to create and implement Dr. Felton's business transition. The plan design will enable him to sell his interest when he reaches his newly-projected retirement at age 50. In sum, Dr. Felton knew **when** he wanted to leave, **how much** he wanted to leave with, and **who** would be the purchaser (a yet-to-be-found key employee/co-owner).

Of course, most of us are not as fortunate as Dr. Felton. He was able to fund his retirement plan account to the tune of $30,000 per year for 18 years and still be only 45 years old. As a result, he won't need that much cash from his business when he leaves it. You, on the other hand, will likely need to have a much higher percentage of your retirement income come from the business when, or after, you leave it. That's unfortunate for you but, I guess fortunate for me. If every owner planned as well as Dr. Felton, no one would buy my books. Thank God for the Harold Averys of the world!

Dr. Felton's objectives, should he die unexpectedly, included: distributing his assets according to his desires with the least amount of tax and expense; providing for a transfer of his practice to his future partners; providing an education for his children; and providing income for his wife and children in the amount of $100,000 per year as long as his wife lived. These objectives are discussed more fully in the next chapter.

The next phase, "Making Assumptions" will instruct you on how to arrive at the amount of income you will need on an after-tax inflation-adjusted basis. This income objective, once quantified, will drive much of your exit strategy.

## Phase II:  Making Assumptions

In order to arrive at a realistic income objective, we make certain assumptions.  These assumptions are the same as those which you and your advisors must consider:

- Anticipated rate of return on investments
- Inflation rate for future years
- Projections regarding the strength of the local economy to support your business prosperity.

When I discuss with owners the amount of money they think it will take to meet their financial security goals, I usually find they've picked a number out of the air: "I need $2 million in cash for my business." This number usually bears little relationship to the client's true needs as we will see later in *The Case of Mark Tedstrom.*

Let's return now to Dr. Felton and the next Phase of the planning process.

## Phase III:  Evaluating the Current Situation

The items that financial advisors examine to determine Dr. Felton's, or any business owner's current situation include:

- Income tax returns from the previous four years
- Current financial statements of the business as well as personal financial statements
- Existing estate planning documents
- Insurance policies
- Estimate of current business valuation

Before you meet with your financial advisor, you will need to collect this information.  So, begin gathering these documents now using the bullets above as a checklist.

## Phase IV:  Making Observations

Like many business owners, Dr. Felton lacked an estate plan and a business continuity plan.  His financial advisor also commented on the amount and type of disability, health, life, and casualty insurance and offered an opinion on whether Dr. Felton's current situation was consistent with his short- and long-term goals.

Dr. Felton's annual income objective of $150,000 would be met if the business sold in five years for $450,000.  The financial advisor observed that the business sale, with principal and interest payments stretched out over seven years would net Felton, before taxes, $100,000 per year.  Additional income was projected from existing investments outside the business and retirement plan.

## Phase V:  Making Recommendations

Always be wary of the financial advisor who is full of recommendations but devoid of the time or skill to assist you, and lead you through the preceding four time- and task-intensive phases. Ask your financial advisor to present her recommendations at the fiscal year-end meeting, so that your other advisors, perhaps less financially interested in implementing the recommendations (such as acquiring life insurance or increasing your investment portfolio), can participate in those recommendations.

A good financial advisor–whether she is an experienced insurance agent, a certified financial planner or an investment advisor– pulls together several areas of concern in developing your personal financial plan and in making recommendations.  These concerns include income tax reduction and business continuity.

### *Income Tax Reduction.*

Despite recent changes in the Tax Code, the ability to defer taxes makes the qualified retirement plan a most viable way to create personal wealth in your business. Witness Dr. Felton's success.

Many business owners believe that they should have only a defined contribution or a profit-sharing plan because those plans are "flexible" while other types of retirement plans require contributions even if the owner can't afford them. Consequently, some owners will take fliers on risky, tax-oriented schemes upon reaching the funding limit of their defined contribution plans.

Owners have better options than that. A good financial advisor will recommend a strategy that allows rapid funding of the plan. Usually, a defined benefit plan will allow more rapid funding for business owners in their fifties. Sometimes, this technique can produce surprisingly high contributions and is tailor-made for owners who suddenly become successful in their later years.

### *Business Continuity.*

Because the issue of business succession can be highly emotional, especially for the older business owner, it's often postponed until the last possible moment. That raises serious problems because ownership transfers are most effective when the seller can participate. This is especially true for service businesses and other companies in which goodwill is associated with the personality of the owner. Goodwill transfers are hard to execute if the owner has already died, become disabled, or retired.

Planning for the succession of your business should begin as early as possible. Ask your financial advisor to introduce you to a former business owner, preferably one in your field, who has gone through the experience. Ask that former owner about the problems he faced when planning the succession process. This should encourage you to act now rather than to procrastinate any longer.

### Phase VI: Implementing the Plan

Implementing a financial plan is a continuous process. Once investments are selected, their performance must be monitored. The plan itself should be reviewed critically on an annual basis at a minimum to make certain it meets your objectives, even as your objectives change.

Earlier in this chapter I promised you an example of how mistaken assumptions can color the entire planning process. I present now for your consideration *The Case of Mark Tedstrom.*

### *The Case of Mark Tedstrom*

*Mark met with me recently to discuss the sale of his overhead door manufacturing business. He was ready, in fact, more than ready, to sell the business. He figured he needed and wanted, $3 million for the business in order to maintain his family's lifestyle.*

*I introduced him to an investment banker for the primary purpose of ascertaining the sale price range of Tedstrom's business. The investment banker analyzed the company's financial information as well as the marketplace's receptivity to the business and determined a likely sale price of $2.3 - $2.6 million. This was not enough for Tedstrom. Anxious as he was to exit quickly, he knew he needed $3 million.*

*I suddenly had one of those blinding flashes of common sense which occasionally strike me. "Why do you feel you need $3 million?" I asked.*

*"Well, I figure taxes will take one-third, leaving me $2 million. I can probably get seven and one-half percent return on my money which leaves me $150,000 - $100,000 per year after income taxes. And that's what I need to live on."*

It sounded to me that Tedstrom had probably thought through his financial needs quite well (which is precisely why I am not a financial planner). Luckily for Tedstrom, I realized my financial planning limitations and introduced him to an experienced financial advisor who:

1.      Determined Tedstrom's financial objectives.

Mark Tedstrom's financial objective was to maintain his family's lifestyle, which he thought to be $100,000 per year because that's what he normally netted–took home–each year.

The financial advisor prepared a budget for the Tedstroms. Analysis of current spending habits established that the Tedstroms needed not $100,000 per year for normal and unexpected expenses, but only $75,000. Post-sale living expenses were not expected to change significantly.

Bottom line: What the Tedstroms thought they needed to maintain their lifestyle was substantially more than what they actually spent or were likely to spend after the business was sold. The financial planning professional provided far more accurate information than that which relied on instinct. The planner took the time to accumulate financial information and then formulate it in such a way as to provide *factual, accurate* information.

2.      Made Assumptions.

Next, the planner patiently explained to Mark that the assumptions he made regarding the seven and one-half percent payout on $2 million were incorrect for two reasons. First, he had ignored the eroding effect of inflation. Inflation even at four percent per year would soon reduce the spending power of Mark's $150,000 per year. Inflation had to be part of the equation.

Second, Mark's assumption that he could earn a seven and one-half percent investment return (an assumption Mark and I thought to be just a bit on the optimistic side) was all wet. A realistic and conservative rate of growth based on a managed portfolio of diversified investments should be at ten percent and likely higher: 12 percent to 13 percent.

The bottom line: Tedstrom's assumptions (with which I concurred) were wrong because he was uninformed.

3.      Evaluated the current situation.

Here Mark's advisor was especially useful because he worked closely with Tedstrom's CPA. In doing so, he discovered two major points. First, the effective tax on the sale of the business would be about eight percent less than Tedstrom anticipated (because Mark's basis was much higher than he realized). And second, Mark had other investments which would contribute to the annual cash flow needed.

4.      Made Observations.

Based on full information and realistic assumptions, the financial advisor concluded that Mark Tedstrom did not need to get $3 million for the sale of his business. He really only needed, before tax, $1.8 million.

Bottom line: In developing your financial objectives and in determining how much money you need from the sale of a business, do not rely on your gut instincts. Use an experienced financial advisor to gather all the information, to make financial assumptions based on historical data and only then to make recommendations.

5.      Made recommendations.

To meet Tedstrom's objectives, the financial advisor recommended a mix of investments designed to spread investment risk while obtaining the needed investment return. The advisor then made the purchases, reported results to Mark on a quarterly basis, and adjusted the mix as Tedstrom's circumstances and investment performances required.

Bottom Line: Leaving the business in style triggers a number of tax and income issues. The financial planning process must take into account all of these issues and your advisor's recommendations must address each of them.

6.      Implemented the Plan.

Tedstrom's financial advisor selected a number of diversified, no-load mutual funds that minimized risk while achieving the pre-determined income stream Mark needed.

Bottom Line: Recall the fiscal year end planning process of Chapter Three. Use your advisors to help implement your plan.

In the Tedstrom case, performing this analysis **before** embarking upon the sale of his business allowed Mark to sell the business now, rather than continuing to work to unnecessarily boost the value of the business to his originally desired sale price. Sometimes, leaving your business in style means leaving sooner rather than later.

Now, I trust you can better appreciate the contributing role played by experienced financial advisors. For advice on how to select the most appropriate such advisor, read on.

### Picking Financial Advisors

You should have no trouble attracting the financial advisor who's right for you, because financial advisors covet business owners as clients. And why not? Financial advisors consider small business owners to be good clients: they've learned important lessons about life and have realistic expectations of the advisor's work. Most owners don't expect their advisors to perform miracles. They understand uncertainties, are appreciative when good work is done, and are willing to pay for it. Moreover, they are willing to become long-term clients.

Since financial advisors perceive you so favorably, you should have no trouble assembling a list of candidates. So how do you go about selecting one? Review these guidelines from The College for Financial Planning, one of the industry's leading educational institutions:

1.  Ask your attorney or accountant; referrals are an excellent source. Also ask friends and business associates for recommendations. Then interview at least three candidates.

2.  Check the practitioner's academic background. Look for a degree in economics, business administration or finance and completion of a professional financial planning educational program indicated by such designations as CFP (Certified

Financial Planner) or ChFC (Chartered Financial Consultant) (and, I might add, CLU–Certified Life Underwriter) as well as evidence of continuing education.

3.    Check the candidate's professional experience. Those who have worked in accounting, banking, insurance or law have the technical background required to offer solid financial planning advice.

4.    Request and examine copies of written plans that the candidate has completed for other clients. A sound plan should include consideration of risk management, investments, tax planning and management, retirement planning and employee benefits and estate planning.

5.    Most importantly, ask for client references and the names of other professional advisors with whom the planner may work. Responsible planners will consult regularly with other professionals who are experts on specific subjects.

6.    Determine how the planner is compensated for his or her services. Let's take a closer look at this item. Financial planners are compensated in one of three ways:
      a.   Some are "fee only" planners who may charge a flat fee or by the hour.
      b.   Others earn commissions on products sold during plan implementation.
      c.   Many charge a combination of fees and commissions. In fact, a study conducted for the College for Financial Planning showed that the majority derive their income from a combination of fees and commissions on investment products they sell to their clients.

The smallest group of planners are "fee only" planners–those who simply charge a fee to develop a comprehensive plan. Their fees are usually scaled to the client's net worth and the complexity of the plan; they sell no investment products.

The idea of financial planners selling investment products is a subject of ongoing debate within the industry. Fee-only planners believe they are more objective in providing professional advice because they are not motivated, either consciously or otherwise, by the need to earn commissions. They advise clients to adopt certain investment strategies without recommending specific products, such as bond or stock funds, real estate investment trusts, commodities, collectibles, or other vehicles. Their clients are free to buy such products anywhere they choose.

Commission-based planners reply that their clients have no problem with the format. "If I can steer my client toward a nice return on his investment, he's not bothered by the fact I earned money on the sale of the product," a planner recently told me.

Advisors who do receive commissions should be willing to reveal how much they earn on the products they recommend. And they should also offer the client a choice of products instead of pushing one over others.

The right compensation method is the one (or two) that makes you comfortable and that provides your financial advisor with the incentive to do the best job for you.

I would add that the financial advisor you select must be an excellent team player. He or she must be able to engage in the important give-and-take sessions with your other advisors–the attorney and accountant. There must be good chemistry among all three.

Another word of caution when selecting your financial advisor: Because of the lack of regulation and standardized credentialing, it's been easy for people to hang out a shingle and call themselves a "financial planner." An estimated 250,000 people have done so. Reports of clients losing their lives' savings to unscrupulous "planners" fill the columns of newspapers and the files of state attorneys general and the Securities and Exchange Commission.

However, while the scam artist and fly-by-night practitioner gets the headlines, the majority of practitioners in the industry goes quietly about business in a professional way, providing important services to satisfied clients. So you need to know there are good ones out there. Follow the guidelines suggested in this chapter, and you greatly increase your chances of finding the advisor who is right for you.

In the end, if you can match a good financial advisor with an equally competent attorney and accountant, you will have assembled a strong advisory team that will provide you with quality support and advice. Such a team will help you achieve your short- and long-term objectives.

## Summary

This chapter could easily have been an addendum to Chapter One: Setting Objectives. Much of this chapter deals with determining what you want and need in the way of financial security.

I suggest that this subject is too important for you to tackle by yourself. Find and use a good financial advisor who will help you develop your Exit Plan as a necessary corollary to your overall retirement estate and financial planning consisting of at least these six phases:

Phase I:      Determining Objectives
Phase II:     Making Assumptions
Phase III:    Evaluating the Current Situation
Phase IV:     Making Observations
Phase V:      Making Recommendations
Phase VI:     Implementing the Plan

# 13

# "Dad Always Liked You Best!"– Part II

### *Estate planning makes sense–and dollars too–for business owners and their families*

*James Keefe sat nervously in my office.*

*Until the day before, he had been president of Keefe Automotive Sales, one of the Rocky Mountain Area's largest new car dealerships. Now he was out of a job and felt he was a victim. Naturally, his first thought was to sue those responsible for his misfortune. The targets of his wrath were his younger sister and his mother. They had forced him out of the business.*

*After his father's death, James had received 49 percent of the stock in the family business. Another 49 percent share went to his sister. The remaining two percent–the swing vote–was held by their mother.*

*James's father had brought him into the business early and taught him well. After the founder's death, James assumed all responsibilities for sales and became the key man in the business. His sister, Susan, handled the bookkeeping and other administrative matters. Her husband managed the service department.*

*Despite the economic slump that hit the Rocky Mountain region in the 1980s, the business persevered under James's stewardship. It had a long-standing tradition of service and good name identity because the elder Keefe had pioneered the new car business in the Denver suburbs.*

*Because of his dedication to the business, James had not spent much time nurturing family relationships. He was less a devoted son to his mother than was his sister a devoted daughter. As their mother aged, she became increasingly susceptible to the influences of her daughter. Family friction continued. A confrontation was inevitable.*

*James had always assumed that his superior abilities and position as president and board chairman in the company would enable him to win any family showdown. He was wrong. At a special meeting of the board of directors, James was removed from his posts, fired as an employee, and given three months' severance pay–after he had worked 25 years in the business.*

*James naturally felt he had been victimized. And he was! But not so much by his sister and mother as by his deceased father. By failing in the most important remaining task in his life–to plan his estate–the elder Keefe made his son an unintended victim.*

If James's father had asked–and answered–five critical questions, he could have assured the future of his business and his family. Instead, a legal battle that would cost $200,000 and tear the family apart was about to ensue. It would forever end the elder Keefe's dream of a close-knit, happy, family-run business.

The questions the elder Keefe should have addressed are listed below. Your thoughtful answers to these questions, followed by appropriate implementation, may well prevent a similar experience in your own family.

1.     How can I provide for an equitable distribution of my estate among my children?

2.     How can I use my business to fuel the growth of my estate outside of my business interests?

3.     How do I provide for my family's income needs, especially those of my spouse and dependent children, after my death?

4.     How can I help preserve my assets from the claims of creditors during my lifetime and at my death?

5.     How can I minimize or eliminate estate taxes?

Before analyzing these questions further, let's first review the techniques we use to avoid giving Uncle Sam more than is necessary.

## Estate Taxation

Did you know that estate taxes are voluntary? Unlike income, social security, or excise taxes, estate taxes can be totally avoided.

After practicing in the estate planning arena for more than 20 years, I've concluded that there are only three reasons for this unnecessary waste, all based on ignorance: first, ignorance of what estate planning is; second, ignorance of the high rate of estate taxation once it begins and, third, ignorance of the ultimate impact of estate taxation on the owner's estate as he accumulates wealth during his lifetime.

In short, estate taxes exist for those who ignore the facts that they have estates, that they will eventually die, and that there is a tax based on the size of their estate when they do die. These folks almost deserve to be taxed.

It is important to know what estate taxes are, know the tools available to minimize or avoid them, and employ those tools to transfer your estate (including your business) to the objects of your bounty upon your death. But first, let's define what an estate is. An estate, for federal estate tax purposes, is everything you own or control at death, including life insurance proceeds and jointly owned property.

### *What Is the Estate Tax System?*

The federal government imposes an estate tax when two conditions are present: (1) You have departed this earth and (2) your estate is worth at least $600,000. (If your estate is worth less than that, you may stop reading here–the IRS has bigger fish to fry.)

At the $600,000 level, your estate will be taxed at 37 percent. The rate quickly rises to 45 percent at $1.5 million and tops off at 55 percent at $3 million.

For example, if your estate is $1 million at your death, the estate tax payable is $153,000 ($1 million less $600,000 equals $400,000 multiplied by almost 40 percent equals $153,000). On an estate of $1.5 million, the tax is $363,000; on $2.5 million, it's $833,000; and on $5 million, the tax is over $2.2 million.

Obviously the government is a major benefactor of your lifelong efforts to increase the value of your business. There, at the end of the line, stands the IRS with its hands out-stretched, palms upward, with all of the enforcement tools and years of experience behind it.

So what chance do you have to avoid or at least to minimize your estate taxes? You must take the following critical path.

### *How to Avoid or Minimize Estate Taxes*

First, you must make full use of the $600,000 unified credit amount that you can leave at your death without paying any taxes. If your total estate, for example, is $1.2 million, the potential estate tax is $235,000.

This $600,000 exclusion is also available to your spouse. Through the use of the marital deduction and a "family trust" (also called a credit trust), a total estate of $1.2 million may pass to your children without any estate tax consequences. Let's examine how this is done.

The marital deduction is the second primary means to eliminate or reduce estate taxes. This is a total deduction from taxation of all amounts passing from a decedent to his spouse (provided he is a U.S. citizen), either as gifts or at death. Even if your estate is worth $50 billion, if you leave everything to your spouse at your death, there are no federal estate taxes. Period.

This sounds great. And it is, at least at the time the first spouse dies. But there's a hidden trap. When the surviving spouse also dies, there is no longer a marital deduction on any property previously passed to her because of the marital deduction. The only deduction that remains is the $600,000 exclusion. In this case the entire estate tax burden then normally falls on the surviving children.

As we've seen, on an estate worth $1.2 million, the total estate tax is $235,000 when the surviving spouse dies. This tax can be completely avoided in estates of $1.2 million or less by making sure that the $600,000 exclusion is used in each estate–both the husband's and the wife's. DeWayne and Connie Smith provide an example.

*The Smiths, in their late thirties, had two young children, and all of their assets were held entirely in joint tenancy. Their business was worth $500,000, their home had an equity of $100,000, outside investments and personal property were worth $100,000, and they each had life insurance of $250,000 payable to each other. Their total estate was valued at $1,200,000.*

*As their estate was initially structured, there would be no taxes when the first spouse died since the surviving spouse would receive everything. However, when the surviving spouse died, there would be estate taxes of $235,000.*

*I explained to the Smiths that the estate tax consequences of not doing any further estate planning was to pay $235,000 of unnecessary taxes. Both insisted, however, that if DeWayne died first Connie should receive the benefit of the entire estate to satisfy her lifetime needs. That was more important to them than saving estate taxes. But then I explained that they could save the taxes and accomplish that goal.*

*First, I recommended that the joint tenancy on all of their assets be severed and the assets be retitled so that each spouse owned approximately $600,000 of assets in his or her own name. For DeWayne this meant the $250,000 of life insurance would remain his as well as $350,000 worth of business interest. For Connie this meant the $250,000 of life insurance on her life would remain in her name along with the remaining business interest of $150,000, the home, and the personal property.*

*In the case of the Smiths, after equalizing the estates, we created wills with trust provisions. (Living trusts work equally well.) The effect of the wills was to place the first $600,000 of a spouse's estate in a family trust for the benefit of the surviving spouse and children. Accordingly, when the first spouse died (it made no difference who died first, since their estates were equalized–a crucial planning point), the $600,000 owned by the decedent would go into a trust for the survivor. As trustee, the surviving spouse would receive all of the income for the rest of his or her life, as trustee, and have significant control over the use of the money in the trust; yet, for estate tax purposes, only the amount of money owned in his or her name would be includable in the estate when the surviving spouse died. This is true because the trust created at the death of the first spouse was designed to place just enough restrictions on the right of access so that the IRS would not consider the amount in that trust to be includable in the surviving spouse's estate as well.*

*The net result? When the first spouse dies, there will be no estate taxes. Instead, $600,000 will go into a family trust and will be deducted under the $600,000 exclusion. If the decedent spouse had more than $600,000, the rest would go to the surviving spouse via a provision in the will or trust document, and this amount would qualify for the marital deduction. So there is never an estate tax when the first spouse dies.*

*When the surviving spouse dies–assuming the combined estates still total $1.2 million–there is still no estate tax, because the surviving spouse's estate consisted of only $600,000. Although the surviving spouse had the use of the $600,000 left in trust, that amount is not part of the surviving spouse's estate for estate tax purposes.*

*The net result is an estate tax savings of $235,000.*

This type of trust typically continues for the benefit of the surviving children and, eventually, is terminated. The remaining amounts are then distributed to the children at ages Connie and DeWayne deemed appropriate.

We've seen how estates worth less than $1.2 million can be transferred to a younger generation without estate taxation. How about larger estates?

The short answer is: If your combined estate exceeds $1.2 million and you don't leave the excess to charity, be prepared to pay an estate tax.

Since most people don't want to leave large chunks of their estates only to charity, they must, during their lifetimes, reduce the size of their estates if in excess of $1.2 million. Or they can minimize growth.

Of course, it usually makes no sense to either reduce your estate or to avoid growth unless that excess amount passes to your spouse and children.

## Reducing the Taxable Estate

As we've seen, the three methods of avoiding estate taxes are: (1) making full use of the $600,000 exclusion in both spouses' estates; (2) using the charitable estate tax deduction to avoid taxes on estates valued at more than $1.2 million; and (3) reducing estates that exceed $1.2 million.

The easiest way to do the latter is to give away an asset–especially life insurance. Let's see how this could have worked with DeWayne and Connie Smith.

Instead of the business being worth $500,000, assume its value is $1 million. The total estate then is $1.7 million, including $500,000 in life insurance. Even if we maximize the use of the $600,000 unified credit at each death, about $200,000 in estate taxes will be due when the second spouse dies.

On the other hand, if we were able to remove the life insurance from taxability we could eliminate all estate taxes while allowing the surviving spouse and children to be the beneficiaries of the life insurance.

This is accomplished by transferring ownership of life insurance out of the estate of the older generation (the parents) to an irrevocable life insurance trust. This is a document that, once signed by you, can never be changed, altered, or terminated. However, if properly set up, it can still be flexible enough to provide benefits among the family members. Yet, it operates just like the family trust used by the Smiths. This means that Connie will have access to the life insurance proceeds on DeWayne's life for her and their children's needs. After both parents have died, the proceeds are distributed to the children tax-free.

Another aspect of not owning assets at death involves giving property away during your lifetime. For a variety of reasons, not all transfers of business interests are completed during the owner's lifetime. The business may be too valuable, making the gift taxes too expensive; the surviving spouse may want to remain active in the business and in control of it for as long as he or she wishes; the owner may have been unwilling to relinquish control of the business until his or her death; or the owner may have been in the process of giving or selling the business to the children.

Whatever the reason, most businesses don't seem to be transferred to a younger generation until the death of the older generation. That's why it's important to have a planned disposition of your business interest. The planning can be expressed in a will or trust, or in a buy-and-sell agreement with offspring who will remain active in the business.

Without doubt, the preferred method of transferring a business interest is by a binding buy-and-sell agreement in which the buyout at death is funded in whole or in part with life insurance on the owner's life. With this agreement in place, several assurances are made.

The children who will remain in the business and control it know that at your death they will become the controlling owners of the business. The agreements obligate your estate to do that. Conversely, you are assured that upon your death cash will be received by the estate in exchange for stock that may otherwise have little value in the hands of a spouse who has never been active in the business.

In short, the buy-and-sell agreement is a covenant between you and the children who will succeed you in business. It is a promise that protects you and the children, and a great benefit to those heirs for whom money is more important than owning stock in your business.

This is what James Keefe's father failed to do. Had he entered into such an agreement with James, James would have received the business and his sister and mother would have received money and other assets.

Historically, a buy-and-sell agreement has also been used to help establish value for the stock when it transfers at the owner's death. The agreement still remains valuable for this purpose, but you need to keep in mind that the IRS will view with suspicion a transfer between a parent and a child as being other than arms length and will therefore subject the stock value to stricter valuation tests. In essence, the IRS forces family business owners to value the business at an arms-length date of death value; not the value placed on the business in the buy-and-sell agreement.

In the absence of a buy-and-sell agreement, stock can be transferred by your will or trust documents. If you do not specifically make a bequest of the stock to your children, it will pass as part of the "residue" of your estate, and each residuary heir will be entitled to an equal portion of the stock–the worst possible distribution of the company's ownership. At the very least, a specific bequest should be made in your will directing the stock to the appropriate person or persons.

In many situations it's simply not appropriate to do this. You may not want the business continued by the family after your death, family members may be too young or inexperienced to assume control, or they may not want to be involved in the business after your death. The primary method of dealing with any of these situations is to place the ownership in trust and direct the trustee to sell the business through the powers and restrictions given him in the trust document.

In a sense you can continue to rule the business from the grave. For example, instead of selling the business you could require the trust to continue to own the business interest until younger children attain maturity, at which time they can be given the option to take over the family business or let it be sold. The  trustee could be instructed to hire or appoint a key employee or group of employees to run the business until a specified date. The trustee can be given the power to sell the business when certain events related to the business occur. A trust can be designed so that the trustees are given only the power to elect a board of directors consisting of a group or category of individuals you describe in the trust instrument.

In short, trusts are flexible and can be designed to account for the specific conditions and circumstances of your business. They normally are not permanent solutions, but can provide for proper management and control until it's time to transfer, sell, or liquidate the stock.

Now let's return to those key questions we raised early in this chapter.

### How Can I Provide For an Equitable Distribution of My Estate Among My Children?

Parents normally want to give equal amounts of their estates to their surviving children, regardless of how active each child was in the business. The problem with including this provision in a will is that each child will get not only an equal amount of the business, but also an equal amount of the nonbusiness assets.

This arrangement ignores the fact the owner may have already given large portions of the business to the business-active child; it also ignores the fundamental objective of giving the entire business interest to those children active in the business while giving the rest of the children a disproportionate share in the balance of the estate.

The problem of providing for fair (notice I did not say equal) distribution to all of the children is illustrated by the Aurora Scaffolding Corporation. This case reflects most of the problems– and opportunities–involved in the estate planning process.

*My law firm had represented Aurora Scaffolding for many years. Aurora rented and installed scaffolding systems on commercial sites. Like many construction-related firms, its economic fortunes rose and fell with unnerving regularity. However, its founder, Mike Fletcher, was a survivor–not only of the ups and downs of his business but of a disabling injury at the age of 51. That experience made him a true believer in the estate planning process. Consequently, I found him in my office shortly after his release from one of our local hospitals.*

*Mike arrived with a list of objectives he had carefully prepared. He wanted to begin an immediate transition of management–and ultimately control–to his youngest son, Patrick, who had been working in the business almost five years. Mike was motivated not simply out of a desire to benefit Patrick, but more importantly to provide a mechanism for getting money out of the business for Mike's own benefit upon his planned departure in five years. There were no other likely candidates to buy his stock, so the fact that Patrick wanted to eventually own the business enabled Mike to make that decision earlier than he had planned.*

*Because Mike had neglected to obtain adequate disability income insurance, his second objective was to ensure that he would have adequate monies available to him in the event of another disabling injury.*

*Mike described his other objectives:*

- *He wanted to provide a comfortable lifestyle for his wife, Sharon, in the event of his death.*
- *Primarily at her insistence, he wanted to provide for an equitable distribution of the estate to his other son after both he and his wife died.*
- *Finally, he was reluctant to pay any estate taxes.*

These concerns are typical. Retirement income. Disability income. Family income for surviving family members. Fair distribution of the family's estate among children. Avoidance of estate taxes. Aren't they your concerns also?

We addressed all of Mike's concerns by first following the steps discussed in Chapter Ten. Again, these steps are:

1. Establish a process.
2. Set goals.
3. Evaluate potential obstacles.
4. Evaluate tools for overcoming obstacles.
5. Determine how to transfer the business while guaranteeing financial security.
6. Determine how to transfer the business while avoiding unnecessary estate taxes.
7. Determine how to transfer the business to children even though they are not prepared to run it.
8. Determine how to transfer the business to children when not all are active in the business while being fair to the non-active children.
9. Determining how to transfer the business when all the children are active in the business.

Other parts of the planning process (and of this book) address these common objectives and concerns. Specifically, we discussed the transition of management and control to the business active child, during lifetime, in Chapter Ten. Providing for income upon disability was discussed in Chapters 11 and 12 (disability buyout provisions of a buy-and-sell agreement).
Mike's other objectives however, are estate planning based:
• Providing financial security to a dependent spouse upon an owner's death;
• Providing for an equitable distribution of assets;
• Minimizing estate taxes.

*In Mike's situation how did we approach these questions? First we quantified Mike's objectives. Mike and his wife lived comfortably, but not lavishly, on his salary of $200,000 per year. He wanted to maintain this income amount as long as he lived. At Mike's* *death, his wife could live comfortably on $120,000 per year. We then reviewed Mike's estate. His simplified balance sheet looked like this:*

> *Fair market value of business ................. $1,000,000*
> *Net equity in building ............................... $200,000*
> *Net equity in residence ............................. $105,000*
> *Outside liquid investments ........................... $20,000*
> *Profit sharing plan ..................................... $300,000*
> *Life insurance .......................................... $600,000*

*Mike's total estate, for estate tax purposes, was $2,200,000. Concentrating on the estate tax issues, Mike decided to give Patrick 49 percent of the business, worth $325,000, (using a minority discount) in order to remove half of the future appreciation of the business from Mike's estate. He also entered into a deferred compensation agreement with the company. The agreement provided for a $50,000 annual payment to Mike if he terminated employment for any reason other than his death. In that case, his estate would receive nothing under the deferred compensation agreement. The agreement was originally designed to run ten years. Notice this payment of $50,000 to Mike and his family in effect replaces the "lost" value of one-half of the business via the gift to Patrick. After the deferred compensation plan was paid off, Mike also agreed to sell his remaining interest in the business to Patrick. They signed a purchase agreement with Mike to receive payments on the installment note for the purchase of his remaining interest–after the deferred compensation has been paid off.*

*Mike then entered into a buy-and-sell agreement with Patrick so that he and the business became obligated to purchase Mike's stock if he left the company for any reason, including death, disability or planned retirement in five years. The purchase price was the fair market value of Mike's remaining stock, worth $550,000 at present.*

*Next, we redesigned the Fletcher family estate plan. We prepared an irrevocable life insurance trust and transferred all of the life insurance into it. The beneficiaries were Mike's wife, Sharon,* *and both children. The oldest son, William, would receive the first $500,000 of the remaining trust estate at his mother's death. Thereafter, the two sons would divide equally whatever amount was left, if any.*

*The $500,000 additional benefit to William is an attempt to equalize the lifetime gift to Patrick. I say "attempt" because if their mother lives for another 35 years (her probable life expectancy), William would not receive any money until then, while Patrick has enjoyed his gift for those 35 years.*

*On the other hand, when William does receive his share of the inheritance, it will likely be in cash or its equivalent, while Patrick receives his share in the form of closely held stock. This will bind Patrick to the family business, including all the risks attendant in owning a small business. His presence will provide the continuity of management required during a buy out of his father's stock as well as the payment of the deferred compensation.*

*Because Patrick is taking more risk, it can be argued that he is earning the stock being given to him since he has agreed to stay on and provide a means for his father to receive money for his retirement or death–either through the stock sale or the deferred compensation payments.*

In looking at equalizing an estate, the business owner is usually faced with the fact that it is desirable to give stock to the child active in the business during the owner's lifetime and to give other assets to the nonactive child or children only after the death of the surviving spouse. This results in a substantial timing difference. However, the child active in the business will find his share of the family estate at risk. It is difficult to quantify these factors. What is critical here is not the exact **amount** of the gift, but what family members perceive to be **fair**.

In an ideal situation, the nonactive child, William in this case, would be given assets along with his business-active brother during their mother's lifetime. In most circumstances, however, this is impractical; the business owner will need all of the income-producing assets available for himself and his spouse.

*The balance of the Fletcher family estate plan was fairly standard. It created marital trusts and family trusts in Mike's estate plan, thereby protecting an additional $275,000 from estate taxation at Mike's death.*

*Note that since Mike gifted $325,000 during his lifetime, he used $325,000 of the unified credit. This allowed only $275,000 to be placed in the family trust at his death, instead of the normal $600,000. His wife still has her $600,000 amount available to her at her death.*

*Because the life insurance trust will avoid estate taxes on the life insurance proceeds, it will protect $600,000 at Mike's death. Without using these standard planning techniques in conjunction with the irrevocable insurance trusts, the total estate tax amount at Sharon's death would have been approximately $500,000 more.*

*As designed, the plan assured that a stream of income would flow from the business directly to the Fletchers for the rest of Mike's life. At Mike's death, Patrick would be responsible for the purchase of his father's stock, but the company would not be under any obligation to pay deferred compensation. That is true because his mother's needs alone would be less than hers and Mike's combined, and her needs could be satisfied from the income of the irrevocable life insurance trust, the income from other investments and the building rentals as discussed below.*

We've seen from the Mike Fletcher/Aurora Scaffolding example how difficult it can be to distribute the business owner's estate equitably between children while providing for the surviving spouse. Equally difficult is measuring the value of the business interest given to the business-active child **today** against that of the value of a bequest given in the **future** to the non-business active child.

The following factors need to be analyzed:

- Is the business-active child, in effect, paying for the business now through "sweat-equity" (lowered compensation, more working hours, and greater risk)? If so, the current gift is not really a gift, but a recognition of that child's efforts.

- Is the business-active child adding to the business's value through his or her efforts? If so, he should not have to pay for that effort by receiving a reduced share of the ultimate estate.

- Has the active child, by continuing in the business after your retirement, become a critical element in your retirement plan by ensuring that the business can pay any deferred compensation or stock purchase fund? If so, the means by which you tie him or her into the business–the golden handcuffs–may be the gifting of stock.

We saw how that happened to Patrick Fletcher. If you are the offspring-owner of 49 percent of the stock of a company, you are likely to work longer, harder and with the ultimate objective of making sure your father leaves the business under terms he has established.

Hopefully, the transfer of the business interest to the business-active child is only one element in the owner's estate planning. A buy-and-sell agreement which factors in the lifetime income needs of the owner and his dependents is fundamental. This requires coordination between the use of traditional estate planning concepts (such as an irrevocable life insurance trust) and the gift of the business interests to create parity among the children.

### Why Should I Use My Business to Fuel the Growth of My Estate Outside My Business Interest?

The **techniques** for using your business to fuel the growth of your estate outside the business are part of your ongoing financial plan described in Chapter 12, but the **reasons** you need to encourage the growth of your estate outside of your business are compelling and worth reviewing.

If you are like most owners, your assets are much like the Fletcher family's. Primarily, your assets consist of your business, a personal residence, a few personal assets and little else. This typical mix has several typical consequences.

1.    Your ownership interest in the business is probably illiquid and therefore, like Mike Fletcher, it will be difficult to get much for your business interest when you retire unless you plan well in advance.

2.    If the bulk of your estate is in the business, it's subject to the claims of business as well as nonbusiness creditors and, of course, to the ongoing risks of any business.

3.    By increasing the value of your nonbusiness estate, assets become available that can ultimately be given to children who are not active in the business.

4.    Transferring wealth from the business to you is a natural part of preparing for retirement or any other type of ownership transfer.

5.    Taking wealth from the business lowers the value of the business and makes it less tax costly to sell it (or gift it) during your lifetime.

And finally, income generated from assets outside of the business will normally not be subject to earned income taxes, such as FICA, and it provides a base for family income.

Mike Fletcher used two primary vehicles to move income from the business to himself–his retirement plan and the purchase of a building outside of the corporation which he then leased to his business. Without that advance preparation he could not be assured of adequate income in the event of his disability, retirement, or death.

Planning makes the difference between living comfortably and living precariously. You have worked too hard not to enjoy the fruits of your labor. Start by planning now.

## How Do I Provide For My Family's Income Needs After My Death?

In addition to planning for your family's income during your lifetime, your spouse and dependent children will have needs after your death. There are several components that address these needs.

One component will be the nonbusiness income-producing assets that you created during your lifetime. Another will be getting the business value to your family by means of a buy-and-sell agreement that, at your death, requires the active children, a co-owner, or a third party to purchase your business interest in exchange for money, ideally funded by life insurance.

The third component is to design your estate plan so that the assets benefit your spouse while ultimately passing to your children with the fewest tax consequences. This is best achieved by creating trusts to take advantage of the unified credit ($600,000) and marital deductions and to use an irrevocable life insurance trust funded with life insurance that is paid for primarily by the business under a split dollar plan.

Split dollar agreements are discussed in Chapter 11. Basically, they require the business to pay the bulk of the premiums while the death proceeds are owned and payable by the life insurance trust. At the death of the insured, the corporation gets back the cash value to compensate it for making the premium payments, while the balance of the death proceeds are paid to the life insurance trust without estate tax consequences. This is a way of having the business and, indirectly, the active children in the business pay for life insurance premiums benefiting the spouse and, perhaps, the other children.

## How Can I Help Preserve My Assets From The Claims of Creditors During My Lifetime and at My Death?

The most frequently asked question I hear (second only to "How much will this cost?") is, "Can I transfer my assets to my wife and avoid my creditors?"

My response is: "It depends. To get the exact answer, it will cost you . . . ."

Just kidding.

Most owners are deeply concerned about the litigation crisis in our society. They are anxious about spending a lifetime building up assets only to have one lawsuit take away everything. For that reason they want to transfer assets from their names to others–usually their spouses, or sometimes to trusts for their children. Then, if they are sued, they reason, they will be "judgment proof"–that is, there will be no assets to seize.

The difficulty with this approach is that creditors, not debtors, make the laws in this country. There is a law in many states known as the Fraudulent Conveyance Act. It provides that if a person transfers property to another with the intent to delay, hinder, or defraud a current or future creditor, then that transfer is void and the asset so transferred is attachable as part of the debtor's estate.

If a transfer is made to a close family member, it is generally presumed that the conveyance was fraudulent. That means that you–the transferor–have the burden of proving that the transfer to your spouse or children was not fraudulent. If litigation had already been threatened or started, any transfer to a family member for less than fair and adequate consideration is suspicious; it is likely to be attacked as fraudulent.

If a transfer to a family member is to be made, then it must be made well before litigation is even threatened. And there must be a reason that can be established–other than creditor avoidance. If you can demonstrate that the transfer is part of your estate and income tax planning, then you **may** have established an acceptable reason.

Estate planning goals are often accomplished by equalizing estates between husbands and wives. Since the husband, who is usually the owner of the business, normally has the bulk of the estate, it makes sense to transfer at least $600,000 worth of assets to the wife. The assets so transferred are, at least arguably, out of your estate for creditor purposes as well.

Finally, another reason to transfer assets is to fund a children's trust for college education purposes. These trusts may be funded with as much as $100,000 or more of assets per child.

## Summary

Estate planning is a process that continues throughout your lifetime. The degree of involvement–or neglect–you pay to this process will be felt by your loved ones long after you are gone. Thorough estate planning should accomplish these goals:

1. To provide for family income needs, especially those of your spouse and dependent children, after your death.
2. To minimize or eliminate estate taxes.
3. To provide for a fair, but not necessarily equal, distribution of your estate among your children, both during your lifetime and at death.
4. To preserve your assets from the claims of creditors during your lifetime and at death.

### Appendix 13.1: Checklist for Minimizing Taxes

| Task | Date Completed |
|------|---------------|
| 1. To minimize estate taxes, create trusts to take advantage of both parents' lifetime exemptions ($600,000 each). This saves at least $235,000 in estate taxes. The cost to prepare these documents is typically $1500-$2500 per family. | _____ |
| 2. Properly divide ownership of assets between husband and wife to ensure that each spouse's trust is fully-funded with the $600,000 exemption upon death. | _____ |

| **Task** | **Date Completed** |
|---|---|

3. Again, to minimize estate taxes, and provide a measure of creditor protection, create an Irrevocable Life Insurance Trust to own and be the beneficiary of life insurance on your life. With estate taxes starting at 37 percent and topping out at 55 percent, the tax savings are dramatic. Instead of having life insurance fully taxable, an ILIT can keep it fully non-taxable. The cost to prepare an irrevocable insurance trust and supporting documents is typically $1,000 to $1,500.        _____

4. Work on moving assets and value out of the business if they are not necessary for operations. And, even if the assets are necessary, consider leasing them to the business via a family partnership or similar vehicle.        _____

5. Recognize the impossibility of transferring your estate **equally** to all children. Instead, strive to provide an equitable distribution by transferring the business to the business active child and other, more liquid assets to the children inactive in the business (usually at a later date). If this seems unfair to the inactive children, remember, they, too, had a chance to work in the business, but chose not to do so.        _____

| **Task** | **Date Completed** |
|---|---|

6. Whatever you do, make specific provisions in your plan to sell or transfer the business at your death. Be as specific as possible because you won't be around to provide explanations. _____

# *14*

# Nine Steps to Success

*Your action checklist for leaving your business in style*

I've packed a lot of information into this book, mindful that sometimes too much information can be discouraging and overwhelming. Therefore, you may be happy to learn that I have no additional facts with which to burden you. Instead, I simply want to conclude by showing you how to integrate the principles we've discussed into your daily business practice.

First, let's review the basic premise of this book:

*At some point, every owner leaves his or her business–voluntarily or otherwise. At that time the owner will want to receive the maximum amount of money in order to accomplish personal financial, income and estate planning goals.*

To that end, I've shown you first how to create and preserve wealth for your business interest by looking at the business from an ownership standpoint rather than from a management or employee standpoint. Then, in Part II, I recognize that eventually you will transfer your ownership interest–most likely the most significant asset you'll ever own. That's why it's necessary to plan for that certainty so that you can exercise maximum control over that outcome. Finally, the last part of this book deals with your relationship to the business as an owner and shows you how to best use the business to 1) accumulate wealth for your personal use, 2) decrease your tax burden, and 3) preserve a valuable estate for your heirs.

## How To Begin Planning

Although I'm pleased that you've come this far in the book, I now encourage you to go even further–to apply your newly acquired knowledge, to put it to work for you. Do this and you will start down the path toward attaining your owner-based objectives.

Listed below are nine essential steps to start you down that path. In essence, these steps summarize what you have been reading, so that if you take these actions now you will be applying what you have learned.

### Step One

Acknowledge to yourself that sooner or later you will leave your business. With that in mind, resolve to establish at least the following owner-based exit objectives:

- Determine the amount of income needed annually to secure your financial independence.
- Set a departure date, even if it is only tentative.
- Decide to whom the business should be transferred: family, key employee(s), co-owner(s) or outside third party.

### Step Two

Determine the value of your business using the same method the IRS employs. Understand that this value is not the same as a sale price.

### Step Three

Form an advisory team consisting of an accountant, a lawyer, and insurance professional or financial planner. Work with your team to fine tune and adjust your exit goals and strategies. Tap this resource while conducting your fiscal year-end meetings. Ask for a legal audit.

Become familiar with the potential litigation traps that lay hidden in your business. Complete the checklists that are part of Chapter Three.

## Step Four

Introduce methods and programs to motivate and keep your key employee(s). This will help create and preserve value in your business as well as build a potential market when you decide to sell. Complete the checklist at the end of Chapter Four.

## Step Five

Don't try to become a tax expert, but familiarize yourself with the fundamentals of the tax laws. Use your advisors to keep your tax burden from impeding your value-building strategies, especially with regard to your retirement plans.

## Step Six

Examine each of the ways you can leave your business. Determine which way will be best for you. If you want to transfer ownership to your child, use the planning process to achieve clear communication and avoid a family dispute. Complete the checklist at the end of Chapter Ten.

## Step Seven

Ask your attorney to draw up the most important document in your business—the business continuity agreement. Complete the checklist at the end of Chapter 11.

## Step Eight

Work with your advisory team to refine the six-phase financial planning process that will help you reach your personal financial goals.

Ask your advisory team to design an estate plan that meets your personal objectives.  Be certain your money will go where you want it to when you die–and that Uncle Sam gets no more of it than his fair share.  (I suggest zero).

## Step Nine

To help with your planning, take a minute now to review the fiscal year-end outline in Chapter Three (page 36).  After each item, I've noted the corresponding chapter(s) in this book.  Thus, as you proceed with your planning, the process itself will continually reintroduce the points raised in this book, reminding you to consider them as you build your plan.

At times one issue may predominate; it might be income tax considerations or concerns about business continuity.  Rather than dealing with these as stand-alone issues, the planning process will allow you to integrate them with all the other elements in your planning.  Furthermore, by using the fiscal year-end review to work on your planning, you automatically receive the benefits that result from working with your advisory team.

### *Can I help?*

Subsequent to the publication of the first edition of this book, I received hundreds of requests to directly represent business owners. I did not expect this type of response in part because I assumed there were hundreds of attorneys and other advisors around the country who did the same type of Exit Planning work as I.  While giving seminars and workshops across the United States I became convinced that other planning professionals do exist, but they are not easy for most business owners to find.

Consequently, my law firm ended up representing many of my readers, often working with legal and other counsel in those states where we are not authorized to practice.  This experience reconfirmed for me the validity of the Exit Planning strategy described in this book and introduced me to dynamic, successful business owners I would never otherwise have met. That has been a great source of professional and personal pleasure.

There were readers, however, who were beyond Exit Planning and were ready to sell their businesses. Their need was immediate and usually, these owners needed the help of a transaction advisor more than that of an Exit Planning attorney.

Based on that experience, I decided that I would provide much more material regarding transaction advisors in the book's next edition than I had included in the first. Secondly, I sought out and found the best investment banker my firm has ever worked with–Joseph Durnford of JD Ford & Associates, Ltd., LLP. JD Ford is designed to help owners–no matter where they are in the United States–to transfer their businesses to third parties, or to help them to obtain financing for transactions involving management buyouts. Finding Joe dovetailed nicely into my desire to provide more information regarding transaction advisors. As you may recall, I asked him to write Chapter Nine on the subject.

If you think I can help you with your Exit Plan or that Joe can help you sell your business, acquire a new business or help you to find financing, please feel free to call us. Rather than send you on the wild goose chase that I unintentionally sent readers of the first edition, here is how you can reach either Joe or me:

Joseph M. Durnford
JD Ford & Company, Ltd. LLP.
650 S. Cherry Street,
Penthouse
Denver, Colorado 80222
(303) 333-3673

John H. Brown
Minor & Brown, P.C.
650 S. Cherry Street,
#1100
Denver, Colorado 80222
(303) 320-1053

If you would like to work through the material in this book in a 40-page workbook format, you may purchase the companion workbook by completing the Request Form at the back of this book or by calling my publisher, Business Enterprise Press, directly, toll free at 1-888-206-3009. Many business owners have found the workbook helpful as they examine their options, work through decisions, record their thoughts and ultimately keep on track to a successful departure.

## A Final Word About Your Advisors

Throughout this book I've constantly referred to your use of an advisory team consisting of an attorney, an accountant, and an insurance or financial advisor. Their work may also be supplemented by a business consultant such as a business appraiser. These professionals cannot increase your sales or lower the production costs of your product or help you locate or become a good manager. But they are the only resource available to help you attain the owner-based objectives I've described. Armed with an expertise based on training, education, and years of experience in dealing with other business owners, they will help keep you focused on your ownership objectives.

Your team members must be compatible, so that they can work together to help you achieve the final victory of transferring your valuable business interest in exchange for money to accomplish your personal goals. They must also be judicious in introducing planning issues at appropriate times. Certainly, it is not necessary to resolve every issue I've raised at the first planning meeting; but over a period of years all of those issues should be addressed, resolved and, if necessary, reconsidered time and again.

To the extent the issues I've identified become overwhelming, your team of advisors must act as counselors and perhaps teachers so that you can see the whole picture, yet focus only on those issues that are timely.

Many professionals have all the skills necessary to help you. Yet they haven't organized those skills in the fashion described here, nor have they worked with other professionals as a team. Because all facets of business, including planning, are becoming increasingly complex, you can no longer allow your individual advisors to work independently of each other. They must provide each other with advice and input to enhance their value to you.

Take the time now to assess your advisors' qualifications as well as their willingness and capacity to work in a planning mode with you and other team members. Use the Advisor Qualification Checklists provided in Chapter Three. If, in the past they haven't helped you with the issues I've raised, ask them to read this book. In the end, if they don't pass muster, it's time to find new team members.

In sum, keep your ownership objectives continually in mind; commit yourself to the planning process; and find and use professionals whose training, experience, and disposition lend themselves to making your ultimate objectives become a reality. Do these things and you will greatly increase your chances to establish a successful business, achieve satisfaction, and eventually leave your business in style.

**Good luck.**

# Index